Peace and Protection in the Middle Ages

EDITED BY

T.B. LAMBERT AND DAVID ROLLASON

That kings, prelates and even lowly freemen were, under certain specified conditions, capable of offering protection or "peace" to others, usually their inferiors, is relatively well known. That a breach of this protection might entitle, or indeed oblige, the protector to take action against the violator is similarly well understood. However, this protective dynamic has rarely received direct scholarly attention, despite its being evident in an extraordinary range of contexts. The emotional aspects of protection – the honour and love associated with the bond it creates, and the shame and anger that accompany its breach – resonate in both heroic and chivalric ideals, whilst in legal fiction at least, the king's protection or peace would come to underpin the common law of trespass. Such a broad sweep, taking in social, legal, religious and cultural elements, suggests that protection as a concept may have a wider significance than its marginal role in current historiography would indicate. Indeed, the influence of protection both in forming social bonds and in providing a framework for the legitimate use of force suggests that the concept could serve as a valuable counterpoint to more traditional "institutional" understandings of power. This book explores peace and protection as a fundamental motor of medieval society, across a broad geographical and chronological span; brings together literary, legal and historical studies making use of a wide range of approaches; and focuses scholarly attention as never before on the concept of peace and protection viewed in relation to kings and lords, charity and mercy, and the action of feud and vendetta.

Durham University

Centre for Medieval and Renaissance Studies

DURHAM PUBLICATIONS
IN MEDIEVAL AND RENAISSANCE STUDIES
General Editor Dr Giles E.M. Gasper

DURHAM MEDIEVAL AND RENAISSANCE TEXTS
Series Editors Professor John McKinnell
and Dr David Ashurst

DURHAM MEDIEVAL AND RENAISSANCE
MONOGRAPHS AND ESSAYS
Series Editors Professor David Rollason
and Dr Alec Ryrie

DURHAM MEDIEVAL AND RENAISSANCE
TEXTS IN TRANSLATION
Series Editors Dr David Ashurst
and Dr Neil Cartlidge

DURHAM-PIMS MEDIEVAL AND RENAISSANCE
REPRINTS FOR TEACHING
Series Editor Dr Andrew M. Beresford

DURHAM MEDIEVAL AND RENAISSANCE
MONOGRAPHS AND ESSAYS 1

Peace and Protection in the Middle Ages

Edited by
T.B. LAMBERT and DAVID ROLLASON

Centre for Medieval and Renaissance Studies
Durham University

Pontifical Institute of Mediaeval Studies
Toronto

Library and Archives Canada Cataloguing in Publication

Peace and protection in the Middle Ages / edited by T.B. Lambert and David Rollason.

(Durham medieval and renaissance monographs and essays, ISSN 2041–2959 ; 1)
Co-published by the Centre for Medieval and Renaissance Studies, Durham University.
Includes bibliographical references and index.

ISBN 978–0–88844–860–6

1. Privileges and immunities – Europe – History – To 1500. 2. Peace – Religious aspects – Christianity – History of doctrines – Middle Ages, 600-1500. 3. Violence – Religious aspects – Christianity – History of doctrines – Middle Ages, 600-1500. 4. Vendetta – Europe – History – To 1500. 5. Literature, Medieval – History and criticism. 6. Law, Medieval. 7. Civilization, Medieval. I. Rollason, D.W. (David W.) II. Lambert, T.B. (Thomas Benedict), 1981– III. Pontifical Institute of Mediaeval Studies IV. University of Durham. Centre for Medieval and Renaissance Studies. V. Series: Durham medieval and renaissance monographs and essays ; 1

D131.P42 2009 909.07 C2009–903544–8

Pontifical Institute of Mediaeval Studies
59 Queen's Park Crescent East
Toronto, Ontario, Canada M5S 2C4
www.pims.ca

MANUFACTURED IN CANADA

Contents

Preface

This book had its conception in the bar of the Hogshead in Saddler Street, Durham City, and what it has in clarity of guiding ideas and approach is a tribute to the efficacy of Black Sheep Ale in stimulating thought, collaboration, and collegiality. The meeting in question was between the yet-to-be-appointed editors of the present volume together with one of the contributors, Helen Lacey, and Christian Liddy and Giles Gasper. As the talk flowed of royal pardons in connection with Helen Lacey's work and especially of protection in connection with Tom Lambert's, the idea emerged of calling together leading specialists in the early and late Middle Ages and in a range of disciplines to consider in the light of their own disciplines and their own periods what seemed to us then, and seems to us even more now, to be a fundamental issue of the nature of power in the Middle Ages, namely the role played in it by peace and protection.

At the meeting, we drew up a series of sub-themes to form the basis of suites of sessions at the International Congress on Medieval Studies at Kalamazoo in 2007 and at the International Medieval Congress at Leeds later in the same year, and we drew up also a dream-list of scholars we should like to involve in exploring peace and protection. Immediately after the meeting, Tom Lambert drew up a statement of the theme and the intellectual questions raised by it, and we used it as the basis for our invitation to our colleagues across Britain and North America. The response was generous and enthusiastic, and sessions at Kalamazoo and Leeds went forward with much enthusiasm, much presentation of innovative work, and much constructive debate. It seemed to all who were involved that here was a new and exciting approach, addressing a fundamental issue, and ranging across periods and disciplines. Hence the collective decision of all concerned to seek publication, and our gratitude to the newly established monograph and essay series of Durham University's Centre for Medieval and Renaissance Studies for undertaking it.

The editors are grateful to the colleagues whose papers are published here, for their enthusiasm in participating, their efficiency in delivering their papers, and their patience with the minutiae of editorial work; and we are all grateful also to those who participated in the sessions, including

Matthew Innes and Andrew Rabin whose papers it has not been possible to publish here. The whole experience has been, for us, a wonderfully inspiring and indeed educative exercise in the merits and value of collaboration, broad-mindedness, and good-will, and in the necessity to look at fundamental concepts boldly and in the wide perspective which collaboration makes possible.

T.B. Lambert
David Rollason
Durham, October 2008

Abbreviations

Citations are from the first source given in each entry; we have also provided cross-references to other sources and translations for the reader's convenicnce.

Abt	Laws of Æthelberht. Edited and translated in Oliver, *BEL*, 60–81 and in Attenborough, *Laws*, 4–17; edited in Liebermann, *Gesetze*, 1: 3–8; partially translated in *EHD* 1, no. 29.
Af	Laws of Alfred. Edited in Liebermann, *Gesetze*, 1: 16–89; edited and translated in Attenborough, *Laws*, 62–93; partially translated in *EHD* 1, no. 33.
[I–VI] As	Laws of Æthelstan. Edited in Liebermann, *Gesetze*, 1: 146–83; edited and translated in Attenborough, *Laws*, 122–69; translated in *EHD* 1, nos. 35–37.
[I–X] Atr	Laws of Æthelred. Edited in Liebermann, *Gesetze*, 1: 216–70; edited and translated in Robertson, *Laws*, 52–133; translated in *EHD* 1, nos. 42–46.
Attenborough, *Laws*	F.L. Attenborough, ed. and trans., *The Laws of the Earliest English Kings* (Cambridge: Cambridge University Press, 1922).
CCR	*Calendar of the Close Rolls Preserved by the Public Record Office* (London: H.M.S.O., 1892–1963).
CIM	*Calendar of Inquisitions Miscellaneous, Chancery, Preserved in the Public Record Office* (London: H.M.S.O., 1916–).
[I, II] Cn	Laws of Cnut. Edited in Liebermann, *Gesetze*, 1: 278–371; edited and translated in Robertson, *Laws*, 154–219; extracts from both codes translated in *EHD* 1, no. 50.
DB	*Domesday Book*. Entries are cited by folio and by the column letter (a and b on the *recto*, c and d on the *verso*), followed by the name of the county. The standard editions of the text are A. Farley, ed., *Domesday Book* (London, 1783), and, on a county

	by county basis, John Morris et al., eds., *Domesday Book*, 39 vols. (Chichester: Philimore, 1975–86).
Downer, *LHP*	L.J. Downer, ed. and trans., *Leges Henrici Primi* (Oxford: Clarendon Press, 1972).
ECf	*Leges Edwardi Confessoris*. Edited and translated in O'Brien, *GPKP*; edited in Liebermann, *Gesetze*, 1: 627–72.
EETS	Early English Texts Society
EGu	The Laws of Edward and Guthrum. Edited in Liebermann, *Gesetze*, 1: 128–35; edited and translated in Attenborough, *Laws*, 102–9.
EHD 1	Dorothy Whitelock, ed., *English Historical Documents*, vol. 1: *c. 500–1042*, 2nd ed. (London: Eyre Methuen, 1979).
EHD 2	D.C. Douglas and G.W. Greenaway, eds., *English Historical Documents*, vol. 2: *1042–1189*, 2nd ed. (London: Eyre Methuen, 1981).
Grið	The anonymous legal text *Grið*. Edited in Liebermann, *Gesetze*, 1: 470–73.
Hl	Laws of Hlothere and Eadric. Edited and translated in Oliver, *BEL*, 126–33, and in Attenborough, *Laws*, 18–23; edited in Liebermann, *Gesetze*, 1: 9–11; translated in *EHD* 1, no. 30.
Hn	*Leges Henrici Primi*. Edited and translated in Downer, *LHP*; edited in Liebermann, *Gesetze*, 1: 547–611; extracts translated in *EHD* 2, no. 57.
Ine	Laws of Ine. Edited in Liebermann, *Gesetze*, 1: 88–123; edited and translated in Attenborough, *Laws*, 36–61; partially translated in *EHD* 1, no. 32.
Lex Ala	K. Lehmann and K.A. Eckhardt, eds., *Leges Alamannorum*, 2nd ed., MGH Legum Sectio I, 5(1) (Hanover: Hahn, 1966); K.A. Eckhardt, ed. and trans., *Die Gesetze des Karolingerreiches 714–911, II: Alamannen und Bayern*, Germanenrechte 2 (Weimar: H. Böhlaus, 1934), 1–71.
Lex Rib	F. Beyerle and R. Buchner, eds., *Lex Ribuaria*, MGH Legum Sectio I, 3(2) (Hanover: Hahn, 1951).
Lex Sal	K.A. Eckhardt, ed., *Pactus Legis Salicae*, MGH Legum Sectio I, 4(1) (Hanover: Hahn, 1962). Idem,

	ed., *Lex Salica*, MGH Legum Sectio I, 4(2) (Hanover: Hahn, 1969).
Lex Sax	K.A. Eckhardt, ed. and trans., *Die Gesetze des Karolingerreiches 714–911, III: Sachsen, Thüringer, Chamaven und Friesen*, Germanenrechte 2 (Weimar: H. Böhlaus, 1934).
Liber Const	Friedrich Bluhme, ed., *Leges Burgundionum*, MGH Leges in Folio, 3(3) (Hannover: Hahn, 1898, repr. 1965), 497–630.
Liebermann, *Gesetze*	Felix Liebermann, ed. and trans., *Die Gesetze der Angelsachsen*, 3 vols. (Halle: Max Niemeyer, 1903–16).
MGH	Monumenta Germaniae Historica
N-K	Gustav Neckel and Hans Kuhn, eds., *Edda. Die Lieder des Codex Regius. I. Text*, 3rd ed. (Heidelberg: Carl Winter, 1962).
Nor Grið	The anonymous legal text *Norðhymbra Ciricgrið*. Edited in Liebermann, *Gesetze*, 1: 473.
O'Brien, *GPKP*	Bruce R. O'Brien, ed. and trans., *God's Peace and King's Peace: The Laws of Edward the Confessor* (Philadelphia: University of Pennsylvania Press, 1999).
Oliver, *BEL*	Lisi Oliver, ed. and trans., *The Beginnings of English Law*, Toronto Medieval Texts and Translations 14 (Toronto: University of Toronto Press, 2002).
Pax	The anonymous legal text *Pax*. Edited in Liebermann, *Gesetze*, 1: 390–91.
PROME	*The Parliament Rolls of Medieval England*, ed. Chris Given-Wilson, CD-ROM (Leicester: Scholarly Digital Editions, 2005).
R	*La chanson de Roland*, cited by line number. For the text, see *La chanson de Roland*, ed. Ian Short, 2nd ed., Lettres Gothiques, ed. Michel Zink (Paris: Livre de Poche, 1990).
Robertson, *Laws*	A.J. Robertson, ed. and trans., *The Laws of the Kings of England from Edmund to Henry I* (Cambridge: Cambridge University Press, 1925).
Rolls Series	Rolls Series (Rerum Britannicarum medii Aevi Scriptores or Chronicles and Memorials of Great Britain and Ireland during the Middle Ages)

T.B. LAMBERT
Durham University

Introduction

Some Approaches to Peace and Protection in the Middle Ages

Peace and protection today are largely separate concepts. Peace, being a passive state – of inner calmness, external tranquillity or, more specifically, the absence of war – is not necessarily connected with the more active idea of protection, the positive prevention of harm. With a moment's reflection, however, we might well start to make some links between the two concepts. Protection is fundamentally about preservation from harm or danger, the preservation of a state of general tranquillity that could easily be termed peace. We can find links in modern terminology: "peace-keepers" today are soldiers whose primary duty is the protection of civilians; people might protect themselves against risks by buying insurance, and so gain peace of mind. Indeed, we might even wonder if the fact that we generally do manage to lead lives free from fear – that as a rule we can expect to be left in peace by our fellow humans – is to some extent the product of protection. Obviously this cannot be said for everyone; many people do live in daily fear of violence or robbery but – in modern, developed states, at least – these are a minority. Our peace has become so familiar, so constant a part of our normal way of life, that we have come to take it for granted. We no longer really even think of ourselves as enjoying peace; our protection by our states and our laws is remarkable to us only when it fails. Peace and protection are so far from our everyday concerns that their conceptual links are far from obvious.

Our medieval predecessors were not so lucky. Connections that we have to tease out were then impossible to avoid, particularly in early medieval societies where legitimate violence was a long way from being the preserve of governments. We need only think of terms such as the Old English *grið* and the Latin *pax*, which were used interchangeably to mean both peace and protection, to see that in certain contexts being in someone else's peace amounted to being under their protection.[1] However, though it was not unusual to talk about protection in terms of peace, it was equally

1 Angus Cameron, Ashley Crandell Amos, and Antonette diPaolo Healey, eds., *Dictionary of Old English: A to G Online*, http://www.doe.utoronto.ca (accessed 1 October 2008), s.v. "griþ." Specifically, "1. protection / security guaranteed by someone (e.g., the king), usually limited to a particular place (e.g. a church) or time period" but also "3. peace, the state of friendly / peaceable relations; absence of

possible not to do so – other terms with no such connotations (like the Old English *mund*) could be used.[2] Likewise, the word "peace" could be employed, as it is today, to mean the absence of war or a state of tranquillity, without any explicit connection with protection whatsoever.[3] Yet, even with these objections noted, the relationship between the two ideas is striking, particularly so where they are amalgamated into a single concept but also in the much looser links between the two ideas that exist even today.

This introduction attempts to investigate these connections and suggest some potentially useful approaches to them. My intention is not to be comprehensive nor yet to draw any firm conclusions, but rather to speculate and, if possible, to stimulate. I hope, to borrow a phrase from Wendy Davies, "to ring bells in your heads and encourage you to think about possibilities."[4]

Peace as Protective Power

The obvious place to start an investigation of peace and protection is the point at which the two words share a single meaning. So, what exactly did it mean to be in someone's peace, to be under their protection? We can, in fact, be rather precise in defining what was conveyed by this. When a word meaning peace (*pax, grið*) is used to mean protection we are generally confronted with a specific type of power, one which I shall here term "protective power," that is defined by specific relationships and obligations. Firstly, we have a "protector" who offers his peace to a "protectee." The protector need not be an individual – it could be a group or an institution, even a supernatural entity such as a saint – but collectively or individually the protector will almost always be the acknowledged superior of the protectee. If anyone then causes harm to the protectee, the protector is entitled, even obliged, to impose some sort of penalty on the attacker. This penalty may be physical, financial, or spiritual, but whatever its nature it is

conflict." R.E. Latham and D.R. Howlett, eds., *Dictionary of Medieval Latin from British Sources* (London: Oxford University Press, 1975–), s.v. "pax": "1. (condition of) freedom from war, enmity, disagreement or sim. (between nations, groups, or individuals), peace" but also "4. freedom or immunity (from liability, interference, or restrictions); b (granted by God, the church, or a saint); c (granted by king or royal official)" and "6. (leg.) breach of the peace (usu. of the king or royal official)."

2 Joseph Bosworth and T.N. Toller, *An Anglo-Saxon Dictionary* (London: Oxford University Press, 1898), s.v. "mund."

3 See, for example, Cameron, Amos and Healey, *Dictionary of Old English: A to G Online*, http://www.doe.utoronto.ca (accessed 1 October 2008), s.v. "frið"; Latham and Howlett, *Dictionary of Medieval Latin*, s.v. "pax."

4 Wendy Davies, "'Protected Space' in Britain and Ireland in the Middle Ages," in *Scotland in Dark Age Britain*, ed. B.E. Crawford (Aberdeen: Scottish Cultural Press, 1996), 1.

the penalty that underwrites the efficacy of the protection. It is the credible threat of a penalty, not any direct use of force, that defines this particular type of protection. This, perhaps, goes some way towards explaining the unity of the two concepts. What this protection provides, in fact, is a guarantee that the recipient will be left in peace, a guarantee whose efficacy depends on the ability of the protector to avenge any breach.

It is important to emphasize that this sort of protection is not based on the physical defence of the protectee by the protector. Being in someone's peace, under someone's protection, does not mean that they will constantly be there physically to prevent any harm from coming to you. This could be done – castle walls and military households obviously offered protection to important places and people – but it is conceptually different in that it depends on the direct application of raw military power. We should, I think, conceive of protection rather broadly as the goal of preventing harm, a goal that can be achieved by the application of a number of different types of power: military power, in the case of fortifications or bodyguards; or protective power, which involves the specific relationship of protector and protectee outlined above. Military power may in fact provide a greater degree of security, but it also makes large and constant demands on the resources of the protector, who must ensure that the protectee can be defended from attack even when there is no obvious threat. Protective power, on the other hand, requires no armed guards or fortifications; indeed the protector does not have to do anything at all unless his protection is violated. This, ideally, will happen infrequently, but when it does happen the protector must make sure that the violator is publicly and severely punished or the deterrent effect of his protection will be diminished. He may, in effect, at this point have to resort to military power, or it may be that its threat is great enough to impose a suitable financial penalty without the use of force. This is the key advantage of protective power: it requires only occasional displays of raw power to be effective. It is a fundamentally more efficient way of offering protection, of converting armed force into a meaningful guarantee of peace.

Protective power, then, is at its very root based on the sanctions that will result from its breach. A penalty of some sort must be inflicted for any breach or else the credibility of the protection will be reduced, and with it the respect in which the protector is held. The breach in itself is a grievous insult, and to allow it to stand would result in shame, dishonour, and exposure to mockery.[5] This type of protection is thus as much an emotional

5 See Wendy Davies, "Adding Insult to Injury: Power, Property and Immunities in Early Medieval Wales," in *Property and Power in the Early Middle Ages*, ed. Wendy Davies and Paul Fouracre (Cambridge: Cambridge University Press, 1995), 137–64, at 144–47.

concept as a legal one. It is a key part of the culture of feud and vengeance that pervaded the early and high Middle Ages and, in some regions, persisted well into modern times. Stephen White's contribution to this volume illustrates this well. He shows how *La chanson de Roland* revolves around this very concept of protective power – in this case termed "warranty" – drawing out how the poet juxtaposes honourable vengeance with shameful inactivity and neatly balances the breaches made and vengeance taken by both sides. Likewise, John McKinnell's paper shows how in the Icelandic literary tradition (though to a much lesser extent in contemporary legal sources) honourable vengeance appears as such a powerful imperative, the power of mockery for inaction so great, that it had to be attempted even when it was tantamount to suicide. Indeed, in the poems he examines so irrational and so irresistible is the pull of vengeance that McKinnell questions the extent to which this concept of peace or protection could in fact provide anything of the sort.

In contrast, Lisi Oliver's detailed exploration of the mechanics of personal injury cases in early medieval law strikes a markedly less bloodthirsty note. She examines how kindreds could come together and exact protective penalties through a court process rather than through any use, or direct threat, of violence. The sharp divergence between the two pictures – legal and literary – highlights how well these different approaches can complement one another. Feud may not always have been as cruel and hopeless as heroic poetry tends to present it, but equally our very limited and generally rather terse legal sources probably do present the more civilized end of the spectrum of medieval disputes. Honour doubtless mattered a lot to early medieval kindreds who felt they had been wronged through violence, and to maintain it they needed to avenge the breach of their protection. However, we should remember that there was frequently more than one way of achieving this: relatively peaceful litigation, with the aim of financial compensation, and violent vengeance were in many ways just two different routes to the same destination.

But what about protection's relationship with peace? We must not be overly taken in by the dissonance between the pictures presented here. The process of litigation Oliver presents is only relatively peaceful; as she notes on a number of occasions, the threat of feud was constantly hanging over such cases. To an extent, early medieval litigation was just feud by other means. Indeed, McKinnell's question of whether a system with such a strong emphasis on vengeance can really be said to provide either peace or protection is a good one. McKinnell, in fact, is not the only contributor to have been struck by the contradiction here; Richard Kaeuper's paper examines the severe tension between the chivalric knight's need to maintain his honour through vengeance and the message of peace and forgiveness that was at the very heart of his religion. The solution he identifies, the

"Romance Compromise," which was essentially vengeance to the point of utter defeat and humiliation for the unfortunate opponent followed by a magnanimous display of mercy by the victor, demonstrates the fundamental inconsistency of an idea of protection, or peace, that almost inevitably leads to violence. Clearly the concept in question is far from identical to the Christian ideal of peace which, to some extent, served to restrain it.

Peace as a Positive

We have thus far been focusing on the ideas that accompany the negation of peace – shame, dishonour, vengeance, punishment – but what about those which are associated with its unbroken presence? What is the active meaning of peace? This is a question that Otto Brunner addressed directly in his seminal work *Land und Herrschaft*:

> Unlike today, when the term peace merely means the absence of enmity, the original meaning was far more active. It included the concept of protection, the security that friends provide each other, the help and support to which they are mutually bound.[6]

Friendship, in the sense Brunner intended, meant more than it would do in a modern context. According to Brunner, "concepts such as peace, feud and retribution must be understood in their original context, that of friendship based on kinship."[7]

Brunner's ideas do now require some considerable caution – particularly when they touch on matters pan-Germanic, as they do here – but used critically they can still prove valuable, as the long-term popularity of his work testifies. In fact, Brunner's observations on this point retain much of their value today. Gerd Althoff's much more recent examination of kinship, friendship, and lordship reaches what are in effect rather similar conclusions, noting that members of kin groups were not only obliged to stay at peace with one another, but also to afford each other every help they could.[8] He also argues, however, that

6 Otto Brunner, *Land and Lordship: Structures of Governance in Medieval Austria*, trans. Howard Kaminsky and James Van Horn Melton (Philadelphia: University of Pennsylvania Press, 1992), 18.

7 Ibid., 25.

8 Gerd Althoff, *Family, Friends and Followers: Political and Social Bonds in Medieval Europe*, trans. Christopher Carroll (Cambridge: Cambridge University Press, 2004), 59.

> [a]s a rule, all bonds in the Middle Ages seem to have been based on the model of the family; the ideas and terminology of kinship even had an effect on the bonds of co-operative associations and the bond between a lord and his men. ... The result was a much larger, broader "family," and bonds like these had one very clear outcome: they drew sharp lines between the people whom a person was to support, help and favour in all areas of life, and those to whom they had no such obligations.[9]

This broad family functioned, as he makes clear elsewhere, as "a larger community of peace and support" for its members.[10] If we follow Althoff, then, we can see peace as a concept defined by positive affective relationships following the model of kinship. At least in theory, then, peace defined a group, a community, with a positive obligation to support and help one another.

This sort of approach marries up well with Paul Hyams's observation that peace settlements ending feuds often went beyond a simple cessation of hostilities and into "the construction of a fresh or revived, positive amity," which could even go so far as the creation of kinship through a new marriage between the opposing parties.[11] Indeed, in one famous Northumbrian feud the chief opponents became blood-brothers in an attempt to make peace.[12] Though reality did not always live up to such high ideals (our Northumbrian example ended in disaster) the conceptual connection between bonds of kinship and a positive understanding of peace seems clear.

The idea of peace as a concept defining a group linked together by social bonds modelled on kinship also resonates with the anthropological model of "peace in the feud."[13] According to this model, "peace" is underwritten by the fact that some individuals might have kinship links with both sides in any potential feud and, as a result, work to avoid the agonizing prospect of being forced to take sides and fight against their own kin. It is the strength of these "cross-linkages" joining two potentially hostile

9 Ibid., 160.

10 Ibid., 100.

11 Paul R. Hyams, *Rancor and Reconciliation in Medieval England* (Ithaca: Cornell University Press, 2003), 16, 201–2.

12 R.A. Fletcher, *Bloodfeud: Murder and Revenge in Anglo-Saxon England* (London: Penguin, 2003), 119.

13 This approach has sometimes been viewed with suspicion by historians but still remains useful. Paul Hyams sums up the historiographical situation as follows: "In the wrong hands, the theory presented itself as just the kind of assumption of an easy, almost automatic equilibrium ('Look! No hands!') that gave functionalist anthropology a bad name. The underlying logic nevertheless retains a compelling power that still merits consideration" (Hyams, *Rancor and Reconciliation*, 15).

groups that prevents an outbreak of violence.[14] In a sense, then, this model brings us to a similar definition of peace to that of Brunner and Althoff: a peace that can only hold within a group that is bound together by links based on the idea of kinship.

However, the peace in the feud model does also lead to a question: did such bonds really, as Althoff argues, "draw sharp lines" between those within and those outside such a peace? The model relies on the existence of cross-linkages, people who have bonds with two potentially hostile parties which would otherwise be unconnected. This surely implies that some degree of peace extends not only to those with direct links, with friends, lords, and kinsmen, but also to the friends of friends, the kinsmen of lords, the friends of kinsmen and so on. We might well expect there to be not "sharp lines" but a substantial grey area between those "whom a person was to support, help and favour in all areas of life, and those to whom they had no such obligations."[15] Might not, in other words, the level of obligation have been proportional to how closely bonded any two individuals were? Might we not expect kinsmen to offer their help and support to one of their number by asking favours of their own lords and friends? Might we, perhaps, want to think of a "peace" in relation to the individual as defined by the people whom he, through a chain of personal contacts, can induce to help him? This does strike me, at least, as a potentially useful way of imagining larger communities defined by a positive expectation of help and support.

How, then, does this positive form of peace based on bonds of kinship, or of what could be termed "artificial kinship," marry up with the concept of peace as protective power that was identified above? Ought we to see the two as intrinsically related? There are some obvious and very good reasons to do so. Firstly, as should be plain by this point, kinship in a feud society fits perfectly into our concept of protective power. The group as a whole protects its members, the killing of an individual obliging the group to maintain its honour by exacting vengeance, or at least a fitting financial compensation. Likewise lordship, as White's contribution to this volume makes abundantly clear, is a protective relationship, lords being expected to "warrant" their men, if needs be by avenging them. The positive bonds that make up the peace that Brunner, Althoff, and to some extent Hyams identify are fundamentally protective.

What we have in this peace, then, is to some degree the other side of the coin to White, McKinnell, and Kaeuper's focus on vengeance. A protective bond, whole and unbroken, creates honour, friendship, and peace; it is only in its destruction that shame, enmity, and violence come to the

14 Ibid., 14–16.
15 Althoff, *Family, Friends and Followers*, 160.

fore. Whether the relationship is as simple as this is hard to say for sure. It may be that some form of peace, in fact, extends beyond those to whom an individual is directly bonded: to friends of friends, kinsmen of lords, and the like. If this is the case, we can still see protective power as fundamental – each link in the chain is a protective relationship, after all – but we should see peace in this context as an amorphous and constantly shifting web, extending beyond the immediate protective bonds of any individual, but diminishing in strength as it does so.

To some extent it is the relationship between this positive peace and protective power that David Rollason is investigating in his contribution to this volume. Rollason's approach to the idea of the hall as a protected place utilizes, it is true, legal texts that outline the protective power they enjoyed, but in drawing on the work of Michael J. Enright (who rather like Althoff sees lordship as, in effect, the patriarchal authority of the head of a "fictive family")[16] and in asking why this protection adhered to such buildings, he moves towards a more positive understanding of peace. Indeed, his suggestion of the "formalized and ritualized use of drink" as a potential explanation for the protected status of the mead-hall fits well with Althoff's understanding of banquets as attempts to "guarantee ... peaceful and friendly relations between the participants in the future."[17] Yet this type of peace – peace as the goodwill that accompanies positive social bonds – is fragile and eminently shatterable; its negation leads to potentially mortal enmity. Hence the importance of the Christian type of peace that, as Kaeuper illustrates to such good effect, was in direct conflict with these violent impulses.

Peace and Charity

Christian peace was a multi-faceted idea. Thomas Renna, in his account of the idea of peace from 500 to 1150, divides it into three main conceptual strands: the monastic or ascetic peace of a pure heart and life devoted to prayer; the episcopal peace, or *pax ecclesiae*, of a properly functioning free and unified church; and the social or imperial peace of the world.[18] The dividing lines between these types of peace were often very blurred, as Renna himself notes, and they were all by their nature imperfect imitations of the celestial peace which good Christians could hope to attain in

16 Michael J. Enright, *Lady with a Mead Cup: Ritual, Prophecy and Lordship in the European Warband from La Tène to the Viking Age* (Dublin: Four Courts Press, 1996), 283.

17 Althoff, *Family, Friends and Followers*, 153.

18 Thomas Renna, "The Idea of Peace in the West," *Journal of Medieval History* 6 (1980): 143–67.

heaven.[19] This is a point also made by Roger Bonnaud Delamare in his substantial monograph on Carolingian ideas of peace. For the purpose of analysis he distinguished between "la paix du cœur," the peace that the Christian finds within his heart, and "la paix sociale," the peace of this world. But, he argued, for some Carolingian authors the two were inseparable: in effect, the aim of the social, worldly peace was the unanimity of all Christian hearts in a single united church, whilst the peace in the heart of the individual was the necessary foundation of any true social peace. The peace was, in fact, one, united in Christ and in the spirit of charity.[20] Indeed, in Bonnaud Delamare's assessment, the concept of charity was crucial to the ninth-century understanding of Christian peace: the true Christian peace consisted of concord with one's fellow man: "la vraie paix ... est assimilée à la charité."[21]

There is a great deal more that could be said about Christian ideals of peace in this period than there is space for here, where our priority is their relationship with protection. For current purposes, it is this idea of peace as a state of charity that concerns us. It is here that we can see the link with the more limited idea of peace as something which accompanies social bonds modelled on kinship. As the "False Capitularies" of Benedict the Levite (a fraudulent mid-ninth-century "continuation" of the capitulary collection of Ansegisus) state, the unity of the Church obliges Christians to live in peace; they have one father in God, one mother in the Church, one faith, and one baptism, and they must therefore live in one peace.[22] Thus, even when it is imagined on the grandest of scales, as encompassing all of western Christendom, we still find exactly the same logic that Brunner identified: peace was the result of shared kinship.

It is this peace, this charity towards fellow Christians, whose interaction with a vengeance culture Kaeuper's paper seeks to elucidate. The rather utopian ideal of Christendom as, in effect, one large family united in peace, could clearly never entirely displace older and much more entrenched ideals of protection and honour, shame, and vengeance, but in the creation of Kaeuper's "Romance Compromise" it seems clear that it had some effect. The outlook, at any rate, is significantly less gloomy than that found by McKinnell in Icelandic heroic poems. Daniel Thiery pursues a similar line of thought in his contribution, examining the extent to which

19 Ibid., 152.

20 Roger Bonnaud Delamare, *L'idée de paix a l'époque Carolingienne* (Paris: Les Éditions Domat-Montchrestien, 1939), 309–16.

21 Ibid., 210.

22 Ibid., 241–42. *Benedicta Capitularia*, Additio III, ch. 26 in G.H. Pertz, ed., *Pars Altera: Capitularia Spuria, Canones Ecclesiastici, Bullae Pontificum*, MGH Leges in Folio, 2(2) (Hanover: Hahn, 1837), 140.

"the sacred obligation of charity" functioned as a force for social peace in later medieval England. Did this ideal of charity among Christians in fact offer any meaningful protection to English parishioners, urging them towards peaceful relations with their neighbours? Thiery's note of restrained optimism puts Stefan Jurasinski's answer to a similar question about the protection of the mentally ill in Anglo-Saxon England into stark relief. Unlike other vulnerable categories of people – such as widows, foreigners, and the clergy – who were protected by Anglo-Saxon kings,[23] the mentally ill received no similar royal protection, nor indeed much by way of sympathy. Neither Christian peace nor Christian charity, he finds, extended to those who committed violence while insane, as insanity was so closely linked with demonic possession and hence with personal morality.

The Social Peace

Peace as charity, then, fits in with all three of Renna's conceptual strands. We have the peace within the individual's heart, the peace of the united Church, and the social peace that emerges as a result. This social peace, however, was more than this. It did not arise simply out of charitable hearts and the unity of Christendom as one large family; it required the legal and political workings of medieval kingdoms. Peace is a pervasive concept in sources concerned with medieval justice and the workings of medieval governments. In Anglo-Saxon legal sources there are repeated references to a general peace (*frið*); the idea of the Peace of God was, as is well known, influential in and around eleventh-century France; in Germany there emerged a tradition of *Landfrieden*, peace legislation covering a specific territory, issued by both emperors and lesser princes; and in later medieval England there was the important legal concept of the King's Peace. In this context peace is associated with temporal justice and good order far more than it is with charity.[24] As Ernst-Dieter Hehl notes, the Decretists of the later Middle Ages had few qualms about dispensing with the wider religious meaning of the term, using peace to mean something like "the safe and orderly existence of a political society."[25]

23 For examples of such protections, see Abt 75–76; V Atr 21; VI Atr 26; VIII Atr 33–34; II Cn 42, 52–52:1; EGu 12; Hn 13:6.

24 Gerd Althoff, *Otto III*, trans. Phyllis G. Jestice (University Park, PA: Pennsylvania State University Press, 2003), 18. Cf. Thomas Head, *Hagiography and the Cult of Saints: The Diocese of Orleans, 800–1200* (Cambridge: Cambridge University Press, 1990), 2–3.

25 Ernst-Dieter Hehl, "War, Peace and the Christian Order," in *The New Cambridge Medieval History*, vol. 4: *c.1024–c.1198, Part I*, ed. David Luscombe and Jonathan Riley-Smith (Cambridge: Cambridge University Press, 2004), 225.

In this worldly context the relationship between peace and protection could vary considerably. Peace could simply be, as Hehl noted, a general sense of good order with no link to protection except in anything but the loose sense that its presence would afford people a degree of safety. This, broadly speaking, seems to be the meaning of the Anglo-Saxon term *frið* when used by kings such as Æthelstan in early-tenth-century law codes – peace was largely about the suppression of theft.[26] Peace could, however, also be closely linked with the mechanisms of protective power, particularly when directed specifically against violence. This was the case with many of the councils of the Peace of God and, indeed, in much royal legislation up to the end of the twelfth century: when Louis VII issued his ten-year peace at Soissons in 1155 it consisted of a number of specific protections covering churches, peasants, merchants, and the like; it was not a general protection covering everyone.[27] Finally, it was also possible for the concepts of peace and protection to unite on a grand scale, the peace covering a kingdom being conceived as royal protective power, a peace that would be breached by any violence towards anyone in any location at any time. This was precisely what Frederick Barbarossa's great *Landfriede* of 1152 was meant to do – it was effectively an attempt to outlaw violence within his kingdom – and, as will be seen, it is possible to look at the later medieval King's Peace in England in a similar light.[28]

Some examples of this interaction between ideas of social peace and the exercise of protective power are examined in this volume. In Claire Taylor's assessment, the Peace of God was not a unilateral clerical attempt to pacify a violent and disorderly lay aristocracy, but rather an alliance between the clergy and the princely class, with the former providing an ideology of peace that served to legitimize the assumption of major protective powers by the latter. My own paper, in a sense, identifies almost the direct opposite development: churches augmenting their own secular power using ideas emanating from the crown. I argue there that in order to keep up with the conversion of numerous specific royal protections into one all-encompassing King's Peace, the churches of Ripon and Beverley may have performed a

26 V As Prol.; II As 20; J. Goebel, *Felony and Misdemeanor: A Study in the History of English Criminal Procedure* (New York: The Commonwealth Fund, 1937), 423–24.

27 Aryeh Graboïs, "De la trêve de dieu à la paix du roi: Étude sur les transformations du mouvement de la paix au XIIe siècle," in *Mélanges offerts à René Crozet*, ed. P. Gallais and Y.J. Riou (Poitiers: Société d'Études Médiévales, 1966), 594–95.

28 Brunner, *Land and Lordship*, 29; Alan Harding, *Medieval Law and the Foundations of the State* (Oxford: Oxford University Press, 2002), 91–92, 128–31. On England, see Frederick Pollock, "The King's Peace," in *Oxford Lectures and Other Discourses* (London: Macmillan, 1890), 87–90, and note 29, below.

similar transformation – converting their Anglo-Saxon sanctuary rights into zones of high jurisdiction. Both papers show, albeit in rather different contexts, that the combination of specific protective powers with more general ideas about social peace could prove a powerful one.

Perhaps the most far-reaching combination of peace and protection is the third of the three options outlined above: when the general social peace covering a kingdom is understood as protective power, with the ruler as protector and the entire population as protectee. In the case of Barbarossa's *Landfriede* this seems to have been more wishful thinking than a realistic effort at reform, but a case certainly can be made for seeing the English King's Peace from the reign of Henry II as a more practical application of the same principle. There is no space here to go into detail on the merits of such a case – in the 125 years since Sir Frederick Pollock's seminal public lecture on the subject there has been little agreement and some confusion[29] – but it does seem clear enough from the thirteenth-century legal text

29 Pollock argued for a general peace emerging out of specific Anglo-Saxon protections shortly, perhaps even immediately, after the Norman Conquest (Pollock, "King's Peace," 87). This basic framework was accepted by F.W. Maitland, though he shifted the transition to Henry II's reign (Frederick Pollock and Frederic William Maitland, *The History of English Law Before the Time of Edward I*, 2nd ed., 2 vols. [Cambridge: Cambridge University Press, 1968], 2: 457–64). This interpretation received a degree of support from Alan Harding's investigation into Scottish protections (Harding, "The Medieval Brieves of Protection and the Development of the Common Law," *Juridical Review*, n.s., 2 [1966]: 115–49) and is now regarded, at least by some, as being well established (see Hyams, *Rancor and Reconciliation*, 224). A surprising number of writers, however, have continued to use Pollock's periodization (David Feldman, "The King's Peace, the Royal Prerogative and Public Order: The Roots and Early Development of Binding Over Powers," *Cambridge Law Journal* 41 [1988], 101–28, at 106; Jack K. Weber, "The King's Peace: A Comparative Study," *Journal of Legal History* 10 [1989]: 135–60, at 135 and 149; David A. Carpenter, "Kingship and the Maintenance of Peace: England in the Twelfth and Thirteenth Centuries," in *England and Germany in the High Middle Ages*, ed. Alfred Haverkamp and Hanna Vollrath [Oxford: Oxford University Press, 1990], 105–25, at 106). All this is in spite of a powerful attack on the idea by Julius Goebel, who questioned the plausibility of specific protections combining into a general peace (Goebel, *Felony and Misdemeanor*, 429–34). Goebel never finished what was intended to be a three-volume work, so we cannot be sure how he would have explained the later King's Peace. A reasonable guess, however, is that he would have interpreted it as an ideological statement whose importance was limited to justifying more significant procedural innovations (this is the approach taken in John Hudson, *The Formation of the Common Law* [London: Longman, 1996], 83). These issues are discussed in detail in my thesis, "Protection, Feud and Royal Power: Violence and Its Regulation in English Law, *c.*850–*c.*1250" (PhD thesis, Durham University, forthcoming).

known as *Bracton* that all homicides and serious assaults did come to be punished, at least in part, as a breach of the King's Peace.[30] This suggests that the Crown was providing a peace that was not just ideological but a functioning protection against violence that covered the entire population.

This vast and uniform peace can be seen (as, broadly speaking, it was by Pollock) as the climax of a process by which a plethora of royal protections merged and expanded until they covered the entire realm, thus making any serious act of violence an offence against the Crown.[31] From one angle, then, it is a triumph of protective power. From another, however, it can be seen as its destruction. Because of this development, the old protective relationships between kinsmen, between lords and men, and maybe even between friends, lost a key element. Violent vengeance was no longer a legitimate obligation: the threat of a penalty, the feature which for centuries had underwritten protective power, became uniquely that of the king. Furthermore, because in theory everyone was protected equally, the fact of being protected lost most of its meaning. What mattered in any given case was not the protected status of the victim but the precise nature of the offence committed. Making law became as it is today, a question of defining prohibited acts rather than protected people; we might say that it became a matter of almost pure "prohibitive power."

The Middle Ages and Beyond

The contributions to this volume, at least, tend to accord with such an interpretation for England. Though Helen Lacey's contribution shows that specific protections did have an afterlife of sorts in later medieval England, they did not function as they had before. Men still acquired personal protections from kings, but much of their value was as protection not from homicide or assault (which were crimes regardless) but from litigation or from interference with property in the protectee's absence. The use of protections was, as Lacey emphasizes, intimately tied up with the symbolic

30 Samuel E. Thorne, ed. and trans., *Bracton on the Laws and Customs of England* (Cambridge, MA: Harvard University Press, 1977), 2: 340, 345, 388.

31 Pollock, "King's Peace," 83, 87. Broadly similar developments have been suggested elsewhere. Harding, for example, sees this as a process that culminated in Scotland in 1357 (Harding, "Medieval Brieves of Protection," 137). For France he identifies a gradual development across the thirteenth and fourteenth centuries (Harding, *Medieval Law*, 240–42), which Brunner believed failed to achieve "true success" until the late fifteenth century (Brunner, *Land and Lordship*, 29). For a more sceptical assessment of the abilities of medieval rulers to claim a genuine monopoly on the legitimate use of force, see Howard Kaminsky, "The Noble Feud in the Later Middle Ages," *Past and Present* 177 (2002): 55–83.

invocation of ancient liberties to affect a rather different legal present. Thiery's paper demonstrates well that ideas of social and religious peace had considerable relevance to the parishioners of the early sixteenth century, but protective power does not feature. Indeed, their disputes seem to inhabit a different world entirely to those dealt with by McKinnell, White, and Kaeuper. The contrast here is, of course, greatly exaggerated by the different types of sources used, but it may also reflect a genuine shift. It is perhaps reasonable to suggest that though ideas of social peace are of perennial importance for reducing the effects of the inevitable conflicts that occur when humans live together, the use of protective power is usually associated with cultures where violence is not effectively monopolized by the state.

Protective power, however, need not be thought of as entirely alien to modern societies. It remains an important concept for the understanding of illegal groups that make frequent use of violence, such as the Sicilian mafia. Indeed, both the Sicilian and Russian mafias have been modelled by sociologists as businesses offering "private protection" as a commodity genuinely valued by their clients, not merely as a euphemism for extortion.[32] Whether we believe this or not, few would deny that the logic of the "protection racket" is as viable today as it was a thousand years ago. As medievalists, we ought not to be surprised at suggestions that such exactions might ripen into custom and acquire a degree of legitimacy. We might, though, want to question the insistence on modelling the mafia as a business in the light of epitaphs such as this one, belonging, bizarrely, to two distinct mid-twentieth-century Sicilian mafia bosses: "With both words and deeds he proved that *his* mafia was not one of delinquency but rather one of abiding by the law of honor, protecting every right; it was greatness of soul, it was love."[33] The parallels with lordship, it seems, go well beyond the provision of protection.

Furthermore, if we trust the judgement of the eminent sociologist, political scientist, and historian Charles Tilly, who once provocatively compared nation-states to protection rackets, we still have to think of modern political power as being to some extent about protection.[34] Though this

32 Diego Gambetta, *The Sicilian Mafia: The Business of Private Protection* (Cambridge, MA: Harvard University Press, 1993), 28–33; Federico Varese, *The Russian Mafia: Private Protection in a New Market Economy* (Oxford: Oxford University Press, 2001), 189–90; see also Henner Hess, *Mafia and Mafiosi: The Structure of Power* (Farnborough, Hants: Saxon House, 1973), 139–43.

33 Gambetta, *Sicilian Mafia*, 248. Emphasis in original.

34 Charles Tilly, "War Making and State Making as Organized Crime," in *Bringing the State Back In*, ed. Peter Evans, Dietrich Rueschemeyer, and Theda Skocpol (Cambridge: Cambridge University Press, 1985), 169–91.

protection need not necessarily be understood as protective power (in the sense that the term is used here), protection as a somewhat broader theme remains a relevant concept in modern discussions of power. Protection is even crucial to some visions of the future. Whether the idea of "cooperative anarchy within the institutional framework of anarcho-capitalism in which private, for-profit agencies offer sets of legal codes and enforcement of these codes," as studied by the economist Daniel Sutter, is in any way realistic is, of course, debatable, but comparisons with certain medieval periods do not give much cause for hope[35] The idea of a society in which the security of the vast majority depended on unregulated competition between a number of powerful protectors would probably not sound too utopian to, for example, historians of millennial France.[36] Whether the game theory models used by scholars such as Sutter could be of any use to medievalists in understanding the functioning of protection remains to be seen.

The point I am trying to make is not so much that medieval historians should familiarize themselves with the sociology of twentieth-century organized crime, or with theoretical models of a potentially utopian anarchic future, but rather that peace and protection are of enduring interest for the study of humanity as a whole, not just the Middle Ages. Some degree of protection, of peace, is ultimately a necessity of society. It need not be perfect, but for humans to live successfully together there has to be some force acting as a deterrent to violence. Whether it comes from kinship, lordship, friendship, guild membership, kingship, the state, the mafia, a "for-profit protection agency," or some combination of these, a form of peace must be provided somehow; for in its complete absence we would, in effect, have the nightmare vision of a Hobbesian state of nature:

35 Daniel Sutter, "Asymmetric Power Relations and Cooperation in Anarchy," *Southern Economic Journal* 61 (1995): 602–13, at 602.

36 For a good flavour of the different approaches historians have taken to this period, see T.N. Bisson, "The 'Feudal Revolution,'" *Past and Present* 142 (1994): 6–42, and the wide-ranging debate that ensued: Dominique Barthelemy and Stephen D. White, "Debate: The 'Feudal Revolution,'" *Past and Present* 152 (1996): 196–223; Timothy Reuter and Chris Wickham, "Debate: The 'Feudal Revolution,'" *Past and Present* 155 (1997): 177–208; T.N. Bisson, "The 'Feudal Revolution': Reply," *Past and Present* 155 (1997): 208–25. Sutter's own view is cautiously optimistic: examining the possibility that "protection agencies" might "degenerate into exploitative gangs," he concludes that the relationship between such agencies and individuals "may not be as one-sided as the division of power" (Sutter, "Asymmetric Power Relations," 602–4, 610).

> There is no place for Industry; because the fruit thereof is uncertain; … no Knowledge of the face of the Earth; no account of Time; no Arts; no Letters; no Society; and which is worst of all, continuall feare, and danger of violent death; And the life of man, solitary, poore, nasty, brutish, and short.[37]

That such a state has never truly prevailed – that humans have always formed groups both for protection against external threats and for the creation of a peaceful social environment in which positive affection is possible – demonstrates, I believe, the universality and importance of the themes addressed in this volume.

37 Thomas Hobbes, *Leviathan*, ed. Richard Tuck, Cambridge Texts in the History of Political Thought (Cambridge: Cambridge University Press, 1991), ch. 13.

PART I

Kingship, Lordship and Protection

DAVID ROLLASON
Durham University

Protection and the Mead-Hall

The aim of this paper is to consider the extent to which in the early Middle Ages some form of protection, in the sense discussed by T.B. Lambert in the introduction to this volume, was assigned to royal and lordly halls, the mead-halls of Old English literature. In addressing this question, the paper will focus on three possibilities: first, that such protection attached to the very fabric of the hall as a building, regardless of who was in it, in much the same way as the protection afforded by sanctuary attached to a church-building; secondly, that the protection offered by the hall was simply derived from the protection assigned to kings or lords, who thus transferred this protection to the hall when they were in it; thirdly, that the protection offered by the hall derived from the ritualized use of alcoholic drink, which took place within it and enjoyed particular protection which could be transferred from it to the hall.

We need to begin with the Old English epic poem *Beowulf*, which is to a large extent a poem about breach of the protection of the hall. This is most notable in the case of King Hrothgar's hall of Heorot, the violation of which by the monster Grendel is of course central to the poem's narrative, but also in the so-called Fight at Finnsburg, which is quoted in the poem and which envisages that violence and killing between two formerly enemy groups will be re-awakened in the hall, at the marriage feast which was supposed to seal their new friendship.[1]

A crucial issue in the huge amount of scholarship devoted to *Beowulf* remains that of whether the poem is to be seen as an echo of an ancient Germanic past, its ideas and attitudes rooted in what was for the poet and his audience a distant past, or whether it should be seen as a reflection of the poet's own contemporary society and culture. On the former side, for example, Michael J. Enright, in his *Lady with a Mead Cup: Ritual,*

1 R.D. Fulk, Robert E. Bjork, and John D. Niles, eds., *Klaeber's Beowulf and the Fight at Finnsburg*, 4th ed. (Toronto, Buffalo, and London: University of Toronto Press, 2008), 2–109, 283–85; for one of many translations into modern English, see Michael Alexander, trans., *Beowulf: A Verse Translation* (Harmondsworth: Penguin, 1973).

Prophecy and Lordship in the European Warband from La Tène to the Viking Age, envisages the poem as reflecting the mechanisms and structures of the age of its literary composition, but in fact constituting in essence an echo of an ancient Iron Age past.[2] On the other, Alain Stoclet in his recent article, "From Baghdād to Beowulf: Eulogising 'Imperial' Capitals East and West in the Mid-Eighth Century," treats the poem as a direct reflection of contemporary Carolingian developments.[3] The date of the poem, of course, remains elusive. Both scholars mentioned here accept the date of the poem as eighth-century, but if we date it as late as the only surviving manuscript it could equally be a reflection of early eleventh-century developments.[4] Can we, then, see *Beowulf*'s image of the protection meant to be offered by the mead-hall as contemporary with the poem's composition, not, indeed, as a hangover from the Iron Age but as something relevant in the context of the exercise of power in the early Middle Ages?

Archaeological excavation and literary and historical writing from the period show that halls like that of Heorot in *Beowulf* were to be found in western Europe in the broad period of *Beowulf*'s composition as a written text.[5] The great sequence of seventh-century timber halls at Yeavering in the Kingdom of Northumbria has often been seen as a parallel in real life to Heorot, and the apparent lack of fortification around these halls might be held to suggest that they benefited from a protective power more effec-

2 Michael J. Enright, *Lady with a Mead Cup: Ritual, Prophecy and Lordship in the European Warband from La Tène to the Viking Age* (Dublin: Four Courts Press, 1996).

3 Alain J. Stoclet, "From Baghdād to Beowulf: Eulogising 'Imperial' Capitals East and West in the Mid-Eighth Century," *Proceedings of the Royal Irish Academy* 105C, no. 4 (2005): 151–95.

4 See Colin Chase, ed., *The Dating of Beowulf* (Toronto: University of Toronto Press, 1981).

5 Bruce Mitchell and Fred C. Robinson, eds., *Beowulf: An Edition with Relevant Shorter Texts, including Archaeology and Beowulf by Leslie Webster* (Oxford: Blackwell, 1998), 186–87; and Rosemary Cramp, "The Hall in Beowulf and Archaeology," in *Heroic Poetry in the Anglo-Saxon Period: Studies in Honor of Jess B. Bessinger, Jr.*, ed. Helen Damico and John Leyerle, Studies in Medieval Culture 32 (Kalamazoo: Medieval Institute Publications, 1993), 331–46; see also Lloyd R. Laing, "Timber Halls in Dark Age Britain – Some Problems," *Transactions of the Dumfriesshire and Galloway Natural History and Antiquarian Society*, 3rd series, 46 (1969): 110–27; Nicholas Reynolds, "Dark Age Timber Halls and the Background to Excavation at Balbridie," in *Settlements in Scotland 1000 BC–AD 1000*, ed. Lisbeth M. Thoms, Scottish Archaeological Forum 10 (Edinburgh: Edinburgh University Press, 1980), 41–60; and Stephen Pollington, *The Mead-Hall: The Feasting Tradition in Anglo-Saxon England* (Hockwold-cum-Wilton: Anglo-Saxon Books, 2003), 65–98.

tive than that of ramparts or stockades.[6] It may be that the great stone halls of the Carolingian palaces on the Continent, although superficially different to the halls of Yeavering or Heorot because of their building materials, were essentially of the same type.[7] The feast which the early ninth-century Frankish emperor Louis the Pious held in the hall of his palace at Ingelheim near Mainz in honour of his (as he hoped) ally on the Danish throne, Harold, suggests a hall of similar function and status to that of Heorot – and indeed the great stone apse of that hall survives for us to see the ambition of its construction.[8] Halls were central also to the Carolingian palaces at Frankfurt;[9] at Paderborn where the emperor Charlemagne entertained the pope, Leo III, to lavish feasting and drinking just as King Hrothgar received his guests and followers at Heorot;[10] and at Charlemagne's greatest palace, that of Aachen, where there was a truly magnificent hall, the dimensions of which are still there to admire, although the building was converted into the town-hall during the Renaissance.[11] As for the Scandinavian world, the contemporary aspects of Heorot as it appears in *Beowulf*, have led some scholars to propose that it was actually modelled on the Scandinavian halls of Lejre, which have been recovered as a sequence of major structures, beginning in the sixth century, with subsequent constructions in 680 and 990.[12] Halls like Heorot, then, were a feature of early medieval reality as well as literature.

Let us now consider the first of our possibilities, namely that protection attached to the hall as a building. The early English law-codes provide a few hints. The seventh-century Kentish Laws of Æthelberht concern the protection accorded to the king's *tun*, which perhaps encompasses a hall:

6 Brian Hope-Taylor, *Yeavering: An Anglo-British Centre of Early Northumbria* (London: HMSO, 1977), 213–37.

7 Günther Binding, *Deutsche Königspfalzen von Karl dem Grossen bis Friedrich II, 765–1240* (Darmstadt: Primus Verlag, 1996), 59–197.

8 Edmond Faral, ed. and trans., *Ermold le Noir: Poème sur Louis le Pieux et Épitres au Roi Pépin,* Les Classiques de l'Histoire de France au Moyen Age (Paris: Honoré Champion, 1932), 180–81; Binding, *Deutsche Königspfalzen*, 99–114.

9 Binding, *Deutsche Königspfalzen*, 117–22; see also Marianne Schalles-Fischer, *Pfalz und Fiskus Frankfurt*, Verröffentlichung des Max-Planck-Instituts für Geschichte 20 (Göttingen: Vandenhoeck and Ruprecht, 1969), 200–237.

10 Binding, *Deutsche Königspfalzen*, 123–30; see also Christoph Stiegemann and Matthias Wemhoff, eds., *799: Kunst und Kultur der Karolingerzeit: Karl der Grosse und Papst Leo III in Paderborn: Beiträge zum Katalog der Ausstellung Paderborn 1999* (Mainz: Philipp von Zabern, 1999), 175–221.

11 Binding, *Deutsche Königspfalzen*, 72–98; see also Wolfgang Braunfels, ed., *Karl der Grosse: Werk und Wirkung* (Aachen: Schwann, 1965), 395–400.

12 John D. Niles, Tom Christensen, and Marijane Osborn, *Beowulf and Lejre* (Turnhout: Brepols, 2007).

> If one man slays another on the king's premises, he shall pay 50 shillings compensation.[13]

In the Laws of the West Saxon king, Ine, of the late seventh century, special protection is offered by the king's "house" (*hus*):

> If anyone fights in the king's house, he shall forfeit all his property, and it shall be for the king to decide whether he shall be put to death or not.[14]

The word *hus* here need not necessarily make us think of a more diminutive structure than a hall, and it is noticeable that in the ninth-century West Saxon Laws of Alfred, which drew extensively on those of Ine, a similar clause, but in a rather more developed form, uses "king's hall" (*cyninges healle*):

> If anyone fights or draws his weapon in the king's hall, and if he is arrested, it shall be for the king to decide whether he shall be put to death, or permitted to live, in case the king is willing to forgive him.[15]

In the same law-code, there is a fine of 120 shillings laid down for breaking into the king's "burh" (that is, fortified place), although it is not certain whether this term would have encompassed a hall such as Heorot.[16]

If "burh" was in some way synonymous with "hall," however, it may be that the most interesting evidence in the Old English laws for our discussion is the relatively late anonymous fragment known as *Pax*, which its editor, Felix Liebermann, dated to *c.*910–*c.*1060, but Patrick Wormald thought more precisely might have been associated with King Æthelred's Wantage Code of 978–1008 (III Æthelred). This reads:

> Thus far shall the peace of the king be from the gate of his burh, where he resides, in the four directions, that is 3 miles and 3 furlongs and 3 acre-widths and 9 feet and 9 handwidths and 9 barleycorns.[17]

13 "Gif in cyninges tune man mannan ofslea, L scill' gebete": Abt 5.

14 "Gwif hwa gefeohte on cyninges huse, sie he scyldig ealles his ierfes, 7 sie on cyninges dome, hwæðer he líf age þe nage": Ine 6.

15 "Gif hwa in cyninges healle gefeohte, oððe his wæpn gebrede, 7 hine mon gefó, sie ðæt on cyninges dome, swa deað swa lif, swa he him forgifan wille": Af 7.

16 "Cyninges burgbryce bið CXX scill.": Af 40.

17 Liebermann, *Gesetze*, 1: 390 (see also 3: 230): "Đus feor sceal beon þaes cinges grið fram his burhgeate, þær he is sittende, on feower healfe his, ðæt is III mila 7 III furlang 7 III æcera bræde 7 IX fóta 7 IX scæftmunda 7 IX berecorna." See Patrick Wormald, *The Making of English Law: King Alfred to the Twelfth Century*, vol. 1: *Legislation and Its Limits* (Oxford: Blackwell, 1998), 371–72.

This very precise formulation of protection sounds almost like a charm, especially with the use of what was possibly the sacral number nine, and certainly suggests the existence of some sort of passive protection attached to the king's burh.[18]

Surveying these clauses, Liebermann argued that the importance of the hall and the penalties for attacking it actually increased during the Anglo-Saxon period, the implication being that, far from being an echo of a distant Germanic past, this sort of protection was of current, perhaps increasing, importance in the early Middle Ages.[19] Liebermann's observation suggests a possible parallel between whatever protection the hall may have offered and the protection offered by churches through their rights of sanctuary. Such rights too seem to have been increased, or at least formalized, in the course of the ninth, tenth, and eleventh centuries, and thus seemingly to have moved in parallel with the increasing protection offered to halls by the laws.[20]

A possible resonance between ecclesiastical sanctuary and the protection offered by the hall may be found in one of the details given by *Beowulf* of the monster Grendel's attacks on Heorot. In Michael Alexander's translation, the relevant lines (166–69) read:

> Again and again the enemy of man [Grendel]
> stalking unseen struck terrible
> and bitter blows. In the black nights
> he camped in the hall, under Heorot's golden roof;
> yet he could not touch the treasure-throne
> against the Lord's will, whose love was unknown to him.[21]

For the present paper, the interest of these lines, as they are understood in this and many other translations, is that the reference to the treasure-throne is reminiscent of the account of rights of sanctuary which is given, in the context of the church of Hexham in Northumberland, by the

18 See William A. Chaney, "Aethelberht's Code and the King's Number," *American Journal of Legal History*, 6 (1962): 151–77 (esp. 155–56), and below, 121–40.

19 Liebermann, *Gesetze*, 2: 553 (s.v. "Königshof").

20 David Hall, "The Sanctuary of St Cuthbert," in *St Cuthbert, His Cult and His Community to* AD *1200*, ed. Gerald Bonner, David Rollason, and Clare Stancliffe (Woodbridge: Boydell Press, 1989), 425–36. See also J.C. Cox, "The Sanctuaries and Sanctuary Seekers of Yorkshire," *Archaeological Journal* 68 (1911): 273–99; Norman Maclaren Trenholme, *The Right of Sanctuary in England* (University of Missouri Studies, 1903); and below, 131–40.

21 Alexander, trans., *Beowulf*, lines 166–69.

twelfth-century writer, Richard of Hexham.[22] David Hall has analyzed the graded system of fines for breach of sanctuary described in this, from the minimum payable for assaulting someone who had taken sanctuary within the "four crosses outside the town" (*infra quatuor cruces extra villam*), to the maximum payable for assault on someone in sanctuary "within the doors of the choir of the church" (*infra valvas chori*). Were a person to be assaulted or killed who had taken sanctuary at the "seat by the high altar" (*cathedra lapidea iuxta altare*), the *friðstol* ("seat of peace") as Richard of Hexham tells us it was called, or at the shrine containing the relics behind the altar, this was an unemendable (*botolos*) crime. The treasure-throne of Heorot enjoyed a protection not unlike that afforded by the *friðstol* of the church of Hexham, and the protection of both was underwritten by the Lord's will.

A parallelism between protection of the hall and ecclesiastical sanctuary seems apparent also in the Laws of Alfred, clause 42 of which relates to a man who "knows his adversary to be residing at home." Such a man, the law lays down, may besiege him in his home but not attack him for a period of seven days. "And if, after seven days, he will submit and hand over his weapons, he shall keep him unscathed for thirty days, and send formal notice of his position to his kinsmen and friends." This seems very close to the fifth clause of the Laws of Alfred, which relates to ecclesiastical sanctuary and lays down that a man who has fled to a church cannot be dragged out for seven days, and when he is brought out shall be held for thirty days while "formal notice of his position" is sent to his kinsmen.[23]

There is, however, a serious difficulty in the way of such an interpretation, in that the lines from *Beowulf* are subject to considerable debate as to their meaning, and in particular with regard to who it was who was prevented from approaching the "treasure-throne." The Old English text reads:

Heorot eardode,
sincfāge sel swveartum nihtum;
Nō he þone gifstōl gretan mōste,
māþðum for metode, nē his myne wisse.[24]

22 James Raine, ed., *The Priory of Hexham, Its Chroniclers, Endowments and Annals*, vol. 1, Surtees Society 44 (Durham: Surtees Society, 1864), 61–62.

23 Af 5: 1–3, 42: 1–3 (note that 42: 2 makes explicit the connection with ecclesiastical sanctuary); see Charles H. Riggs, *Criminal Asylum in Anglo-Saxon Law*, University of Florida Monographs, Social Sciences 18 (Gainesville: University of Florida Press, 1963), 29–34.

24 Fulk, Bjork, and Niles, eds., *Klaeber's Beowulf*, lines 166–69.

Aside from the problem of whether the words *gifstōl* and *māþðum* can be brought together to yield the meaning "treasure-throne," there is the more serious problem for our discussion of to whom "he" is referring in the third line of the above quotation, whether to Grendel (as most translators, including Alexander, have assumed) or to King Hrothgar, the builder of Heorot and therefore the principal party injured by Grendel's attacks. The most obvious reading of the text is indeed that "he" was Grendel, but Jane Roberts has recently argued that the use of the word *swā* two lines before introduces a section which draws "the elements together by contrasting the positions of Grendel and Hrothgar," and thus opens the possibility (probability in Roberts's view) that "he" is Hrothgar. Roberts translates:

> and he [Hrothgar] could not approach that noble seat, [his] treasure, because of the Creator, or know His purpose.[25]

It would then have been Hrothgar who was prevented by Grendel's hostile presence in Heorot from approaching the throne, a circumstance which had arisen as a result of Hrothgar's ignorance of God; so the point of the lines would be to emphasize the humiliation of Hrothgar. Roberts is not the first to have put this forward, although it has not hitherto commanded any scholarly consensus, and the meaningfulness of her translation of these lines is open to question.[26] If we accept her view, however, we cannot accept the interpretation that God was preventing Grendel from approaching the throne because of some special protection attaching to it, so there would be no grounds for perceiving the protection offered by the *gifstol* in Heorot as similar to that offered by the *friðstol* in Hexham.

Let us now consider the second possibility to be explored in this paper, that is that the protection attaching to the hall derived not from the building but from the presence of particular persons in it. A hint in this direction may be found in the fourth law-code of King Æthelstan, which reads in translation from the Old English fragment of this code:

25 Jane Roberts, "Understanding Hrothgar's Humiliation: *Beowulf* Lines 144–74 in Context," in *Text, Image, Interpretation: Studies in Anglo-Saxon Literature and its Insular Context in Honour of Éamonn Ó Carragáin*, ed. Alastair Minnis and Jane Roberts (Turnhout: Brepols, 2007), 355–67.

26 Roberts, "Understanding Hrothgar's Humiliation," 357 n. 8, citing Stanley B. Greenfield, "'Gifstol' and Goldhoard in Beowulf," in *Old English Studies in Honour of John C. Pope*, ed. Robert B. Burlin and Edward B. Irving, Jr. (Toronto: University of Toronto Press, 1974), 107–17, and David Clipsham, "*Beowulf* 168–169," in *In Geardagum: Essays on Old and Middle English Language and Literature*, ed. Loren C. Gruber and Dean Loganbill (Denver, Colorado: Society for New Language Study, 1974), 19–24.

> If any thief or robber has fled to the king, or to any church and to the bishop, he should have respite for nine days.
>
> If he flees to an ealdorman, or an abbot or a thegn, he shall have respite of three days.[27]

This does not of course necessarily refer to the hall as such, but rather to the presence of the king or lord as the source of protection. If we suppose that the law-maker envisaged that the king or the ealdorman or the thegn would be found in his hall, however, the implication may nevertheless be that that protection was in some sense transferred to the hall. We should note also that the parallels to ecclesiastical sanctuary seem close. The clauses deal with a fugitive from justice, and the respite from pursuit offered is a time-limited one in just the same way that the respites offered by sanctuary were time-limited.

Let us now turn to our third possibility, that is that the protection offered by the hall derived from the ritualized use of alcoholic drink within it. It is at this point that we should turn again to Enright's *Lady with a Mead Cup* of 1996, and the article preparatory to it published in 1988.[28] Enright's thesis, as it concerns the present paper, is essentially that the power wielded by an early medieval king, which Enright envisages as being focused on what he calls the warband but which we might also think of as the court, has two possible sources, which he defines as "military" and "domestic." Where the source of power was military, the king or lord was the "leader over followers who voluntarily join his warband and who grant obedience because it is their unfettered will to do so"; where the source of power was domestic, the lord was the "head of a household who exercises patriarchal authority over wife, minor sons, daughters, slaves and dependants whose desires need not be taken into account since they are not themselves free to make decisions but depend on him for protection and are, therefore, under his guardianship or *munt*." Enright argued that the source of power in early medieval lordship, royal and non-royal, was domestic, and he presented what seem to me to be very interesting philological arguments that even the quintessentially military warband owed its subordination to its lord to the conception of it as a domestic institution. Joining it was the equivalent of being adopted into the lord's family and thus, as a

27 "Gif hwilc þeof oððe reafere gesohte þone cing oþþe hwylce cyrican 7 ðone biscop, þæt he hæbbe nigon nihta fyrst. 7 gif he ealderman oððe abbud oþþe ðegen sece, hæbbe ðeora nihta fyrst": IV As 6: 1–2. I owe this reference to T.B. Lambert.

28 Michael J. Enright, "Lady with a Mead-Cup: Ritual, Group Cohesion and Hierarchy in the Germanic Warband," *Frühmittelalterliche Studien* 22 (1988): 170–203; Enright, *Lady with a Mead Cup*.

family-member, coming under his patriarchal authority or guardianship. This familial character of the warband was, Enright argued, formalized through ritualized use of alcoholic drink in the hall. His starting-point was that the role of Hrothgar's queen Wealtheow in *Beowulf* in distributing drink was a crucial aspect of power; in his words "weapons and liquor bind the follower to the *comitatus*."[29]

In Enright's intepretation then, ritualized drinking was crucial to the power which the hall's lord exercised over his warband. Did this ritualized drinking then entitle the hall to special protection? A series of clauses in the early English law-codes relate to drinking and to the particular protection attached to it. The earliest is a clause from the early seventh-century laws of King Æthelberht of Kent, which reads in translation as follows:

> If the king drinks at a person's home (*ham*), and a person should do anything seriously dishonest there, let him pay two[-fold] restitution.[30]

In chronological sequence, there then follow clauses in the somewhat later code of the Kentish kings Hlothhere and Eadric, issued between 673 and 685, which concern the penalties attaching to fighting where drinking is taking place, and which read:

29 Enright, *Lady with a Mead Cup*, 38–96, esp. 70–71. Enright's book was not widely reviewed. Alexander Callander Murray, "[Review of Michael J. Enright, *Lady with a Mead Cup*]," *Speculum* 74, no. 4 (1999): 1055–56, made what seem to me subjective judgments on Enright's interpretation of the tone of the passages in *Beowulf* concerning Wealtheow's role in the distribution of mead, and he was dismissive of Enright's handling of the philological evidence for the relationship between warband membership and marriage. The book, he wrote, was useful in that it discussed so many published writings, but he really had no time for what he called "this sort of scholarship." Pauline Stafford, "[Review of Michael J. Enright, *Lady with a Mead Cup*]," *Early Medieval Europe* 7 (1998): 133–35, was affronted by Enright's handling of the queen as essentially subordinate to the king, and she declared that the warband context discussed by Enright could have no relevance for royal courts of the Carolingian period and later. For all its problems, Enright's cross-period, cross-disciplinary scholarship deserves better than this, and part of the purpose of this paper is to generate debate about it, not least because the issues that it raises seem to me to have real significance. For a much more positive comment on Enright's work, see Donald A. Bullough, *Friends, Neighbours and Fellow-Drinkers: Aspects of Community and Conflict in the Early Medieval West*, H.M. Chadwick Memorial Lectures 1 (Cambridge: Department of Anglo-Saxon, Norse and Celtic, University of Cambridge, 1991), 13 n. 22.

30 Abt 3: "Gif cyning æt mannes ham drincæþ 7 ðær man lyswæs hwæt gedo, twibote gebete" (in the work from which this translation is taken, Oliver, *BEL*, this is clause 9).

> If a person takes a cup from another where men are drinking without [the man from whom the cup was taken being at] fault, according to the established right let him give a shilling to him who owns the house (*flet*), and 6 shillings to him from whom the cup was taken, and 12 shillings to the king.
>
> If a person should draw a weapon where men are drinking and no harm is done there, a shilling to him who owns that house (*flet*), and 12 shillings to the king. If that house becomes bloodied, let him pay the man [the price for violation of] his protection and fifty shillings to the king.[31]

Between 688 and 694, in Wessex, we find in the Laws of King Ine of Wessex a clause similarly dealing with conflict in the context of drinking:

> If two quarrel over their cups and one bears it with patience, the other must pay a fine of 30 shillings.[32]

We should not exaggerate the significance of this, since it occurs at the end of a series of clauses relating to fighting in various buildings. Indeed, there is nothing concerning drink in the West Saxon Laws of King Alfred from the late ninth century, although there are clauses about fighting in a house.[33] Seen alongside the other texts cited here, however, it may seem more significant.

Moreover, in the early tenth century there is a remarkable clause in the sixth law-code of King Æthelstan of Wessex, also known as "the ordinance of the bishops and reeves of the London district." This concerns the appropriate times and perhaps rituals which should accompany meetings of "the officials of the hundred-groups (*hyndenmenn*) and those who have charge of the bodies of ten (*þa þe ða teoþunge bewitan*)." According to the clause in question, they will meet every month "if we have leisure and can do so – whether it be when the butts are being filled (*byttfyllinge*), or on any

31 Hl 12–14: "Gif man oðrum steop asette ðær mæn drincen, buton scylde, an eald riht scilling agelde þam þe þæt flet age, 7 VI scilling þam þe man þone steap aset, 7 cynge XII scillings. Gif man wæpn abregde þær mæn drincen 7 ðær man nan yfel ne deþ, scilling þan þe þæt flet age, 7 cyninge XII scillings. Gif þæt flet geblodgad wyrþe, forgylde þem mæn his mundbyrd 7 cyninge L scillings" (in the work from which this translation is taken, Oliver, *BEL*, these are clauses 8, 9, and 9: 1).

32 Ine 6: 5: "Gif ðonne on gebeorscipe hie geciden, 7 oðer hiora mid geðylde hit forbere, geselle se oðer XXX scill. to wite."

33 Af 39.

other occasion that may be convenient to us."[34] The butts were presumably being filled with an alcoholic beverage and, although this is not stated as essential to meetings, it is very striking that it should be mentioned in connection with them in this way.

The only other clause in pre-Conquest English law-codes referring to alcoholic drink is in King Æthelred of England's code, issued at Wantage between 978 and 1008. This code, which is intended for the area of the Danelaw, sets the peace granted to the meeting of the borough and the wapentake alongside that granted to the alehouse (*ealahuse*):

> And the peace which is given in the meeting of one borough is to be atoned for with six hundreds; and that which is given in a wapentake, is to be atoned for with a hundred, if it is broken; and that which is given in an alehouse, is to be atoned for, if a man is killed, with six half marks, and if no one is killed, with twelve ones.[35]

Finally, and perhaps most interestingly, there is a clause in the early twelfth-century code known as the *Leges Henrici Primi*, which refers at some length to the King's Peace (*pax regis*) attaching to a drinking assembly (*potatio*). The clause reads:

> Concerning the granting of the king's peace during a drinking assembly. In the case of every drinking assembly which has been set up for the making of any gift or purchase or guild meeting or for anything of this kind, the peace of God and of the master of the house is first of all to be established, by a public announcement previously made, among those who have assembled, and the demand is to be made that if anyone brings a charge against another there for whatever reason, if he is agreeable he shall do this publicly, and security shall be given to him for the doing of justice at an appropriate time, as and where it is just.[36]

34 VI As 8: 1: "Þæt we us gegaderian à emban ænne monað, gif we mágon 7 ǽmton habban, þa hyndemenn 7 þa þe ða teoþunge bewitan, swa mid byttfyllinge swa elles swa us tóanhágie, 7 witen hwæt ure gecwydræddene gelæst sy."

35 III Atr 1: 2: "And þæt grið, þæt man sylleð on I burhgaþinðe, bete man þæt mid VI hundr̄; and þær man sylle on wæpentake, bete man þæt mid hundr̄, gif hit man brecð; and þæt man sylle on ealahuse, bete man þæt æt deadum menn mid VI healfmarce 7 æt cwicon mid XII oran." On this code, see Wormald, *Making of English Law*, 322–23, 326–27.

36 Hn 81–81: 1: "De pace regis danda in potatione. In omni potatione, dationi uel emptioni uel gilde uel ad quidlibet in hunc modum preparata, primo pax Dei et domini inter eos qui conuenerint publica prenuntiatione ponenda est, et rogandum ut siquis alium ibi quacumque deuocet occasione, si placet, palam faciat, et rectum ei uadietur competenti termino peragendum, sicut et ubi iustum erit."

Neither Bullough nor anyone else seems to have considered these clauses in connection with Enright's arguments, although Bullough did note the clause from the Laws of Æthelred about the alehouse.[37] Enright's interpretation can be brought into stark relief, however, by comparing it with the approach taken by Liebermann, who connected the clauses in question with the condemnation of drunkenness in Anglo-Saxon writings, noting for example Boniface's condemnation of alcoholism as the English vice, the prohibitions on drunkenness paired with those on gluttony in the Laws of Æthelred, and the suspension of drunken priests in the Penitential of Theodore.[38] Liebermann recognized the importance of drink itself, noting for example the frequency in Old English poetry of the use of the words *ealu* 'ale', *beor* 'beer', *medu* 'mead', *win* 'wine', and *drincan* 'to drink', and the various compounds of them which are impressively numerous in the case of *beor* and *medu*;[39] and he noted too that Old English *gebeorscipe* can be translated by Latin *convivium* 'feast, banquet', as the Old English translator of Bede's *Ecclesiastical History of the English People* rendered the word in Bede's account of the feast at Whitby when Caedmon received his gift of song.[40] But he essentially interpreted drinking as a social activity, and sometimes a troublesome one owing to the effects of drunkenness. Although he acknowledged that beer-feasts were also the scene of gifts, purchases, and guild-meetings, for which of course he drew on the clauses of the *Leges Henrici Primi* cited above, he was not willing to suggest a possible connection, distant as it would be, with the famous passage in Tacitus's *Germania* to the effect that the Germans made decisions during feasts:

> They often make a feast an occasion for discussing such affairs as the ending of feuds, the arrangement of marriage alliances, the adoption of chiefs, and even the choice of peace and war.[41]

37 Bullough, *Friends, Neighbours and Fellow-Drinkers*, 26.

38 Liebermann, *Gesetze*, 2: 312–13.

39 Cf., for more recent studies, Christine Fell, "Old English *Beor*," *Leeds Studies in English* 8 (1975): 76–95; Bill Griffiths, "The Old English Alcoholic Vocabulary: A Reexamination," *Durham University Journal* 47 (1986): 231–37.

40 Angus Cameron, Ashley Crandell Amos, and Antonette diPaolo Healey, eds., *Dictionary of Old English: A to G Online*, http://www.doe.utoronto.ca (accessed 8 September 2008), s.v. "gebeorscipe," gives "feast at which (alcoholic) drink is served." See also Hugh Magennis, *Anglo-Saxon Appetites: Food and Drink and Their Consumption in Old English and Related Literature* (Dublin: Four Courts, 1998), 31; and Pollington, *Mead-Hall*, 55–64.

41 Rudolf Much, ed., *Die Germania des Tacitus*, 3rd ed. (Heidelberg: Carl Winter, 1967), ch. 22: "Sed et de reconciliandis invicem inimicis et iungendis affinitatibus et adsciscendis principibus, de pace denique ac bello plerumque in conviviis con-

It is clear from the context that a "feast" was synonymous with a "drinking-bout." Tacitus too seems bothered about the practice he describes, and remarks rather implausibly in succeeding sentences that the Germans then revise the decisions when they are sober the next day;[42] and his embarrassment seems in a sense to be echoed by Liebermann's, when that scholar awkwardly admits that the beer-feast can fulfil such serious functions as a sort of incidental by-product of social enjoyment.

There was clearly a tension beneath the surface of Liebermann's interpretation of drinking as a social activity. He was concerned about the clause quoted above from the Wantage code of Æthelred, in which he notes that the fine for breaking the peace enjoyed by the ale-house is too high to be a private fine, and is mentioned in one breath with fines for breaking the peace of borough, wapentake, and hundred courts.[43] Why should an ale-house have been treated in the same sort of way as a legal court? Why, in the Laws of Æthelberht, should particular protection (for breach of which twofold compensation was exacted) have been granted to someone's home when the king was drinking there? Liebermann maintained that it was the king's presence which was the source of protection and that the drinking was an irrelevance; elsewhere he adds that in this clause and in the clause from the Laws of Hlothhere and Eadric drinking just means "being a guest of someone's hospitality." Insofar as he recognized more serious aspects of drinking, he believed that these arose from the association between drinking and guild-meetings. Thus he commented that the protection which the Laws of Æthelberht seemed to extend to drinking with the king in one's home was somehow to do with the fact that this was in reality a guild-feast. That was how he also interpreted the clause quoted above from the *Leges Henrici Primi*, which does indeed refer to guild-feasts but only as one aspect of what it was legislating for. For Liebermann, however, it was solely concerned with laying down rules for a guild-feast, and the rubric about the king's protection was somehow a confusion on the part of the twelfth-century compiler. In general, Liebermann proposed that the many citations of "beer-feasts" in the laws were in fact to do with guild-feasts. Drinking itself was not what was at issue; what mattered was the organization of guilds.[44]

---

sultant." The translation is from H. Mattingly and S.A. Handforth, trans., *Tacitus: The Agricola and the Germania*, rev. ed. (Penguin Classics, Harmondsworth: Penguin, 1970).

42 It should be noted that this was also said of the Scythians and the Persians by earlier writers such as Herodotus (Much, *Die Germania*, 311).

43 Liebermann, *Gesetze*, 2: 312 (paragraph 7e).

44 Liebermann, *Gesetze*, 2: 312–13 (s.v. "Biergelage"), 445–48 (s.v. "Genossenschaft").

Liebermann was thus advancing a particular interpretation, with some points of tension visible and acknowledged in it, but an interpretation nevertheless, and one which had no truck with attempts to relate Tacitus's *Germania* or *Beowulf* to the early English laws. Those works scarcely figure in Liebermann's commentary. That he has generally carried the day is evident in the failure of such a widely used reference work as the *Blackwell's Encyclopaedia of Anglo-Saxon England* to do more than devote a paragraph to alcoholic drink treated as nothing more than just another beverage,[45] or indeed in Alban Gautier's excellent book on feasting, where drinking is treated as a sign of social distinction but nothing more.[46] It is evident in a more specific way in the translation of the Old English word *flet* in the Laws of Hlothhere and Eadric as "house," which is what we find in both Attenborough's, Whitelock's, and Oliver's translations.[47] This makes the clauses about fines payable to the owner of the *flet* when there is quarrelling or weapons are drawn sound a very private affair, and the clauses seem just about disturbances in anyone's house where a party happens to be going on. But *flet* of course could equally be translated "hall" as in Latin *aula*, and that seems to be its meaning in *Beowulf*, as when (in line 1024):

> Bēowulf geþah ful on flette.
> Beowulf drank with the company in the hall.[48]

We might then be dealing with something much grander and more important. The protection offered to those drinking in the hall could in reality be

45 Debby Banham, "Food and Drink," in *The Blackwell Encyclopedia of Anglo-Saxon England*, ed. Michael Lapidge, et al. (Oxford: Blackwell, 1999), 190–91. One notable exception, already cited, is Bullough, *Friends, Neighbours and Fellow-Drinkers*, who refers to a very stimulating, if somewhat tongue-in-cheek, study of the importance of alcohol in *Beowulf*: Paul Edwards, "Art and Alcoholism in Beowulf," *Durham University Journal* 72 (1980): 127–31. An interesting study of the role of alcohol in Welsh literature is Marged Haycock, *"Where Cider Ends, There Ale Begins to Reign": Drink in Medieval Welsh Poetry*, H.M. Chadwick Memorial Lectures 10 (Cambridge: Department of Anglo-Saxon, Norse and Celtic, University of Cambridge, 1999). (I owe this reference to Richard Gameson.)

46 Alban Gautier, *Le Festin dans l'Angleterre Anglo-Saxonne (Ve–XIe siècle)* (Rennes: Presses Universitaires de Rennes, 2006). See, however, Magennis, *Anglo-Saxon Appetites*, 21–36, where the significance of drinking in Old English poetic and prose accounts of feasts is discussed.

47 Attenborough, *Laws*, 21; Dorothy Whitelock, ed., *English Historical Documents*, 2nd ed., vol. 1: *c.500–1042* (London: Eyre and Spottiswood, 1979), no. 30; Oliver, ed., *Beginnings of English Law*, 133.

48 Fulk, Bjork, and Niles, eds., *Klaeber's Beowulf*, line 1024; Alexander, trans., *Beowulf*.

a protection for just the sort of decision-making meetings with alcoholic drink which Tacitus described.

Should the clauses from the early English laws be viewed in the context of Enright's argument that drinking was a ritualized process, closely bound up with the means by which power was expressed and made effective, and bound up with the projection of that power as rooted in the protection and hospitality offered by the *paterfamilias* to those who were either real members of his family, or adopted members as the warriors of his warband were? As in the early eleventh-century Old English poem, the *Battle of Maldon*, drink is what seals undertakings to act, as the warriors refer to "the words that we uttered many a time over the mead," that is to what they have undertaken during drinking in the hall.[49] Likewise in the Old Welsh, possibly seventh-century poem, *The Gododdin* by Aneirin, the warriors are entertained before they set out to battle in a hall at Edinburgh, the "defining characteristic" of which, Marged Haycock observes, is mead. "Mead in early Welsh poetry," she continues, "is the central symbol of sustenance of the warband, its solidarity and community of purpose."[50]

It is instructive to think about the clauses from the early English laws in this way. We have already referred to the Laws of Æthelberht's penalty for perpetrating an evil deed where the king is drinking. The scale of the penalty, a two-fold one, could surely suggest that we are dealing here with the disruption of a formal meeting which was an affront to established power. We should be impressed by the regulations of the Laws of Hlothhere and Eadric on taking away the stoup of a drinker and the drawing of weapons "where men are drinking." The prominence of these clauses in the code and the scale of fine imposed surely suggests that the offences being penalized are more than rowdiness at a drinking party. When we consider that Gautier has shown how formal feasts were in their organization and seating-plan,[51] we might well be more inclined to think that taking a stoup from someone else was a formal offence in a context where drink was literally the fuel of decision-making.[52] Indeed, we might begin to think that the word *gebeorscipe*, "beer-ship" as Bosworth and Toller translate it,[53] is more than just "beer-drinking" and means something closer to "member-

49 Donald Scragg, ed., *The Battle of Maldon AD 991* (Oxford: Blackwell, 1991), lines 212–14.

50 Haycock, "*Where Cider Ends*," 13.

51 Gautier, *Le Festin*, 83–117, 254–55.

52 For a thought-provoking discussion of the possible symbolism of seizing a stoup of wine in connection with Celtic mythology, see Lisi Oliver, "Spilled Wine and Lost Sovereignty in Chrétien's *Perceval*," *Neuphilologische Mitteilungen* 97 (1996): 91–102.

ship of those who drink beer because that is part and parcel of the decision-making process in English political life."

But above all we should, with due regard to all the problems and difficulties inherent in the use of that text, revisit clause 81 of the *Leges Henrici Primi*. Let us by way of conclusion look at it again. First there is the rubric which so worried Liebermann: "De pace regis danda in potatione." As the most recent editor, L.J. Downer, noted, Pollock had treated the word *regis* here as an error for *domini*, and Liebermann himself argued that the rubric just meant the "preservation of a general peace in the community."[54] But, whatever the truth of this (and the text of the clause does indeed refer to the lord rather than the king), the clause is nevertheless about the giving of a protection to *potationes*, "drinking sessions." The *potatio* could be for guild-business, as the clause states, but it could also be for buying and selling; and it is clear from what follows that it also served as the context in which one brought "a charge against another for whatever reason." The peace of the *potatio* was established by "a public announcement previously made," and it was the "peace of God and of the lord." This formal and much more important aspect of the *potatio* is further emphasized by the follow-up clause:

> If after peace has been established in this way there is any misconduct by those who are drinking together in the house, amends must be made by payment of the fine for *ouerseunessa* to the lord of the house or to the person to whom it is appropriate, if the offender is charged and held after being seized on the spot, or even though he may be subject to the lordship of another person.[55]

The aim of this paper has been not to reach any definite conclusion, but rather to suggest the potential of pursuing the three ways in which the early the medieval hall may have enjoyed protection. The first of these, that that protection of the hall derived from its status as a building, just as sanctuary rights pertained to the very fabric of a church, carries the implication that the hall enjoyed protection even when there was no one in it (as – if we reject Roberts's argument for the moment – Grendel was prevented from approaching the throne when Heorot was deserted). The references in

53 Joseph Bosworth and T. Northcote Toller, eds., *An Anglo-Saxon Dictionary* (Oxford: Oxford University Press, 1898).

54 Downer, *LHP*, 401.

55 "Si, postquam pax ita posita sit, a combibentibus in domo quid agatur, ouerseunessa est emendandum domino domus (uel cui proueniet), si crauatus et retentus sit ibi, et sit alterius dominii": *Leges Henrici Primi* 81.2. On the meaning of *ouerseunessa*, which was a fine, see Downer, *LHP*, 435–37.

the laws to the protection of houses without reference to the presence of the owner or anyone else may point in this direction, and we need to hold the possibility open. The second possibility, that protection depended on the presence of a person whose status determined the extent of it, carries the implication that it may not be exclusively connected to the hall at all, although some of the references in the laws can be read in this way. The third possibility, that protection attached particularly to the drinking taking place within the hall, is more specific to halls. It carries the implication that the hall only enjoyed whatever protection this was while the drinking was going on, which seems consistent with the texts, and especially with the passage quoted from the *Leges Henrici Primi.* The hall would thus only have enjoyed this protection during the formalized use of drink which played a crucial role in meetings and the decision-making process which took place in halls. Drinking conferred status on such meetings and was the reason that they and the halls in which they took place benefited from a particular level of protection. It is perhaps this third possibility which offers the most promising lines of thought. If drinking was in this way crucial to the very status of the hall at least while the drinking ritual was taking place, it is clear why Old English poetry refers to the hall as the "mead-hall," or indeed "beer-hall," or "wine-hall."[56] The drinking which took place in it made it what it was, at least from the point of view of the protection it enjoyed.

These possibilities are, as has been stressed already, no more than that, and nor need they be mutually exclusive ones. Protection was clearly a complex concept, and the hall may have benefited from different levels of it in different circumstances. Neither the evidence nor our understanding of it permits anything more definite; but it is hoped that enough has been presented to convince readers that the mead-hall is a subject worth pursuing in the context of the nature of protection in the early Middle Ages.

56 Magennis, *Anglo-Saxon Appetites*, 23, citing *Beowulf*, lines 484, 482, 695 (Fulk, Bjork, and Niles, eds., *Klaeber's Beowulf*).

CLAIRE TAYLOR
University of Nottingham

Royal Protection in Aquitaine and Gascony by *c.*1000: The Public, the Private, and the Princely

Introduction

T.B. Lambert's schema of themes to be addressed in considering the subject of royal protection raises some very interesting issues for the study of the early medieval West.[1] Especially thought-provoking is the contrast between the equality in forms of protection that all free people could, at least theoretically, expect from Carolingian public authority,[2] and the inequality in protection afforded through the granting of royal privileges, almost exclusively to the Church.[3] To François-Louis Ganshof, the privilege represented "certain legal rights derogatory to the common law, more favourable than it [to the party receiving the privilege]."[4] Privileges distinguished between who could and who could not be legitimately exploited by those in a position to use force to compel them. Two types of protection offered by kings are important here, therefore, and they operated in different ways legally. In essence, whereas the king was supposed to protect all of the free from personal violation and theft, the privileged were also protected from legal forms of economic exploitation, such as rents, tolls, and taxation.

The context of the drawn-out decline in Carolingian royal power is also something that makes a discussion of royal protection in *c.*1000 of interest. To Ganshof, Carolingian public authority derived in large degree from the Carolingian family's assumed imperial role as promoter and defender of the Church.[5] If this was undermined, how might it affect the

1 See above, 1–16.
2 See, most influentially, Marc Bloch, *Feudal Society*, trans. L.A. Manyon, 2 vols. (Chicago: University of Chicago Press, 1961), 2: 361, 368; Chris Wickham, "Debate: The 'Feudal Revolution,'" *Past and Present*, 155 (1997), 196–208, at 198.
3 Bloch, *Feudal Society*, 2: 362.
4 François-Louis Ganshof, "The Institutional Framework of the Frankish Monarchy: A Survey of its General Characteristics," in idem, *The Carolingians and the Frankish Monarchy*, trans. Janet Sondheimer (London: Longman, 1971), 86–110, at 93.
5 Ganshof, "The Institutional Framework," 88–89.

practical operation of royal protection of clerics and Church property? He suggested that one of "the several factors that explain the spreading of the privilege was the inadequate protection guaranteed to persons and possessions by the irregular and ineffective action of officials,"[6] because "the monarchy was not even in a position to maintain the public peace to a satisfactory level, that is to provide normally effective protection."[7]

Ganshof's interpretation of the decline of the Carolingians and its implications has been severely undermined, for example by Simon MacLean.[8] The king needed men who were powerful in the regions, MacLean argues, because he could not act there himself. The marquises (*marchiones*) under Charles the Fat were indeed both powerful locally and capable of independent action, but did not necessarily use their power to act autonomously. Logically, therefore, the issue of how the privilege worked to protect might need re-evaluating too. In Ganshof's schema, defiance of privileges incurred the exercise of the *bannum*, the right to command and prohibit, on the part of counts, to whom it was delegated by the king. In other words, a king could not guarantee that no harm would be done to those enjoying privileges, but there would be consequences, enacted by his representatives on his behalf, if harm was done. This system too, it follows, relied on locally and independently powerful counts who could be understood as able to enforce royal prerogatives without needing the immediate protection of kings themselves; whereas authority could be delegated, actual power to enforce the *bannum* had, logically, to be independent to some degree.

However, in the case of Aquitaine and Gascony, locally powerful princes do not seem to have been engaging with the centre in this way. Ganshof offers no examples, even from the period of the peak of Carolingian power, of the operation of royal courts of immunity presided over by an advocate (*advocatus*), such as operated elsewhere.[9] Whereas some Church lands remained royal protectorates – most notably the archdiocese of Bourges – as lay abbots the princes of Aquitaine and Gascony became

6 François-Louis Ganshof, *Frankish Institutions under Charlemagne*, trans. Bryce and Mary Lyon (New York: Norton Library, 1970), 45 and see idem, "The Institutional Framework," 93.

7 Ganshof, "The Institutional Framework," 90.

8 Simon MacLean, *Kingship and Politics in the Late Ninth Century: Charles the Fat and the End of the Carolingian Empire* (Cambridge: Cambridge University Press, 2003). For another example of traditional literature suggesting the rise of regional princely power as the antithesis of centrally strong Carolingian royal authority that it usurped from the ninth century, see Jan Dhondt, *Études sur la naissance des principautés territoriales en France, IXe–Xe siècle*, Rijksuniversiteit te Gent Faculteit van Letteren en Wijsbegeerte, Werke 102 (Bruges: De Tempel, 1948), esp. 231–58.

9 Cf. Ganshof, *Frankish Institutions*, 46–48.

masters as well as protectors of both monks and dioceses, by forcing acceptance of their own candidates over the heads of royal nominees.[10] This was taking place even in the ninth century, when Aquitaine was still viewed by the Carolingians as one of their kingdoms.

Taking this further, some historians have asserted that there followed a decline in public authority at a more local level, leading to the collapse of judicial institutions and the rise of private arrangements in the later Carolingian era. In the Mâconnais, as studied by Duby and Bois, and in Catalonia, as studied by Bonnassie, the degradation of comital, or public, courts arguably accelerated *c.*1000.[11] The Carolingian concept of protection of the free by the free, what Wickham characterizes as the Carolingian "dialectic of public and private ... normative behaviour,"[12] was being seriously undermined. The disappearance of these courts apparently exacerbated the descent of the vulnerable laity into servitude.

This aspect of the traditional interpretation is also being challenged and does not entirely hold for the far south-west, as will be discussed later. Princely power, that of the dukes of Gascony and Aquitaine, was in the ascendant, and was not necessarily even in opposition to that of the viscounts and castellans, who were in fact being bound more closely to the princes by *c.*1000 rather than slipping from their control.

We might therefore expect to find delegated royal authority in operation in judicial contexts, but we do not. Instead, "bishops substituted themselves for the king in the mission to defend the churches and the 'poor' free men."[13] Thus, the council called at Charroux in Poitou in 989[14] has come to be viewed as the first meeting of the Peace of God movement, a clerically orchestrated judicial innovation in which the abbeys and their saints cast

10 See Dhondt, *Études sur la naissance des principautés*, 53, 231–58; Yves Sassier, "De l'ordre seigneurial à l'ordre féodal (fin x^e^–début xiiie siècle)," in *Pouvoirs et institutions dans la France médiévale, des origines à l'époque féodale*, ed. Olivier Guillot and Yves Sassier (Paris: A. Colin, 1994), 171–298, at 234.

11 Georges Duby, "The Evolution of Judicial Institutions," in idem, *The Chivalrous Society*, trans. Cynthia Postan (Berkeley: Edward Arnold, 1977), 15–58; Guy Bois, *La mutation de l'an mil: Lournand, village mâconnais de l'Antiquité au féodalisme*, Nouvelles études historiques (Paris: Fayard, 1989); Pierre Bonnassie, *Le Catalogne au tournant de l'an mil: croissance et mutations d'une société*, L'Aventure humaine (Paris: A. Michel, 1990). Preceding these and agreeing, although less rigid chronologically, was Bloch's *Feudal Society*, 2: 359–74.

12 Wickham, "Debate," 205.

13 Jean-Pierre Poly and Eric Bournazel, *The Feudal Transformation, 900–1200*, trans. Caroline Higgitt (New York/London: Holmes and Meier, 1991), 151.

14 Joannes Dominicus Mansi, ed., *Concilia*, introduction and 53 volumes (Graz: Akademische Druck- u. Verlagsanstalt, 1960–61; reprint of idem, *Sacrorum conciliorum nova et amplissima collectio*, 53 vols., Venice, 1759–98), 19: 89–90.

themselves as protectors of the ordinary free laity. The canons of the Peace of God councils suggest that livestock and crops were being stolen from peasants, peasants themselves were imprisoned and ransomed, and knightly wrong-doers were protected by their lords.[15] The movement quickly spread throughout Aquitaine and the Midi to Narbonne (990), Limoges, Anse, and Le Puy (all in 994), Poitiers (*c.*1000) and continued on into the eleventh century.

The implication of this tenth-century phase of the Peace of God is therefore that lay rulers, supposed to be the enforcers of social peace and defenders of those oppressed as royal representatives of public power, did not fulfil this role. If it was not the case in the south-west that they were unable to do their job, because there was no real collapse of local lay authority, why did the Peace of God movement begin here? The Peace of God, it will be argued, was part of the growth in princely power, and was not prefiguring it and certainly not operating in spite of it.

Royal power and protection in Aquitaine and Gascony

Before arriving at 989 we need to explore the historical relationship between the Carolingians and the south-west. We should note that the early histories of Aquitaine and Gascony are quite distinct. This is so even though Gascony was considered by the Franks to be part of the Kingdom of Aquitaine. We should also note that the concept of royal protection operated at different levels in these histories.

(a) Aquitaine[16]

By the end of the ninth century, Aquitaine was marginal to key Carolingian territorial and governmental activity. Probably as a result, we have relatively few Frankish sources for it, either narrative or legislative.[17] Flodoard

15 See below.

16 The accounts of Aquitaine by Jean Dhondt, Charles Higounet, and Léonce Auzias are a little dated but thorough: Dhondt, *Études sur la naissance des principautés*, esp. 169–229; Higounet, "Le groupe aristocratique en Aquitaine et en Gascogne (fin x^e^–début xiie siècle)," in *Les structures sociales de l'Aquitaine, du Languedoc et de l'Espagne au premier age féodal* (Paris: Centre National de la Recherche Scientifique, 1969), 221–37; Auzias, *L'Aquitaine carolingienne (778–987)*, Bibliothèque méridionale 28 (Toulouse/Paris: Privat, Didier, 1937).

17 François-Louis Ganshof, "The Use of the Written Word in Charlemagne's Administration," in idem, *The Carolingians and the Frankish Monarchy* (London: Longman, 1971), 125–142, at 125–26; and idem, "The Institutional Framework," 90.

of Reims tells us most of what little we know because there was no local chronicler of the tenth century until Adhémar of Chabannes.[18] The early-Carolingian impact on Aquitainian political structures had been profound, however. Counts were established at Poitou, Limoges, Saintes, Périgueux, Angoulême, and Bourges by Pippin and Charlemagne, and the latter also installed loyal abbots at Poitiers and Saint-Maixent, granting them significant immunities as royal protectorates. Charlemagne then created the Kingdom of Aquitaine for Louis the Pious in 778 and intervened directly in its government and political structure, issuing a special set of instructions for *missi* in the region in 789.[19]

Ganshof identifies a special kind of landed vassal created by Charlemagne in marcher regions or where he felt he had less authority, in order to establish "a kind of military colony." He gives Aquitaine as an example, observing that such benefices as there were were typically created out of Church, not royal land, and that clerics were compensated for this through rents and extra tithes from the 790s. Royal vassals in Aquitaine were therefore typically landed as a result of their protective military function. By the time of Louis the Pious they were tied to the crown as counts and begin to be recorded as *vassi* and *vassalli*. But by this stage Ganshof cannot give examples for Aquitaine, let alone of the mobilization of such men, unlike for the region between the Seine and Loire, and unlike Dhondt's examples for the eastern Pyrenees.[20]

Louis passed to his son Pippin II (817–38) the title to a kingdom including Aquitaine, Gascony, the Toulousain, and Septimania. It was not disputed in the negotiations of the 840s that Charles the Bald's rights to west Francia included Aquitaine, and these were taken to include all the dioceses, abbeys, and counties, as well as royal domain.[21] In other words,

18 Steven Fanning and Bernard S. Bachrach, eds. and trans., *The Annals of Flodoard of Reims, 919–966*, Readings in Medieval Civilizations and Cultures 9 (Peterborough, ON, Plymouth, and Sydney: Broadview Press, 2004); Jules Chavanon, ed., *Adémar de Chabannes, Chronique publiée d'après les manuscrits*, Collection de textes pour servir à l'étude et à l'enseignement de l'histoire 20 (Paris: Picard, 1897).

19 Alfredus Boretius et al., eds., *Capitularia Regum Francorum*, MGH, Sectio 2, Legum Sectio II, 1 (Hanover: Hahn, 1883), no. 24; Ganshof, *Frankish Institutions*, 30–31, 40; Auzias, *L'Aquitaine carolingienne*, 68–70; Dhondt, *Études sur la naissance des principautés*, 169–71; Rosamond McKitterick, *The Frankish Kingdoms under the Carolingians, 751–987* (London/New York: Longman, 1983), 17–18, 33–34, 50–53; and Ganshof, "The Use of the Written Word," 127 and n. 16.

20 Cf. Ganshof, "The Institutional Framework," 95, 103 and idem, *Frankish Institutions*, 51–52, 60 (and n. 13); Dhondt, *Études sur la naissance des principautés*, 171–89.

21 Ernestus Müller, ed., *Nithardi Historiarum libri IIII*, MGH, Scriptores rerum Germanicarum (Hanover: Hahn, 1907), 43, 45; *Annales Bertiniani* as cited in Ganshof,

the benefices included in these were those of the crown, not those of the occupant, who was therefore under royal protection as well as obligation. Along with Burgundy, Aquitaine became part of the south-western double kingdom of Carloman II, king of West Francia (879–84).

But Aquitaine still saw very little at all of its kings or manifestations of their authority. It was becoming quite distinct. Abbo of Saint-Germain demonstrates that the Aquitainians were not part of a generalized west Frankish political consciousness, being described by him as cunning and sharp-toothed in contrast with the "Franks" (*Francigeni*).[22] But MacLean also shows that Bernard Plantevelue, count of Auvergne, whose descendants would transform some of the central territories of Carloman's double kingdom, most significantly the county of Auvergne, into what would be the Duchy of Aquitaine, was no usurper but a close ally of Charles, chosen as such because he was locally powerful.[23] After Charles was deposed, however, Aquitaine, now a distant fragment of the old Carolingian realm, passed into independent local hands. In the 890s Count Ramnulf of Poitou, not Bernard's heir, became King of Aquitaine, although the title died with him.[24] In 898 William "the Pious," count of Auvergne and Gothia, acknowledged Charles the Simple as king of West Francia but not of Aquitaine, and took the title Duke of Aquitaine (*dux Aquitanorum*).[25] He and his successors William II and Ebles Manzer did not act as though they understood their counties as being within royal jurisdiction. With William III "Towhead," count of Poitou-Auvergne 932–63, would come the decisive shift in the powerbase of Aquitaine from Auvergne to Poitou. His successors would prove even less willing to support the non-Carolingian kings of West Francia than their predecessors had been to acknowledge the ancient line.

Flodoard's first reference to Aquitaine is for the year 923, when William II successfully fought the Northmen of the Loire as they attacked Aquitaine.[26] For 924 he tells us that the duke had "delayed making his personal submission" to King Radulf of Francia (923–36), but that he now

"The Genesis and Significance of the Treaty of Verdun (843)," in *The Carolingians*, 289–302, at 290–91, 292, 294–95.

22 As cited in MacLean, *Kingship*, 60.

23 MacLean, *Kingship*, 69–70, 72, 75.

24 Auzias, *L'Aquitaine carolingienne*, 424–48; Dhondt, *Études sur la naissance des principautés*, 22, 190–93, 201; MacLean, *Kingship*, 76; McKitterick, *The Frankish Kingdoms*, 262–63.

25 Fanning and Bachrach, *Flodoard of Reims*, xxii; Auzias, *L'Aquitaine carolingienne*, 449.

26 Fanning and Bachrach, *Flodoard of Reims*, vii, xvii, xxi, 7, and see 5 for the location of the Northmen; McKitterick, *The Frankish Kingdoms*, 51.

"committed himself" because Radulf brought a force to the Loire to threaten him.[27] Radulf then returned to him the county of Berry. This had been confiscated by Radulf and Count Robert of Paris, along with the *civitas* of Bourges (they retained the latter). It was not until 941, five years into the reign of Louis IV d'Outremer, king of West Francia (936–54), that William III acknowledged him as king. The duke performed homage again in 944 and 950, but he and King Louis IV were estranged in 951 when the latter threatened to cross the Loire. When the king died in 954 the powerful men (*proceres*) of Aquitaine were involved in electing his son Lothar as king of West Francia (954–86), and in 955 Hugh the Great, who controlled the young King Lothar, was given Aquitaine and made its duke (*dux*). As Count of Poitou-Auvergne, William III was therefore effectively Hugh's vassal, and yet Hugh never had any real power in the Duchy of Aquitaine. In fact Hugh and Lothar were reduced to besieging William in Poitiers for two months in 955, and when they broke off the siege to return north William actually pursued them. The crown had thus failed to exert Carolingian control within Aquitaine by the time of Hugh's death in 956, although his son, Hugh Capet, was nevertheless given the *pagus* of Poitou in 960 by Lothar.[28]

Léonce Auzias argued that Hugh Capet limited his ambitions in Aquitaine to the title of Count of Poitou because he wished to have other southern magnates as allies, notably Raymond of Toulouse, Boso of La Marche, and Guy, viscount of Clermont. Nonetheless the Auvergne fell to William III by 955. Then, taking advantage of the discord between Lothar and Hugh by 962, William co-operated with the latter, correctly anticipating that Hugh would agree to relinquish the Poitevin title as a result. However, William then submitted to the king, and was thereby master of Aquitaine at his death in 963.[29]

From this time the ducal line established itself as the leading dynasty in the south-west of France in defiance of King Lothar. Crucially, Duke William IV "Iron-Arm" (963–96) established a better relationship with Hugh Capet, and in 968 married his daughter Emma to Count Thibault of Chartres, Hugh's most important vassal. Hugh in turn married William's sister Adelaide in 969. In 970, Hugh abandoned rights in Aquitaine to William IV against the wishes of Lothar. In retaliation, the king sought an alliance with the duke's Angevin neighbour Count Geoffrey Greymantle,

27 Fanning and Bachrach, *Flodoard of Reims*, 10–11, at 10.

28 Fanning and Bachrach, *Flodoard of Reims*, xvii, xxi, xxii, 5, 10–11, 36, 60, 61, 65; McKitterick, *Frankish Kingdoms*, 313, 319–23; Auzias, *L'Aquitaine carolingienne*, 329–30, 476–500, 502–3.

29 Auzias, *L'Aquitaine carolingienne*, 503–8; Dhondt, *Études sur la naissance des principautés*, 223. See also Fanning and Bachrach, *Flodoard of Reims*, 65.

installing Geoffrey's brother, Abbot Guy of Cormery, as Bishop of Le Puy in 975, with the comital powers associated with the title. In 979 Lothar tried to re-establish Aquitaine as a sub-kingdom under his infant son Louis, marrying him to Greymantle's daughter Adelaide at Brioude in the heart of the Auvergne, where they were also crowned king and queen of Aquitaine. The marriage and restoration ended with their quick divorce, the upshot being an even closer Poitevin alliance with Hugh Capet against Lothar and Louis. The Poitevins were then involved in Capet's election as king of West Francia in 987,[30] and William V "the Great" (993–1030), duke of Aquitaine, inherited an almost independent principality.[31]

In the context of early-Carolingian ambitions in the region, it is surprising to note how little administrative evidence remains. Pippin's *Capitulare Aquitanicum* established that Aquitainians had the right to appeal to the crown and to be judged according to the traditional law-codes of the Frankish or Roman peoples, as had been the case under the Merovingians, and contains instructions for the support of the Church.[32] Many of Charlemagne's legal measures were intended to apply to Aquitaine as elsewhere.[33] However, the only actual examples of royal immunities in Carolingian Aquitaine are of limited exemptions from tolls on boats for Noirmoutier and a concession of immunity to the patrimony of Charroux.[34] In contrast to the rest of Charlemagne's realm, examples of advocates or courts of immunity are likewise hard to find, as is evidence for the activity of *missi*, *scabini*, or of the county court (*mallus*) actually sitting, or of other trials and judgements, or of kings presiding over *placita* (the traditional jurisdictional assemblies of the Carolingian free), even though these still took

30 Louis Rédet, ed., *Documents pour Saint-Hilaire de Poitou (768–1300)*, 2 vols., Mémoires de la société des Antiquaires de l'Ouest 14–15 (1847–52), 1: 36; Chronique de Saint-Pierre-du-Puy, cited in Auzias, *L'Aquitaine carolingienne*, 510–11, and see 508–10, 511–17, 518 n. 35; Ferdinand Lot, *Fidèles ou vassaux? Essai sur la nature juridique du lien qui unissait les grand vassaux à la royauté depuis le milieu du IXe jusqu'à la fin du XIIe siècle* (Paris: Bouillon, 1904), 70; McKitterick, *Frankish Kingdoms*, 323, 326, 328.

31 On William the Great see D.F. Callahan, "William the Great and the Monasteries of Aquitaine," *Studia monastica* 19 (1977): 321–42; Claire Taylor, *Heresy in Medieval France: Dualism in Aquitaine and Agenais, 1000–1249* (Woodbridge: Boydell, 2005), 12–17. Cf. Bernard S. Bachrach, "Towards a Reappraisal of William the Great, Duke of Aquitaine (995–1030)," *Journal of Medieval History* 5 (1979): 11–21, and "A Study in Feudal Politics: Relations between Fulk Nerra and William the Great, 995–1030," *Viator* 7 (1976): 111–22.

32 Boretius, *Capitularia regum Francorum*, 1, no. 18; McKitterick, *The Frankish Kingdoms*, 52; Ganshof, "The Use of the Written Word," 91–92, 125–26.

33 Ganshof, *Frankish Institutions*, 71–72.

34 Ganshof, *Frankish Institutions*, 47 n. 347.

place.[35] The closest we get to direct royal intervention is when Hugh the Great held a *placitum* in 945 as a royal representative.[36]

But we should consider royal protection in its broadest terms. There is evidence of a relationship between the crown and the rulers of Aquitaine in terms of protection from external forces. Flodoard makes a connection between royal protection, or its absence, and the fate of Aquitaine in his accounts of the events of the years 923 to 930. In 924, Duke William II and King Radulf did a deal with the Norse invaders, establishing a "security pact for their lands."[37] When Radulf defeated the Northmen attacking Aquitaine in 930, "the king then made the Aquitainians submit themselves to him."[38] Auzias says of this intervention by the king on behalf of the Aquitainians in 930 that Radulf entered Aquitaine not as an enemy but "en auxiliaire, en protecteur."[39] Flodoard notes that Magyars too attacked Francia in the early 950s, including Aquitaine in 951, in which year Louis IV threatened to attack the duchy. He retreated after William III was reconciled with him.[40] They were still in the west by 955, in which year Louis IV indeed attacked Poitou, a campaign resulting in a battle in which the duke's army was destroyed and in which, Floadoard asserts, the duke barely escaped.[41] Is Flodoard making another connection between the royal protection, or its absence, and the fate of the duchy? If so, by the end of the tenth century this was scarcely an issue. The political and administrative relationship between the counts of Poitou and the crown had become polite and dignified but distant.[42] McKitterick cautions against taking literally Gerbert of Aurillac's statement of 980 that not King Lothar but Hugh Capet was the real ruler of West Francia.[43] But, although she notes that "the regional structure of Carolingian administration was preserved" in the county of Poitou, amongst other places,[44] kings found it difficult to dismiss counts and the office had become hereditary.[45] Adhémar

35 Fanning and Bachrach, *Flodoard of Reims*, 11–12, 13, 65; McKitterick, *Frankish Kingdoms*, 332.

36 Fanning and Bachrach, *Flodoard of Reims*, 41; McKitterick, *Frankish Kingdoms*, 332.

37 Fanning and Bachrach, *Flodoard of Reims*, 12; Auzias, *L'Aquitaine carolingienne*, 457.

38 Fanning and Bachrach, *Flodoard of Reims*, 19.

39 Auzias, *L'Aquitaine carolingienne*, 47.

40 Fanning and Bachrach, *Flodoard of Reims*, 55 and 56.

41 Fanning and Bachrach, *Flodoard of Reims*, 61.

42 See, for example, the portrayal of the sources in Sassier, "De l'ordre seigneurial," 232, 237–39.

43 McKitterick, *Frankish Kingdoms*, 305.

44 McKitterick, *Frankish Kingdoms*, 332.

45 Ganshof, "The Institutional Framework," 91; McKitterick, *Frankish Kingdoms*, 329.

of Chabannes may indeed have attributed too much to Duke William "the Great" in terms of his personal achievements, but whatever power historians come to agree that he did wield, the duke owed the king little if anything.[46]

(b) Gascony[47]

The rule of William "the Great's" contemporary Bernard William, duke of Gascony (999–1010), was an unfortunate blip in the gradual rise in power of the rulers of Gascony, that is south of the Dordogne, who in the ninth century were free men entirely in possession of their lands.[48] All in all, it is astonishing how little is recorded about them even in the tenth and early-eleventh centuries. We know that the Gascons as a people descended from the Pyrenean Basques, and whilst they had nominally submitted to Merovingian authority as early as 602, and in 769 Duke Lupus recognized the Frankish kings, they had a turbulent relationship with the later Carolingians. Sancho-Lupus, Lupus's descendant, was perhaps the most obviously Carolingian-allied Gascon ruler, serving in the court of Louis the Pious from 781, and in *c.*800 this was in the context of a campaign against Islamic Iberia.[49] On the other hand the Gascons rebelled against Pippin and most famously against Charlemagne. It is they rather than Muslims who should have featured in *La chanson de Roland* as having attacked the

46 Bernard S. Bachrach, "Potius rex quam esse Dux putabatur: Some Observations concerning Adhémar of Chabannes' Panegyric on Duke William the Great," *Haskins Society Journal* 1 (1989), 11–21; cf. Callahan, "William the Great"; Sassier, "De l'ordre seigneurial," 235–36.

47 For Gascony in this period, Higounet, "Le groupe aristocratique," 223–25, is very useful. Some of the conclusions in Dhondt, *Études sur la naissance des principautés*, 96–99, 226–27, have been partly superseded with regard to Gascony by modern works such as Benoît Cursente, "La Gascogne," in *Les sociétés méridionales autour de l'an mil*, ed. Michel Zimmermann (Paris: Centre Nationale de la Recherche Scientifique, 1992), 257–93; idem, *Les castelnaux de Gascogne médiévale*, Études et documents d'Aquitaine 5 (Bordeaux: Fédération historique du Sud-Ouest, 1980); Renée Mussot-Goulard, "La Gascogne," in Zimmermann, *Les sociétés méridionales*, 295–326; and Renée Mussot-Goulard, *Les Princes de Gascogne (768–1070)* (Lectoure: CTR Éditeur, 1982).

48 Charles Higounet, "Structures sociales, *castra* et castelnaux dans le sud-ouest aquitain (x^{e}–xiiie siècles)," in *Structures féodales et féodalisme dans l'occident méditerranéan (X^{e}–XIIIe siècles)*, ed. Toubert et al., Collection de l'École française de Rome 44 (Rome: École Française de Rome, 1980), 109–117, esp. 109–110.

49 Mussot-Goulard, *Les Princes*, 76–77 and n. 49, 77–81.

rearguard of the royal army in the Pyrenees in 778,[50] and their leader Adelgar (or Adalric), who was duke in 781, deserted his Frankish allies at Toulouse in 787, for which he was exiled and tried at Worms in 790.[51]

The status of the ninth-century Gascons within the *regnum Francorum* is obscure. There is no record of the issuing of royal diplomas for Gascony in the late Carolingian documents. Rebellions certainly occurred if the Franks attempted to impose non-Gascon rulers on the region, for example in *c.*836. But Gascon dukes also allied with the early Carolingians: Lupus with Charlemagne against Hunoald, duke of Aquitaine, and Sancho-Lupus with Louis the Pious against the Muslims. To Renée Mussot-Goulard it seems that the Gascons were "well integrated" into the Carolingian realm because of a story from Nithard that they took part in a jousting tournament in front of King Charles the Bald at Worms in 842, in which they were pitted against other peoples (*generis*), Saxons and Bretons. In the same year, Charles the Bald was at Agen on the River Garonne in Gascony. Yet at some point between 848 and 850, Sancho Mitarra, duke of Gascony, revolted against the Carolingians and ceased to acknowledge them until the end of his rule, in 864. Gascon independence was in the ascendant as the Franks lost administrative control. Mitarra's grandson, Garciá Sánchez, duke of Gascony (886–920/1), acknowledged Carolingian rulers but, like the Poitevins, not Count Robert of Paris when he claimed the throne of West Francia in 922.[52]

It is perhaps best to understand the early Carolingians' relationship with Gascony as being intrinsically connected to the matter of protection against Islamic Iberia, entailing defence of the Frankish heartlands from Islamic invasion through political and military control of the Gascon marches. This is most evident in Charlemagne's sidelining of the Gascon leader Lupus in the 778 Iberian campaign and the founding of La Réole (then Squirs), Saint-Savin de Lavedan, and Sorde in the same year, on the road to Roncevaux.[53] Saint-Savin received privileges from Charlemagne at

50 Robert Fawtier, *La Chanson de Roland: étude historique* (Paris: E. de Boccard, 1933), 177; Mussot-Goulard, *Les princes*, 54, 59, 60, 67–68, 72, 74–75; McKitterick, *The Frankish Kingdoms*, 34, 53.

51 Astronome, *Vita Hludowici Pii Imperatoris*: G.H. Pertz, ed., *Ludovici Pii ... vita per anonymum quendam et incertum, sed tamen coætaneum fidumque scriptorem*, MGH, Scriptores II (Hanover: Hahn, 1829), 609; Ganshof, *Frankish Institutions*, 84; Mussot-Goulard, *Les princes*, 25, 72.

52 Müller, *Nithardi Historiarum libri IIII*, 38; Sassier, "De l'ordre seigneurial," 232; Dhondt, *Études sur la naissance des principautés*, 197; McKitterick, *The Frankish Kingdoms*, 53; Higounet, "Structures sociales," 109–10; Mussot-Goulard, *Les Princes*, 16, 30–32, 37, 66, 72, 87–90, 92–94, 126, 170–71.

53 Mussot-Goulard, *Les Princes*, 21–22, 74.

the 817 Council of Aachen, where it was placed under the protection of the viscounts of Lavedan and Bigorre. Charlemagne was simultaneously protecting both Francia and the religious life through his patronage of Gascon abbeys.

But it was the Northmen who posed the major problem in Gascony by the 800s. In 840–45, 848, and on three further occasions between 850 and 864 they wreaked havoc, attacking monasteries in particular. Most of the episcopal seats in Gascony also fell and the archdiocese of Auch collapsed almost entirely. From bases in Gascony, the Garonne being a particularly important and vulnerable artery, they attacked both Francia and Navarre. Charles the Bald could do little if anything to prevent this, being hard-pressed by the same problem further north. The protection of Gascony was therefore the task of local powers, and they came to flourish as a result. We see a change in Gascon strategy under Duke William Sánchez (d. *c.*996), who went on the offensive for the first time. The decisive battle, at Taller on the banks of the Adour, was fought in 981 or 982. Under him we can most clearly see the relationship between local power and the ability to protect. He revived the title of duke autonomously, and the later Carolingians certainly did not recognize the Gascon ruler as representing their authority.[54]

We can see this shift from royal to local influence in patterns of minting. Whilst Carolingian coins were once minted at Dax, Agen, and Bordeaux for Charlemagne, Louis the Pious, Pippin, Charles the Bald, and possibly also Lothar, the dukes started minting their own from the late tenth century (William Sánchez, from 977 to *c.*999, Bernard William from 999 to 1010, Sancho William and Odo from 1036 to 1039). Stronger ties were then formed with Aquitaine in the eleventh century in a process leading to the absorption of Gascony into the growing sphere of influence of the counts of Poitou. Duke Sancho William visited Aquitaine in 1014 or 1017 to celebrate the feast of St John the Baptist with the Duke of Aquitaine and the King of France, at Saint-Jean-d'Angély. This was the first time a ruler of Gascony met a Capetian king. There was no question of the performance of homage, however. As Mussot-Goulard astutely points out, Sancho William had everything in practice that the king could only nominally have delegated to him.[55]

Thus the interpretation of the tenth-century Carolingian world according to which there existed a very weak relationship between kings and princes holds to a great extent in south-western France. Public authority, and thereby the responsibility of protection within the region, had not been

54 Mussot-Goulard, *Les Princes*, 98–100, 100–102, 134–36.
55 Mussot-Goulard, *Les Princes*, 50–51, 170.

willingly delegated by the crown even if, certainly in the case of Aquitaine, it had once derived from imperial rule. However, this does not illustrate a collapse in Carolingian power in the way that Ganshof and after him Dhondt understood it,[56] but was the result of an enduring absence of the king from the region.

Having considered the relationship between kings and dukes in south-western France, we should examine the nature of authority within the duchies themselves, not least to evaluate who protected whom.

The collapse of public power

(a) Aquitaine

There is no evidence for the duchy of Aquitaine as a whole demonstrating that a "feudal revolution" took place there in *c.*1000, but such a phenomenon is often assumed to have occurred and there is some local evidence for it, not least in Charente, as studied by André Debord, and in conflicts between the viscounts of Limoges and the lords of La Marche in the late tenth century.[57] Castles proliferated in Poitou in the same period. They were of three categories essentially: those built by ancient, locally powerful viscomital families, such as the lords of Thouars and Aunay; those built by the Count of Poitou himself, such as Lusignan and Maillezais; and those perhaps built by new lords such as at Saint-Maixent and Niort. But whatever their origin, they were by the late tenth century increasingly within the sphere of the Counts of Poitou, who were recovering from their loss of control over Anjou and Angoulême in the 970s and from the influence of Geoffrey Greymantle of Anjou within Poitou itself. Furthermore, comital provosts with vicarial powers were installed at Poitiers, Niort, Talmond, and other places.[58] Stephen White observes that the arguments of those who maintain that a collapse of public power took place "would be more compelling if they did not depend so much on the assumption that when allegedly public institutions disappear uncontrolled violence necessarily breaks out."[59] However,

56 For example, in Dhondt, *Études sur la naissance des principautés territoriales*, *passim*.

57 Chavanon, *Adémar de Chabannes*, 146–50; André Debord, *La Société laïque dans les pays de la Charente: Xe–XIIe Siècles* (Paris: Picard, 1984). See also Sassier, "De l'ordre seigneurial," 177–78, 183–84, 197, 205; Thomas Head, "The Development of the Peace of God in Aquitaine (970–1005)," *Speculum* 74 (1999): 656–87, at 658, 662–66.

58 Higounet, "Le groupe aristocratique," 221–23; Head, "Development of the Peace," 660.

59 White, "The 'Feudal Revolution,'" 221.

it is not difficult to show that under Duke William Iron-Arm local wars did proliferate in *c.*970. Yet whatever the case elsewhere in the Frankish realm, the concept of a "feudal revolution" does not apply neatly to Aquitaine as a generalization by the time of the Council of Charroux in 989.[60]

Furthermore, William the Great improved on the achievements of Iron-Arm, exerting a good deal of control over the viscounts of Limoges and the counts of Angoulême, making alliances with and between them as his father had done, and in terms of influence within Poitou successfully bringing his troublesome castellan vassals to heel.[61] Some of these lords – those of Lusignan, La Marche, Thouars, and Gençay – were embroiled in local wars against each other in *c.*1020. Because they were already divided against each other, they proved that much easier to dominate. As part of bringing them to heel, the duke appears to have adopted a strategy of alternating unpredictably between showing them favour (protection) and ambivalence (abandonment). The source allowing us this insight, known as the *Conventum*, is a unique narrative of the turbulent relationship between the duke and his vassal Hugh of Lusignan. Although problematic as a source, it indicates clearly that William was understood as being able to protect cooperative vassals *should he wish to*, and that they considered that he should indeed do so. When William drags a reluctant Hugh all the way to Blaye as part of his court, he reassures him that his castles will not be attacked because he has arranged a truce between Hugh and his enemy, Bernard of La Marche. When Hugh duly hears a rumour that his castle is being attacked, he is reassured by William that, were this the case, he would come to Hugh's aid. The castle is indeed lost, yet William does nothing. Hugh protests, not because William *could not* protect him, but because he *did not*. And ultimately Hugh cannot rebel. He has no one else to protect him, and so has to swallow his humiliation.[62]

But William the Great had little such influence in the Auvergne, where his ancestors had lost a good deal of power. This region too was affected by endemic local warfare,[63] which makes it important for our understand-

60 Regional differences as a problem in terms of the *mutationniste* model was first suggested by Timothy Reuter in "Debate: the 'Feudal Revolution,'" *Past and Present* 155 (1997): 177–95, at 187–95.

61 See, for example, Chavanon, *Adémar de Chabannes*, 150, 156–57, 162; Head, "Development of the Peace," 666, 679–80.

62 George Beech, Yves Chauvin, and Georges Pon, eds., *Le Conventum (vers 1030): un précurseur aquitain des premières épopées*, Publications Romanes et Françaises 212 (Geneva: Librairie Droz, 1995), 131–32.

63 Chavanon, *Adémar de Chabannes*, 163; Geoffrey of Vigeois, *Chronica*, in: Philippe Labbé, ed., *Novæ Bibliothecæ Manuscript. librorum tomus primus: historias, chronica sanctorum, sanctarumque vitas, translationes, miracula, stemmata genealogica,*

ing of the protection of churches and the development of the Peace of God. Sassier notes that the Capetians did not issue charters in favour of southern churches until the twelfth century.[64] This is more surprising in the case of the archdiocese of Bourges because, unlike those of Auch and Bordeaux, it remained technically a royal protectorate, and this included the churches of Le Puy and Clermont.[65] Laurenson-Rosaz criticizes the dukes of Aquitaine for their inactivity in the context of *advocati*, defenders of abbeys in the Auvergne.[66] This is perhaps to miss the point. They could not be especially active there in *any* capacity.

The Auvergne had been withheld from the dukes of Aquitaine when Berry was returned to William I. But where all free subjects and all royal officials had once sworn fealty to Charlemagne, by the tenth century oaths were sworn to counts and other regional potentates, and not all great Auvergnat magnates were royal vassals or noted as *fideles* in royal charters.[67] Bishop Stephen of Clermont performed homage to the king in 950, but he was probably the last bishop to do so in this period.[68] But whereas we know that *placita* continued to be held in the Auvergne, as will be discussed, the last convened by a count was in *c.*945.[69] Chris Wickham has argued that the disappearance of comital *placita* denotes the end of the old regime, in which local lords implemented public authority, and the beginning of the new in which the implementation of justice, and we might add the concept of protection, became private.[70] Thus it is only in the Auvergne that we find an Aquitainian county undergoing anything like a "feudal revolution," in that both royal and princely authority declined in the late-Carolingian world. For such reasons, Christian Lauranson-Rosaz and Frédéric de Gournay are able to read the region as undergoing feudal revolution and note examples of unrestrained violence by the lesser aristocracy against

---

ac similia antiquitatis, præsertim Francicæ, monumenta, ... repræsentans. (Tom. 2. Rerum Aquitanicarum, præsertim Bituricensium, ... collectio, etc.), 2 vols. (Paris, 1657), 2: 279–342 (esp. 281). Geoffrey wrote in the twelfth century, but recorded the vicecomital wars, about which Adhémar is uninformative: Michel Aubrun, "Le Prieur Geoffrey de Vigeois et sa chronique," *Revue Mabillon* 68 (1974): 313. See other sources for William V above.

64 Sassier, "De l'ordre seigneurial," 232.

65 Sassier, "De l'ordre seigneurial," 234.

66 Christian Lauranson-Rosaz, "Peace from the Mountains: the Auvergnat Origins of the Peace of God," in *The Peace of God: Social Violence and Religious Response in France around the Year 1000*, ed. Thomas Head and Richard Landes (Ithaca and London: Cornell University Press, 1992), 104–34, at 109.

67 McKitterick, *Frankish Kingdoms*, 329.

68 Lauranson-Rosaz, "Peace from the Mountains," 107.

69 Lauranson-Rosaz, "Peace from the Mountains," 107–8.

70 Wickham, "Debate," esp. 203, 205.

abbeys.[71] The significance of this will be addressed after discussion of comparable characteristics in Gascony.

(b) Gascony

In Gascony, even more viscounties were under ducal control by *c.*1000 than in Aquitaine because the dukes had increased their authority over the great Gascon allodialists in south-eastern Gascony through activity in the context of the Norse attacks. William Sánchez was able to create a new network of viscounts in the mid-tenth century. The seats of Dax, Oloron, and Marsan were based on the older episcopal centres destroyed by the Northmen, and dominated river traffic for defensive as well as economic reasons. We first hear of a viscount of Levedan in 945; Lomagne was revitalized politically in this context; and a viscount of Gascony was also created, based at Lectoure. We know of this because he was murdered by an ally of the count, Lupus the Strong of Serres, and replaced by another comital ally, Odat. No money appears to have been minted in Gascony independently of the duke, i.e., by lesser nobles or bishops, aside from the Bishop of Agen, until the later eleventh century.[72]

Some viscounties do seem to have become hereditary under Duke Bernard William, who brought lesser men into his curia whom the sources call *milites*, and gave these men castles. But it is not until later in the eleventh century that we encounter castellans independent of the duke, and few at that, and the *miles* is not common until the twelfth. The majority of castles were in fact held by the higher nobility, typically within the ducal sphere, and either owed their titles and fortifications to the duke in the tenth and earlier eleventh century, or were built by the dukes as monastic fortifications.[73]

Abbeys protected by the Gascon dukes in turn protected Gascony, and this became more and more a feature of ducal patronage in the duchy. In 876 Garciá Sánchez was, fairly traditionally, *adjutor* and *defensor* of Sorèze and, in 902, *custos* and *defensor* of its priory at Saramon where, to cite Mussot-Goulard, he behaved in the manner of a king, becoming holder of one of the essential regalian prerogatives, which was the protection of its churches. The refoundation of Condom was part of this same project. Having been all but destroyed and abandoned after Norse raids, it was rebuilt early in the 900s. William Sánchez is said to have vowed that if he

71 Lauranson-Rosaz, "Peace from the Mountains," 109; Frédéric de Gournay, *Le Rouergue au tournant de l'an mil: de l'ordre carolingien à l'ordre féodal (IXe–XIIe siècle)* (Toulouse: Université de Toulouse–Le Mirail, 2004).

72 See Mussot-Goulard, *Les Princes*, 50–51, 129, 140, 141–42.

73 Mussot-Goulard, *Les Princes*, 164–66; Higounet, "Structures sociales," 110–11.

was able to defeat the Northmen he would build a magnificent new abbey for the monks of Saint-Sever. Its charter records the victory at Taller and the protective intervention of the saint himself. The abbey of Palastrion, modern Morlanne, was built accordingly, on the site of a small church and land bought from two knights, and was already overshadowed by a comital castle, which was garrisoned by *milites* under direct comital control. It dominated the Garonne, which was essential in defending not only Gascony but the whole of southern France should a Norse flotilla return.[74]

At La Réole we also find a ducal fortified abbey. Its cartulary refers to its foundation by Charlemagne, submission to Fleury, attack by Northmen, and refoundation in 977 under the custodianship of Bishop Gombaud of Gascony, when it was granted immunities by his brother William Sánchez.[75] We know that La Réole had good natural and man-made defences, because Abbot Abbo of Fleury was very impressed by them in 1004.[76] Saint-Sever was placed under the protection of Cluny and La Réole under Fleury.[77] These abbeys were, in several senses, "fortified."

Nonetheless, we can see that under Bernard William localized dissent and disorder did sometimes manifest itself. Shortly before he was murdered by a mob in 1004 at La Réole, Abbo of Fleury supposedly remarked, "I am more powerful than our lord the king of the Franks within this territory, where no one fears his power."[78] Marcus Bull observes, "perhaps Abbo should have been less sanguine about the remoteness of secular authority in that part of the world ... King Robert the Pious was not there to help him. ... More to the point, perhaps, neither of the princes who dominated the region, Duke William V of Aquitaine and Duke Bernard William of Gascony, was present and able to save the abbot."[79]

It is the ducal ability to protect that is the pertinent concept here. After Abbo's death, the surviving Frankish monks of Fleury, presumably traumatized and still endangered, were given shelter by Viscount Amalvi of Bézaume and his wife Rosemberga. Amongst them was Aimoin, Abbo's biographer. According to Mussot-Goulard, Bernard William's swift re-

74 Mussot-Goulard, *Les Princes*, 108–9, 111.

75 Paris, Bibliothèque Nationale de France, MS lat. 5652, published in Luc d'Achery, ed., *Spicilegium*, 2 vols. (Paris, 1723), 2: 580–602.

76 See below.

77 Archives Départementales des Landes, MS H.14, fol. 23; Mussot-Goulard, *Les Princes*, 138, 155. The story may be sixteenth-century.

78 *Vita s. Abbonis abbatis Floriancensis*, in J.-P. Migne, ed., *Patrologiae cursus completus ... Series latina*, vol. 139 (Paris, 1853), cols. 407–12, at col. 410.

79 Marcus Bull, "Conclusion," in *France in the Central Middle Ages*, ed. Bull (Oxford: Oxford University Press, 2002), 198–99.

prisals against the murderers, of which we hear from Adhémar of Chabannes, may have been to counteract the moral superiority that Amalvi now had as the protector of Fleury's embassy.[80] Around the same time a new, independent viscounty emerged, Montaner. Its first named viscount is Odon-Doat (1010). The family annexed the abbey of Saint-Orens-de-Larreule in 1009 and the new abbot was a member of it.[81] Little observed is the fact that this was therefore the second abbey Bernard William had failed to protect from illegitimate force.

Social disorder was to be the death of Bernard William. According to the cartulary of Sainte-Marie-d'Auch, he was murdered by a knight, Raymond Paba, to whom possession of one of the first mottes in Gascony is attributed.[82] Paba sought the protection of the count of Fézensac, probably Aimeric I, who gave him the villa of Vic-Fézensac, the implication being that he was acting under his orders. The personal ties of vassalage between Paba and Aimeric were stronger than legal codes which might have led to the former being given up to justice. Certainly the Bishop of Auch thought this wrong, and excommunicated Paba. However, before Paba left for Jerusalem, a pilgrimage he undertook to redeem himself but on which he died, Bernard William's half-brother and successor, Sancho William, gave him the fief of Buzet-sur-Baïse, where Garciá Sánchez had built a *castellum* to protect the abbey.[83] Castles such as Buzet, and others with a more secular function, were in fact typically held by the higher nobility, firmly within the ducal sphere and owing their titles to him in the tenth and earlier eleventh century. It therefore possible that both Sancho William and Count Aimeric had conspired against the hapless Bernard William. The 1031 canons of a council at Limoges indeed assert that Sancho William had had his brother murdered by a knight.[84] But we nonetheless have to understand a growth in princely power in relation to subordinates overall. Bernard William and Raymond Paba remind us that this process was not always uninterrupted or peaceful, in particular from 1004, but by the late tenth century Gascony was pretty firmly under ducal control.

In discussing ordinary people in Gascony, the more vulnerable free, it is difficult to explore whether or not their freedom was being protected in *c.*1000 or eroded according to the "feudal revolution" model, because there is little direct evidence for society at its lower levels in Gascony. However, we do have some evidence that primitive commercial activity was

80 Chavanon, *Adémar de Chabannes*, 159–60; Mussot-Goulard, *Les Princes*, 167–68.

81 Mussot-Goulard, *Les Princes*, 164–66.

82 Higounet, "Structures sociales," 111.

83 According to the Condom cartulary (Higounet, "Structures sociales," 111).

84 Mansi, *Concilia*, 19: 507–48.

being protected within the duchy. There were several ducal mints, as noted. Viscounts of Oloron, drawn by William Sánchez from a powerful local family with established interests in the area, represented the count-duke in providing protection for pilgrims crossing the Pyrenees, and Oloron became a modest commercial centre but a significant one for Gascony. It seems likely that Bordeaux and La Réole also had markets, and so the fortification of the abbeys dominating them needs to be understood in an economic context too. Significantly, the articles of La Réole's charter of 977 refer to warriors stationed at the abbey for its defence at the abbot's command.[85]

The Peace of God[86]

This paper has so far explored the nature and extent of royal influence in the south-west in the tenth century, arguing that it had indeed declined; by *c.*1000 it was all but ignored and had little or no protecting influence, either directly or through accountable delegates, through either privileges or public courts. But it does not follow that ducal authority had likewise declined. There is little non-partisan (i.e., non-monastic) evidence[87] to demonstrate that things were actually getting worse for the vulnerable free, clergy themselves or lay people, in Aquitaine or anywhere else except perhaps in the Auvergne.

So, what really lay behind the Peace of God movement, which supposedly replaced private justice with a new form of public authority, that of the clerics? This is problematic to those assuming that a feudal revolution was general. If throughout Francia by *c.*1000 litigants often preferred private agreements to the chaos or absence of public courts, as Marc Bloch had observed,[88] why did the Peace of God begin in Aquitaine? It is also problematic to a revised account of the late-Carolingian world such as the above. If public and ecclesiastical protection was in safer hands in Aquitaine than it perhaps was elsewhere, why was the Peace of God needed there at all?

Christian Lauranson-Rosaz, of the former school, answers that Roman concepts of freedom and also the distinction between public and private

85 Mussot-Goulard, *Les Princes*, 156.

86 The most important work on the Peace of God in recent years is the collection *The Peace of God*, ed. Head and Landes. But very important also in the present context is Head's "The Development of the Peace of God," for a revised narrative for the movement within wider regional politics.

87 For discussion of the nature of French monastic sources for the "feudal revolution" see Wickham, "Debate," 198.

88 Bloch, *Feudal Society*, 1: 359–74.

justice remained strongest in the south, and so their loss was most resented and most resisted there. Furthermore, diocesan assemblies of peace in the south were already enshrined in Roman tradition. The clergy was able to revive these as a means of restoring order where princes could not. The councils in *c.*1000 further link southern practice to the Peace of God because Roman assemblies had often involved the clergy. In the Auvergne the so-called Landeyrat Charter of 972 notes the jurisdictional authority of the Abbot of Aurillac and makes it clear that bishops as well nobles should hold legal assemblies. Lauranson-Rosaz has demonstrated this by showing that the Peace of God was prefigured by localized Auvergnat assemblies from 958, in which the Bishops Stephen and Guy played an important role. These non-royal and non-comital *placita* were at Clermont (958), Aurillac (972), and Saint-Germain-Laprade (978 x 980). They were followed chronologically by the first Peace of God council at Charroux, and maybe by those at Narbonne, Limoges, Anse, and more locally Le Puy as noted above, and then by further, although still localized, councils in the Auvergne at *Coler* (989 x 994) and Saint-Paulien (in 993 or 994).[89] In other words, neither kings nor counts and dukes could protect the vulnerable free of Auvergne, and so the clergy and the poor (*pauperes*) revived a traditional regional practice whereby they could influence political and social affairs themselves.

But we can alternatively view this same evidence as resonating with recent critiques of the "feudal revolution" model which do not see the operations of episcopal or abbatial courts as indicating a breakdown in public authority, but simply as an alternative embodiment of public protection. In this context we can view the early Peace of God councils as a continuation rather than a revival of tradition. It is only if we view the undertaking of peace and protection as exclusively lay prerogatives in the Carolingian world that it makes sense to see the convening of these councils as indicating weak princely rule and the inventing of new judicial *fora*. As Jeffrey Bowman's work on Catalonia has shown, justice in lay affairs was not the prerogative of lay rulers in the Romanized south, and also that tradition was an important characteristic of the Peace of God. This suggests that courts seen as public, whether they were comital or episcopal and without much distinction between their competences, had a specific role in defending the vulnerable. Indeed, free men, *boni homines*, were involved in reaching judgement into the later eleventh century. "Sharp distinctions

89 Lauranson-Rosaz, "Peace from the Mountains," and idem, "La romanité du Midi de l'an mil," in *La France de l'an mil*, ed. Robert Delort (Paris: Éditions du Seuil, 1990), 49–74. On the scholarship of this aspect of the south, see Jeffrey A. Bowman, *Shifting Landmarks: Property, Proof and Dispute in Catalonia Around the Year 1000* (Ithaca and London: Cornell University Press, 2004), esp. 57–59.

between public and private," he concludes, are "difficult to trace in this period."[90] Further scholarship influential on both sides in the debate around the "feudal revolution" adds weight to such an interpretation, not least because Thomas Bisson suggested that the distinctions between public and private are "modern statist conventions."[91] This is echoed in Stephen White's observation that we should not conceptualize the Carolingian state as having the same functions as a modern state.[92]

Just as the distinction between public and private justice can be undermined, so too can the concept of the Peace of God as entirely novel. Elizabeth Magnou-Nortier stresses that familiar terminologies were used in the new type of councils, and Thomas Head notes allusions in the record to fourth-century authority as a basis for their authority.[93] Perhaps most usefully, when Wickham observed that the cessation of *placita* "marks an important change in the framework that legitimized social action" and that the Peace of God "competed" with seigneurial justice "quite consciously," he recognized it at the same time as the "crystallization of previously informal action."[94]

We also allow ourselves to be misled into attributing the origins of the Peace of God to the clerics if we see it as unifying their interests with those of the *pauperes*. Stressing violence by both encouraging peace and undertaking protection was greatly in the interests of those with power and wanting to legitimize it. Those offering protection where the king could not by *c.*1000 were the beneficiaries of the Peace of God more than were the peasants (*rustici*). They were, most immediately, the Gascon ducal family in the shape of Archbishop Gombaud of Bordeaux, who was Duke William Sánchez's brother, Dukes William IV and William V of Aquitaine, and Bishops Stephen II of Clermont and Guy of Auvergne. It should be noted that the very first act of the very first council, at Charroux, was against attacks on Church property, and the third of the three acts condemned violence against clergy. Only the second speaks of attacks on the peasantry, and Letaldus of Micy's account of the council is concerned solely with sins against the Church.[95]

90 Bowman, *Shifting Landmarks*, 219.

91 Bisson, T.N., "The Feudal Revolution," *Past and Present* 142 (1994): 6–42, at 12.

92 Stephen White, "From Peace to Power: The Study of Disputes in Medieval France," in *Medieval Transformations: Texts, Power and Gifts in Context*, ed. Esther Cohen and Mayke B. de Jong, Cultures, Beliefs, and Traditions: Medieval and Early Modern Peoples 11 (Leiden: Brill, 2001), 203–18, at 218.

93 Elisabeth Magnou-Nortier, "The Enemies of the Peace: Reflections on a Vocabulary, 500–1000," in Head and Landes, *Peace of God*, 58–79; Head, "Development of the Peace," 656.

94 Wickham, "Debate," 204, 205.

95 "Delatio corporis s. Juniani ad synodem Karoffensem," in Migne, *Patrologiae Cursus, Series Latina*, 137: 823–26.

This is most in evidence when we consider that as well as making pronouncements about predation against the peasantry, many Peace of God canons and oaths in fact specify something along the lines of "except where this is justified," for example on the oath-taker's own land, or in time of war.[96]

The growing consensus about the Peace of God is thus that it was a means whereby clerics and lay lords legitimized the servitude they were in any case extending to the peasants on their own estates.[97] Yet again this is not exclusively a characteristic of the Peace of God. Bowman shows that even the most traditional and conventional public courts of Catalonia tended to favour the monks over other vulnerable litigants in disputes.[98] The interests of the vulnerable rustics were very soon sidelined after the Council of Charroux, in fact. Looking back on the Millennial era from *c.*1033, Ralph Glaber remarked that bishops and also princes had initiated the Peace of God from the outset, and that the people attended after they had begun. The popular involvement he describes is one that goes along with rabble-rousing by the bishops, not one that is initiated by *pauperes* themselves.[99] In other words, the Peace of God was part of a consolidation of seigneurial rights, be they lay or clerical.

However, even this cannot necessarily be seen as part of a recent revolution in social relations. Rather, the Peace of God cemented social bonds established in previous decades and served to legitimize the protecting parties. In 994, Adhémar of Chabannes tells us that peace was agreed between William the Great and his men as the major business of the Council at Limoges.[100] By *c.*1000, the revised dating of the Peace of God council at Poitiers, the party threatening protective violence was the duke, who asserted anew his right and ability to judge, and indeed summoned the council. The threat was of harm to hostages given over to him to ensure the cooperation of his inferiors.[101] Head argues that ducal and viscomital charters, for example in favour of Saint-Cyprien in the decades around *c.*1000,

96 For example, in the oath of Beauvais of 1023 (Vatican City, Bibliotheca Apostolica Vaticana, MS Vat. Reg. lat. 566, fol. 38v).

97 See, for example, the chapters in Head and Landes, *Peace of God*. The evidence and scholarship is further surveyed along these lines in Taylor, *Heresy in Medieval France*, 28–32.

98 Bowman, *Shifting Landmarks*, 99.

99 Neithard Bulst, ed., and John France and Paul Reynolds, trans., *Rodulfus Glaber, The Five Books of the Histories*, Oxford Medieval Texts (Oxford: Clarendon Press, 1989), 195–99 (3: 14–17); cf. Loren C. Mackinney, "The People and Public Opinion in the Eleventh-Century Peace Movement," *Speculum* 5 (1930): 181–206.

100 Chavanon, *Adémar de Chabannes*, 158.

101 Mansi, *Concilia*, 19: 265–68. The dating is Thomas Head's (see "The Development of the Peace," esp. 681–86).

denote new coercive powers of the dukes over their vassals that had taken shape within the framework and language of the Peace of God.[102] He notes most importantly that even the first council, Charroux, an entirely clerical affair, itself brought together both allies and enemies of William Iron-Arm in a period of peace following the death of some of his major rivals, and that the episcopal-ducal alliance was secured at his court immediately following the council.[103] Recent interpretations of the Peace of God therefore regard ducal activity early in the movement as being in harmony with the clerical agenda. Monastic privileges obtained from princes are in evidence in Aquitaine as in other regions where the Peace of God had been enacted.[104] Their existence further suggests that the collapse of princely power is a myth.

We understand the Peace of God best if we see it as a process rather than an institution, and as a collection of local, if related, initiatives, rather than as regionally uniform. If we do this we can understand the Auvergne as experiencing more of a "feudal revolution" than Poitou or other counties in the south-west, and read this evidence in the context of what had become of royal protection. The situation in the Auvergne was different to that in western Aquitaine not least because there was an absence of royal protection, and ducal power was less in evidence also. Neither the Archbishop of Bordeaux nor the duke controlled the Peace of God in the Auvergne, and they were in no position to do so. We must now accept that as well as not being entirely novel, the Peace of God began in the Auvergne in the absence of protection from above. Whether the Peace of God was in favour of the *pauperes* or aimed at taming local warriors, the bishops of Clermont and Le Puy were indeed responding to an absence of public security. Gombaud of Bordeaux, in fact a relative of Bishop Guy,[105] must certainly have been inspired by the Auvergnat councils, but he had not initiated them and thus the Auvergnat church defended itself.

Thus, if the majority of Aquitainian churches were no longer royal protectorates, this does not mean that they were not protected, even in the Auvergne, or that protection was understood as deriving from the crown. Rather, existing and effective networks of authority and protection operating at the top levels of society in Aquitaine enabled the clergy and the dukes to consolidate their role as protectors of a social order of which they were the beneficiaries. But the question of whether this protection was *perceived*, by any party, as either deriving originally from the crown or being a reac-

102 Head, "Development of the Peace," esp. 670 and 683.

103 Head, "Development of the Peace," 669–73; see also Callahan, "William the Great."

104 Observed in Sassier, "De l'ordre seigneurial," 213.

105 Head, "Development of the Peace," 667.

tion to its absence is something of a red herring. There is nothing in the legislation of the Peace of God to indicate that it was viewed like this, and it is surely in such legislation that we would expect to find such a view expressed. More significant is that in *c.*1000 ducal authority was strong ideologically and in practice, in spite of being eroded in Gascony under Bernard William. What characterized the south-west was that it lay far beyond royal protection and had done so for far longer than other supposedly anarchic regions of Francia. The Peace of God was therefore the culmination of an alliance between the most physically powerful – the dukes – protecting the most spiritually and morally powerful – the clerics – and receiving legitimization in return. Being looked to for protection was therefore a convenient burden for either party to bear.

LISI OLIVER
Louisiana State University

Protecting the Body in Early Medieval Law

The objective of this paper is to investigate how the laws of early medieval Europe addressed assault and battery.[1] One of the defining features of Germanic laws was the list of compensations required for personal injury, payable by the perpetrator or his kin to the victim or his kin. These clauses thus provided peace both by initially discouraging assault due to the substantial fines that would be incurred, but also by subsequently protecting the person who had inflicted the injury from bloodfeud waged by the injured person's kin. The following discussion examines how redress for injury was obtained in the legal systems of the barbarian territories, drawing upon the meagre records scattered throughout the Germanic regions. The first part of this paper describes the parameters of legal procedure. Crucially, these varied both from region to region and through time; the reconstruction that follows presents a blueprint upon which individual courts constructed specific procedures to which we unfortunately no longer have access. The second part of the discussion presents the very few recorded cases regarding personal injury. Unfortunately, none of these suits describe the litigation process in detail. The concluding section thus provides hypothetical cases and their possible outcomes.

Reconstructing process

The first issue to be considered is who can bring a case to court. The plaintiff must be a free man, generally of property and of local standing. As a general rule a woman cannot plead for herself in court, although she can have an advocate.[2] Slaves are usually represented by their masters. A mandate written in the second half of the eighth century in Tours allows a

1 I would like to thank Stefan Jurasinski and Andrew Rabin for their generous comments on previous drafts of this paper. Also the editors, David Rollason and Tom Lambert, for their help and their patience.

2 Janet L. Nelson, "Dispute Settlement in Carolingian West Francia," in *The Settlement of Disputes in Early Medieval Europe*, ed. Wendy Davies and Paul Fouracre (Cambridge: Cambridge University Press, 1986), 58.

litigant to name a substitute as his representative in a public hearing in the event that illness would prevent his own attendance: the equivalent of modern power of attorney.[3]

What constitutes the court itself is variable, although there are certain common features. In the Salian territories, the judicial assembly was called the *mallus*: the noun is related to, for example, the Old English verb *mælan* ("to speak"), indicating that the function of the gathering was to speak to the legal facts of the matters brought before it. This convocation (similar to the Icelandic *Thing*) was a local meeting of freemen. In Merovingian Francia, those freemen who actually sat on the judgement panel were called *rachimburgii* ("judgement-finders"), but were also referred to as *boni homines* or *boni viri* ("good men") in terminology borrowed from Roman law. They would be summoned to address a variety of administrative business including, but not limited to, legal hearings. The early laws of Kent use the cognate term *mæþel* ("assembly, deliberative or judicial meeting, council") for *mallus*, which implies a comparable institution. Any crime committed during its sitting incurs a double fine, the same penalty which applies to disruption of Church services. (Both Saxony and Brittany prohibited convocations on Sundays, and it seems likely that similar stipulations held elsewhere in early Christian Europe. Although early Kentish law distinguishes the peace of the *mæþel* from that of the Church, the fines for disturbance are the same.) The verbs of judging and settlement used in records of Anglo-Saxon legal procedures are nearly always in the plural, demonstrating the communal nature of the judicial process in England as we can see it also in Francia.[4] The number of freemen who made up the court was not fixed: although in the Frankish court records there can be as few as seven, a case in later Francia is attested to by fifty-two *boni viri*.[5]

Although it originally meant "brave," the term "Frank" later came to mean "free." The nature of this freedom was to perform military service and to participate in public justice; if for some reason a man could no longer perform as a warrior, he concomitantly lost his judicial identity.[6]

3 Rudolf Hübner, *Gerichtsurkunden der Fränkischen Zeit, Erste Abtheilung: Die Gerichtsurkunden aus Deutschland und Frankreich bis zum Jahre 1000. Zeitschrift der Savigny-Stiftung für Rechtsgeschichte: Germanistische Abteilung* (1891), B. 12, sec. 150.

4 Patrick Wormald, "Charters, Law and the Settlement of Disputes in Anglo-Saxon England," in *Settlement of Disputes*, ed. Davies and Fouracre, 149–168, at 164.

5 Werner Bergmann, "Untersuchungen zu den Gerichtsurkunden der Merowingerzeit," *Archiv für Diplomatik, Schriftgeschichte, Siegel-und Wappenkunde* 22 (1976): 1–186, at 167–69.

6 See Patrick J. Geary, *Before France and Germany: The Creation and Transformation of the Merovingian World* (Oxford: Oxford University Press, 1988), 113.

The members of the court were expected to be men of property and of good character, and conversant with legal custom. Several manuscript collections of barbarian laws appear to have been well-used; Rosamond McKitterick believes this may stem from actual use during legal proceedings.[7] However, even given the sporadic nature of the medieval evidence that has come down to us, it is highly unlikely that most local courts would have had access to a written version of the laws. Tellingly, Visigothic law actually fines the members of the court who fail to arrive at a verdict in a case which has no written precedent, thereby preventing a litigant from avoiding a fine on the claim that there is no punishment stipulated in writing for his precise delict.[8]

In preliminary hearings, then, those sitting in the court will not only call upon knowledge of past legal practice, but also serve as impartial witnesses to the hearing. A case from Lombardy implies that an acceptable court-witness must have property worth 150 *solidi*, the wergild of a Lombard freeman.[9] We do not know who determined the composition of any particular group of *boni viri*. Both Visigothic law and a later capitulary of Charlemagne prohibit those convicted of certain crimes to serve as part of the court.[10] Between 769 and 775 Carolingian law seems to have enumerated those who could validly function as one of the *boni homines*, although it is not clear whether this list applied at the lowest local levels.[11]

The *rachimburgii* were expected to come expeditiously to a solution: they could be fined three *solidi* each if they did not reach a fine by the end of the first day, and twelve more if the sun set on an undecided case a second time.[12] Furthermore, if the defendant could prove that they had

7 Rosamond McKitterick, "Some Carolingian Law-Books and their Function," in *Authority and Power: Studies on Medieval Law and Government Presented to Walter Ullmann*, ed. Brian Tierney and Peter Linehan (Cambridge: Cambridge University Press, 1980), 13–27, includes among these Paris, Bibliothèque Nationale de France, MSS lat. 4404, lat. 4417, lat., 4628, and lat. 4788. See discussion in Adolf Schmitt-Weigand, *Rechtspflegedelikte in der fränkischen Zeit*, Münsterische Beiträge zur Rechts- und Staatswissenschaft 7 (Berlin: Walter de Gruyter, 1962), 112–14, 118–19.

8 Schmitt-Weigand, *Rechtspflegedelikte*, 119–20.

9 Chris Wickham, "Land disputes and their social framework in Lombard-Carolingian Italy, 700–900," in *Settlement of Disputes*, ed. Davies and Fouracre, 105–21, at 106, 111.

10 Wendy Davies, "Disputes, their Conduct and their Settlement in the Village Communities of Eastern Brittany in the Ninth Century," *History and Anthropology* 1 (1985): 309, n. 18; Julius Goebel, Jr., *Felony and Misdemeanor: A Study in the History of Criminal Law* (New York: Commonwealth Fund, 1937, repr. Philadelphia: University of Pennsylvania Press, 1976), 79.

11 Schmitt-Weigand, *Rechtspflegedelikte*, 26.

12 Schmitt-Weigand, *Rechtspflegedelikte*, 10–11.

arrived at a judgement which did not accord with the law, they could be charged fifteen *solidi*. Conversely, if such a charge was proven unfounded, the accuser would have to pay each of the *rachimburgii* fifteen *solidi*.[13] This surely protected the jurors by serving as a formidable deterrent against false claims; even if there were as few as seven *rachimburgii* involved in the judgement, the fine would equal 105 *solidi* – more than a half a freeman's wergild – if the ruling was unanimous.

The court was overseen by a presider, whose function at the preliminary presentation of the case was to ensure that both procedure and penalty concurred with written law.[14] He would establish the evidence required and call for it to be produced. At the subsequent sitting his job was: to supervise any necessary oath-swearing; to pronounce on the procedures for judgement; to establish the required waiting period in the case of a delinquent litigant; to ensure that the verdict was in compliance with the law; and, in the event the verdict was divided, to determine the evidence to be brought to the higher court of appeal.[15] The judgement as to guilt and fine was arrived at communally by the participants in the court, and ratified by the presider: what Davies and Fouracre call "collective judgement in an atmosphere of public witness."[16]

The presider (except, apparently, for local cases in Lombard Italy) could not be a priest, although churchmen could serve in the legal affairs of lay people.[17] Commonly he was the local nobleman, *comes* or *grafio* in Francia, *dux* in Lombardy, often also termed *iudex* ("judge"), although as time went on more and more cases were heard by a *missus* ("envoy") of the king.[18] Like the *rachimburgii*, he was enjoined to bring his cases to quick and just conclusions: Lombard law demanded payment of half a wergild if the presider delayed judgement for three months after the finding, and various Carolingian decrees warned against either speeding up the hearing or delaying the court in order to enjoy the hunt or other pleasures.[19]

13 Schmitt-Weigand, *Rechtspflegedelikte*, 13.

14 Bergmann, "Gerichtsurkunden," 24–28. One instance in Brittany shows the approximately equivalent position of *machtiern* being held by a woman (Davies, "Disputes," 294).

15 Bergmann, "Gerichtsurkunden," 27–28, 149.

16 *Settlement of Disputes*, ed. Davies and Fouracre, 216.

17 See *Settlement of Disputes*, ed. Davies and Fouracre, 272–73; Paul Fouracre, "'Placita' and the Settlement of Disputes in Later Merovingian Francia," 32–33; Wendy Davies, "Disputes in ninth-century Brittany," 79; Wickham, "Land disputes," 105, 110; all in *Settlement of Disputes*, ed. Davies and Fouracre; Oliver, *BEL*, 84–85.

18 For this role, see Schmitt-Weigand, *Rechtspflegedelikte*, 27.

19 Schmitt-Weigand, *Rechtspflegedelikte*, 28. Some details for the presider differ in Lombardy; see Schmitt-Weigand, *Rechtspflegedelikte*, 44–51. For example, the half-

In earliest times, the court met out of doors, often either in a grove or around a hill – the *berg* of the *mallus*, or *mallberg*;[20] an exact parallel is found in Modern English *Mettle Hill* "the hill of the *mæþel*."[21] The advantage of a raised barrow was that it might serve as a point for proclamation of judgements. The assembly in which Wihtred's laws were set took place in Bearsted in 695; as late as 1897 the vicar cited local lore that "sessions were formerly held on a moated mound, which has tiers of seats above it, near this village."[22] Later, it seems that some of these meetings may have been held in churches: several extant cases call for the defendant to appear with his witnesses before the altar, although it is also possible that an altar was especially erected outdoors in the court precincts. In 809 Charlemagne ruled that the place of judgement should be covered with a roof, so it could be used in all weathers. In the seventh-century Anglo-Saxon laws of Hlothhere and Eadric, the king seems to have had a permanent hall in London in which cases could be heard.[23]

The *mund*, or protection, of the court was taken very seriously. As stated above, in Anglo-Saxon England any offence committed in the *mæþel* required twice the penalty normally stipulated. At a case in later Francia the defendant was fined fifteen *solidi* for contempt of procedure: ten of these were given to the plaintiff *in exfaida*, literally "to avoid a feud because his word had been wrongly challenged."[24] In this case, the remaining five went to the king, as the dispute cited took place in the king's court. At a lower level the fine would have been paid to the *comes*.

More personal protection was also provided: in Burgundian law a litigant must pay a triple fine for each blow struck at a member of the court. This ruling was clearly inserted to prevent altercations arising when judge-

---

wergild fee for delay was later raised in Lombardy to a full wergild and loss of position. In regard to penalties for false judgement or delay in Visigothic law, see Schmitt-Weigand, *Rechtspflegedelikte*, 70–76.

20 *Lex Salica* contains several Frankish terms or phrases set off from the surrounding Latin text by the term *mallbergo* 'by mallberg'. These represent the vernacular legal terms as they would have been spoken in the meeting which took place on the *berg* of the *mallus*, although they are often so garbled in scribal transmission as to be unintelligible.

21 For discussion of the geographic features of Anglo-Saxon assembly places, see Aliki Pantos, "The Location and Form of Anglo-Saxon Assembly Places: Some 'Moot Points,'" and "'In medle oððe an þinge': The Old English Vocabulary of Assembly," both in *Assembly Places and Practices in Medieval Europe*, ed. Aliki Pantos and Sarah Semple (Dublin: Four Courts Press, 2004), 155–80 and 181–201 respectively.

22 W. Bright, *Chapters in Early English Church History*, 3rd ed. (Oxford: Oxford University Press, 1897), 427, n. 3.

23 Oliver, *BEL*, 141–44.

24 Fouracre, "'Placita,'" 34.

ment was pronounced.[25] A ruling from Carolingian Francia in 820 states that a litigant who has been ordered from the court but refuses to go must pay the king's *bannum* of sixty *solidi* for disruption.[26] Like the *boni homines*, the presider is individually protected from physical assault: a capitulary of 803 declares that a claimant who approaches the presider with clenched fist must be reported to the king, and he also must pay a ten-fold fine of 600 *solidi* (three times a freeman's wergild!) for disturbing the peace.

At his first appearance in court, the plaintiff announces his intention to bring the case. Rulings on bruises, which fade over time, imply that this first appearance must occur shortly after the incident.[27] As a rule, an adjournment would be granted while necessary evidence was gathered – in the case of personal-injury claims, proof would rely on witnesses rather than written documents. In some territories the respite may have served a secondary purpose: it was still possible that the disputing parties could reach out-of-court settlement in the intervening period. (This was not universally true: a case from seventh-century Francia implies that in that region once a procedure was set in motion it must be carried through.[28] The public nature of the proceeding eliminates the possibility of bloodfeud erupting later.)

Sometimes the process even involved two postponements if the evidence produced in the second hearing was deemed insufficient or if the verdict of the first finding was divided.[29] At the first appearance, then, the court would establish who would hear the trial, the means of proof, and the period within which the evidence must be brought to a second hearing.[30]

A formula for a preliminary hearing in a case of self-defence from Sens around 770 provides a good depiction of this process:

> Notice: In what manner and before whom present a certain man named X coming in district X, in the place which is called X, in the

25 Schmitt-Weigand, *Rechtspflegedelikte*, 105.

26 Schmitt-Weigand, *Rechtspflegedelikte*, 105.

27 *Lex Ala* 60: 21; *Liber Const* (Burgundian) 5; Abt 61: 3–4; *Lex Rib* 71: 4; *Lex Sal* 17: 8. For this insight, see Mary Richards, "The Body as Text in Early Anglo-Saxon Law," in *Naked Before God: Uncovering the Body in Anglo-Saxon England*, ed. Benjamin C. Withers and Jonathan Wilcox (Morgantown, WV: West Virginia University Press, 2003), 97–115, at 103.

28 Wood, "Disputes," 27–35, particularly 35.

29 See Fouracre, "'Placita,'" 35; Wickham, "Land Disputes," 106; Richard Sharpe, "Dispute Settlement in Medieval Ireland," 181, all in *Settlement of Disputes*, ed. Davies and Fouracre; Bergmann, "Gerichtsurkunden," 14.

30 F.L. Ganshof, "La preuve dans le droit franc," *Receuils de la Société Jean Bodin pour L'Histoire Comparative des Institutions* 17 (1965): 71–98, at 75.

> public *mallus* before the *comes* X himself or other good men, who have signed below, with his hand placed on the sacred altar, thus the sworn one said: "Here I swear by this sacred place and God the highest and his sacred power: a certain man named X, stirred with rage, came upon me with his arms and struck me blows; and thus God allowed me forthrightly, that I myself with my arms gave him such blows that he died; and what I did I did for my protection. And today I guarantee myself for exculpation and expiation within forty-two nights, as is the law and our custom, with three landholders (*aloarii*) and twelve oath-swearers (*conlaudantes*)." They swore and directed their tongues according to the laws.[31]

The past tense shows that this was based on an actual case; the ruling has been generalized by the substitution of X for all names. In the event of a similar case arising later, the appropriate proper names and locations can be inserted. In this ruling, the defendant has forty-two days to muster his case. This same terminus is found in the Frankish Edict of Chilperic, which states that the adjournment to collect evidence is forty-two days when the accused is a slave, with a possible additional forty-two in the case of excused absence (presumably of the slave's master) from the court due to illness or incapacity.[32]

In a case from Tours in the middle of the eighth century, an accused killer is given forty days to find the necessary witnesses to support his claim of self-defence.[33] This period, established in Salic law, overwhelmingly appears elsewhere: for example, in the case of a divided verdict, the litigants have forty days to bring additional evidence. Furthermore, the regulation on payment for homicide in early seventh-century Kent is that the first 20 shillings of the wergild must be paid at the open grave, but the kin group then has forty days to pay the remaining eighty.[34] (The forty-day time period might be Biblically inspired.) The variant terminus of forty-two days may imply that in those territories the court met every six weeks. On the other hand, the extension of two days to the forty-day terminus could allow for the possibility that the assigned date fell on a Sunday. Finally, Bavaria may have had a larger number of troublemakers than other territories: its law requires the court to meet every month, or more often if nec-

31 Karl Zeumer, ed., *Formulae Merowingici et Karolini aevi*, MGH, Legum Sectio V, Formulae (Hanover: Hahn, 1886), 191–92; translation mine.

32 Ian Wood, "Disputes in Late Fifth- and Sixth-Century Gaul: Some Problems," in *Settlement of Disputes*, ed. Davies and Fouracre, 7–22, at 11.

33 Hübner, *Gerichtsurkunden aus Deutschland und Frankreich*, no. 68.

34 Oliver, *BEL*, 66–67, 96–97. Other examples of the forty-day terminus can be found in Ganshof, "La preuve," 72, 75 and Bergmann, "Gerichtsurkunden," 12, 78, 84.

essary. No other Germanic region seems to have held such frequent meetings of the *mallus*.

A day would be appointed for the second hearing, to which the two claimants were remanded to appear with the required evidence. The meeting of the *mallus* seems to have been a lively local event, in spirit probably not unlike a regional market and perhaps even associated with it. On the appointed day, both accused and accuser – with their respective witnesses – were expected to show up at the court. Failure to do so is finable in *Lex Salica*, which also describes processes for "enforcing judgement on recalcitrant witnesses." Frankish cases include both a terminus of evening and a period of three days within which the defendant must appear.[35] If the accuser does not present himself, the defendant is declared innocent and the case is dismissed.[36] Burgundian law imposes a fine of 6 *solidi* for non-attendance, unless the participant is detained by sickness or business. If he does not come by the sixth hour of the day, the case is concluded in his absence. Extrapolating from a case in which the plaintiff was fined court-costs for presenting a losing case, one can speculate that in some instances he would be similarly charged for bringing a case which he does not appear to prosecute further.[37] Conversely, if the defendant fails to appear, he is considered guilty and assessed the appropriate fine.[38]

At this second assembly the litigants arrive with the proofs specified at the preliminary hearing. In the earliest recorded cases only the accused was allowed to bring witnesses in his defence; as Ganshof indicates, in some sense these trials were all criminal hearings in which the defendant had to clear himself of the accusation.[39] Later in the Merovingian period, the responsibility of bringing witnesses was expanded to the accuser, which puts defendant and plaintiff on more equal ground. In Lombard Italy, a litigant would also need to find a guarantor who pledged for the participant's ability to pay any assessed fine.[40]

In a personal-injury case (which would be unlikely to involve documentation), the crux of proof would rest on the witnesses (*cojuratores*), a group which fulfils two functions. One is to provide eye-witness testimony

35 Bergmann, "Gerichtsurkunden," 112.

36 Further explanation of the points addressed in this paragraph can be found in Wood, "Disputes," 11, 15. See also Hübner, *Gerichtsurkunden aus Deutschland und Frankreich*, secs. 151 and 197.

37 Hübner, *Gerichtsurkunden aus Deutschland und Frankreich*, sec. 158.

38 Hübner, *Gerichtsurkunden aus Deutschland und Frankreich*, secs. 48 and 49 (the citation is from the latter); Zeumer, *Formulae*, 67. Similar rulings can be found in Hübner, *Gerichtsurkunden aus Deutschland und Frankreich*, secs. 197 and 151.

39 Ganshof, "La preuve," 76.

40 Wickham, "Land Disputes," 109.

if possible. The other is to support the oath (of innocence in the case of the defendant, or of just accusation in the case of the plaintiff).[41] In this regard, they essentially serve as character-witnesses. Unique to the personal-injury hearings would be the presence of a doctor, whose testimony under oath established how severe the wound was. As Mary Richards points out, in the case of injury the results

> occur with varying degrees of severity. Someone must render an opinion based upon the examination of the witness and then, with an understanding of what long-term effects such an injury carries in their society, the arbitrator hearing the case can award the damages.[42]

The witness-group is generally composed of members of the expanded family, and particularly close friends. Burgundian law requires a freeman rebutting an accusation to be supported in his oath by twelve relatives including his wife and children, or father and mother. This core can be augmented by concerned friends and neighbours.[43] The usual number is twelve, or some multiple thereof. Less commonly the plaintiff or defendant can bring eleven *cojuratores*, using himself to make up the dozen.[44] The oath is sworn on a *res sacra*: an altar, relics, or the like.[45]

Once the verdict is reached, the proper fine is assessed. Although all laws list the tariffs in *solidi* or shillings, payment could be made in kind, substituting livestock, weaponry, or even land.[46] Upon the payment of this fine, the recipient would often issue a quitclaim, which brought the litigation to an end.

Early medieval law suits involving assault

Unfortunately, we have little historical information about how personal-injury suits were handled in the early medieval courts. Rudolf Hübner's compilations of Frankish and Lombard legal hearings lists 276 cases before 814.[47]

41 Ganshof, "La preuve," 78; Nelson, "Dispute Settlement," 45–64.

42 Richards, "The Body as Text," 113.

43 See Oliver, *BEL*, 75, note e.

44 Ganshof, "La preuve," 77. In the Kentish laws of Wihtred, the number of oath-swearers for a priest or a freeman is only four.

45 Ganshof, "La preuve," 77. See also Oliver, *BEL*, 174–76.

46 See *Lex Rib* 40: 11; *Lex Sax* 18: 1–3.

47 Hübner, *Gerichtsurkunden aus Deutschland und Frankreich*, and Hübner, ed., *Gerichtsurkunden der Fränkischen Zeit, Zweite Abteilung: Die Gerichtsurkunden aus Italien, bis zum Jahre 1150. Zeitschrift der Savigny-Stiftung für Rechtsgeschichte: Germanistische Abteilung* (1893), B. 14.

These deal overwhelmingly with property disputes; a mere fourteen concern homicide and only five deal with assault. Of these, only one case involving assault and two involving homicide provide us with insight into legal process.

The assault case comes from the Frankish town of Ende in the later part of the seventh century. A layman is accused of ambush with intent to steal; this attack caused heavy bruising. The case is adjourned until the first day of the following month, thus for less than the usual forty days, to give the accused time to prepare his defence. The defendant does not appear at the hearing and is fined *in absentia* according to "the law of your place."[48]

The first pertinent homicide took place in Tours in the middle of the eighth century. A *iudex* arrives in a location where a man has just been killed. Those who were actually present or hurried to the place of the incident support the defendant's version of the facts: the killed man intended to rob the defendant, coming against him with unsheathed sword, and striking blows. The killer swears that he acted in self-defence; furthermore, he exhibits his bruises. He thus claims to have acted according to law in killing his assailant. His swearing is accompanied by twelve men, with himself as the thirteenth. The *iudex* sets in that place the requirement that the slayer appear in church forty days later with thirty-six oath-supporters, himself as thirty-seventh, to repeat his claim of self-defence. "And if he is able to do so, [the case of] that death should remain at rest." Three interesting points arise from this unsatisfactorily brief contemporary record. First, the *iudex* did not rule independently, even though this case appears to be relatively clear-cut: there is no indication that anyone challenged the claim of self-defence, and the killer even demonstrated his bruises. The public hearing was, however, necessary to compel the slain man's kin to accept the judgment that the killer was not guilty of homicide so as to ward off later feud. Secondly, even though the *iudex* might not pronounce a verdict, he did set the evidentiary requirements for the case, thus effectively by-passing the preliminary hearing. Thirdly, although twelve men supported the killer's contention of self-defence at the scene of the slaying, he was required to triple that number to thirty-six when he appeared formally at the altar. A purely speculative hypothesis is that the *iudex* stipulated a large number of oath-supporters in lieu of the preliminary hearing.

The second homicide case comes from Sens around 770. A woman falls upon a man and wife, and wounds the man in the knees. Then she kills their daughter. The woman is unable to deny her guilt, and is assessed the required wergild to be paid to the husband and wife. Presumably this fine must have included payment both for the injury to the husband's knees and

48 Hübner, *Gerichtsurkunden aus Deutschland und Frankreich*, secs. 48 and 49; Zeumer, *Formulae*, secs. 29 and 37.

for the death of the daughter, although the document is silent as to the amount and constitution of the fine.[49]

Speculative construction of personal-injury cases

The reconstruction of process and procedure set out above has been based on a variety of facts from a variety of locations; it endeavours, however, to include only those elements which apply in some form to a majority of the barbarian territories. The examination of roughly contemporary hearings demonstrates how very little we actually know about how personal-injury cases were resolved in court. However, the accumulated evidence gives us the possibility of creating informed hypotheses as to how such litigation might have proceeded.

The present section, thus, moves to the realm of fiction, constructing two very different cases, and indicating how they might have been resolved depending on circumstances. The amounts of restitution are based on those stipulated in the laws of Æthelberht of Kent, promulgated in about 600;[50] although the actual monetary fines may differ according to region, the underlying principles remain the same. The second study is more complex than the first, as it involves rulings on payment for medical fees and lost work which are specific, albeit not unique, to Æthelberht's laws.[51] These cases are hypothetical, and details of procedure would have varied both regionally and chronologically. Nonetheless, these docufictions attempt to recreate routes that personal-injury cases may have followed through the legal system. Both cases thus present a range of possible resolutions, and both move from least to most disputative.

(i) The Case of the Missing Hand

The particulars of this case are as follows:

> *Francis and Joseph, both right-handed lumberjacks, go into the woods to chop down trees. Both carry their axes. When they emerge, Francis*

49 Hübner, *Gerichtsurkunden aus Deutschland und Frankreich*, sec. 108. Zeumer footnotes this case with the disclaimer: "I would have preferred in this outrage the accused to have been a man, but as the manuscript consistently uses the feminine gender in that role, we are not able but to accept a feminine villain for the crime" (Zeumer, *Formulae*, sec. 51).

50 See Oliver, *BEL*, 34–51, for discussion on dating of these laws, and in particular the personal-injury tariffs.

51 See Lisi Oliver, "Sick-Maintenance in Anglo-Saxon Law," *Journal for English and Germanic Philology* 107.3 (July 2008): 319–42.

is missing his left hand: only a bloody stump remains at his wrist. Joseph is seen by several witnesses carrying his axe, the blade dripping with blood. Francis claims that Joseph struck off his hand in the woods.

(a) Possible Resolution

Joseph admits to having struck off Francis's hand, whether intentionally or not. They decide mutually on an appropriate amount of restitution, which Joseph pays. There is thus no need to take this case to court.

Scenario 1

Joseph admits to the act, but claims that the common practice is to set a penalty for the right hand. In fact, none of the barbarian laws makes a distinction between the right and left hand (or for the predominant and non-predominant hand in the case of left-handers). Two possibilities present themselves. The simplest is that the two parties settle privately on a lesser restitution, as it was Francis's left hand that was struck off. If, however, they are unable to come to an agreement, they must take the case to the assembly.

Scenario 2

Joseph admits to the act, but claims it was an accident. Francis and Joseph cannot agree on a proper compensation. Two possibilities arise here. (a) They agree that the injury was accidental, but differ on the appropriate amount of restitution. (b) Francis insists that the blow was not accidental, but deliberately struck. Under either scenario, this dispute must go to the assembly.

Scenario 3

Joseph admits to the act, but asserts that he acted in self-defence. Joseph claims that Francis threatened him with a raised axe. Francis denies this allegation. This dispute must go to the assembly.

Scenario 4

Joseph claims that he did not, in fact, strike off Francis's hand. He left Francis in the woods unharmed and headed home. On the way, he was attacked by a wild boar, which he fended off, thereby causing his axe to become bloodied. He does not know how Francis's hand was severed from his wrist (although perhaps it was a further attack by the boar he had driven away?). Francis insists that Joseph did indeed strike off his hand in the woods. This dispute must go to the assembly.

(b) Process and Procedure in Disputed Claims

First appearance: Presentation of the case

Francis claims in the *mæþel* that Joseph struck off his hand, and that he is liable for full compensation – fifty shillings, which equals half a wergild – for the loss of his hand.

A. In the event that Joseph has admitted the act but is unwilling to pay the legally mandated restitution, as it was the left hand which was struck off (Scenario 1), the assembly will rule as to whether or not a lesser penalty should be applied for the non-predominant hand. Similarly, if the two parties agree that the blow was accidental but Francis demands restitution (Scenario 2a), the assembly will determine the appropriate amount of the fine.

B. If Joseph denies culpability, claiming that the blow was accidental, or that he acted in self-defence, or that he never struck Francis at all (Scenarios 2b, 3, 4), the court grants an adjournment of forty days to give the contestants time to seek out witnesses. The assembly determines what supporting evidence should be brought to the next hearing.

This adjournment may allow the possibility that Francis and Joseph will still find a way to settle out of court.

Second appearance: Presentation of witnesses

The witnesses are produced before the presider and the assembled group of local freemen who constitute the court. If there are eye-witnesses, they can be called for sworn testimony, either on behalf of one of the parties in the suit, or as impartial witnesses of the court. If there are no eye-witnesses, each litigant swears an oath as to the veracity of his version of the incident. His oath-supporters serve as character-witnesses. Local politics undoubtedly play a large role at this point in the proceedings, with each side striving to bring the most influential witnesses.

Once the assembly arrives at a verdict, it is ratified by the presider. If the court rules against Francis, it seems harsh if any further payment were exacted: the loss of his own hand is penalty enough. Nonetheless, it is possible that Francis is assessed a fee for bringing a false accusation. This penalty would be rendered to the presider as a representative of the public coffer. If Joseph is found guilty, he will be assessed a fine payable to Francis. Since the legal penalty for the loss of a hand is half a wergild in almost all barbarian law, the fine would be fairly stiff if the court allowed no mitigation for the loss being that of the non-predominant hand. Joseph is given forty days to produce the money (or goods of equal value). He gives surety that he will pay.

(c) The Conclusion of the Case

If Joseph is found guilty, he pays Francis the stipulated penalty, and Francis gives him a quitclaim. The process is completed, and peace has been restored.

(ii) The Case of the Damaged Skull[52]

The circumstances of this case occur in two stages. The particulars of the first of these are fairly straightforward.

> *Francis and Joseph, both right-handed lumberjacks, go into the woods to chop down trees. Each carries his axe. Over lunch, they get into a dispute. Joseph strikes Francis with the side of his axeblade, fracturing the outer layer of Francis's skull. Both are aghast, and the fight immediately comes to an end. Joseph offers to pay Francis for the damage, but they are uncertain how to settle on a suitable amount.*

The diagram on the following page demonstrates the nature of Joseph's injury. Francis and Joseph amicably go to the assembly, where they are informed that the legal ruling is ten shillings for damage to the outer layer of the skull. Joseph pays Francis, Francis gives Joseph a quitclaim, and the case seems to be closed.

The particulars of the second part demonstrate complex variations.

52 The outlines of this case were presented to me by my neighbour Ben Guelfo, whose career as a trial lawyer in Louisiana has encompassed cases even more unusual.

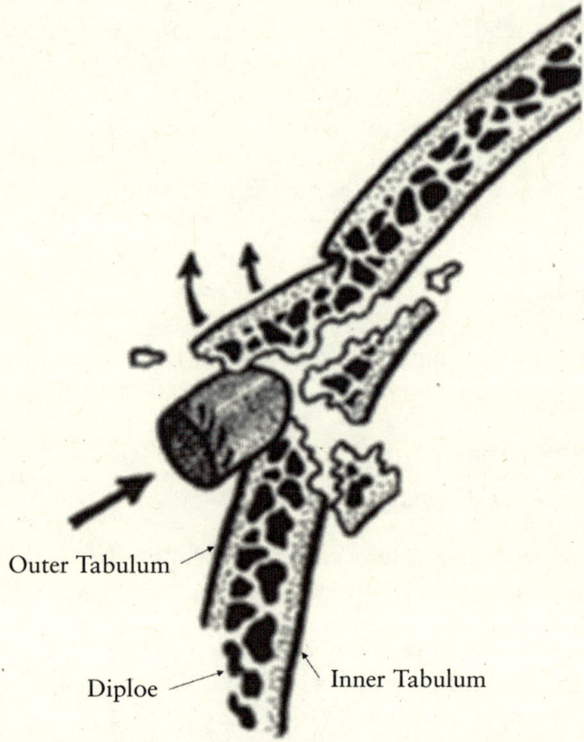

Diagram of a bullet striking the skull tangentially, showing the two bony layers (the *tabula*) separated by spongy tissue (the *diploe*). It is the outer layer that Joseph has fractured.

Diagram from O.C. Smith, E.J. Pope, and S.A. Symes, "Look Until You See: Identification of Trauma in Skeletal Material," in D.W. Steadman, ed., *Hard Evidence: Case Studies in Forensic Anthropology* (Upper Saddle River, NJ: Prentice Hall, 2003), 142, used with permission from Pearson Education, Inc., a division of Prentice Hall.

> *Two months after the incident, Francis begins to be subject to painful headaches. Eventually he passes out at work one day, and has to be carried home. Here he is confined to his bed, but the headaches do not stop. Finally his wife summons a doctor who performs a trepanation to release pressure on the brain. Francis claims that the swelling of the brain was a result of the earlier accident. Joseph replies that there is no proof of this. He also points out that Francis gave him a quitclaim for the injury. Francis counters that the quitclaim was only good for the visible damage to the skull, and did not include the hidden injury to the brain that resulted from the blow. They take the case to the* mæþel.

This case presents a wide range of problems upon which the assembly of men knowledgeable in law must deliberate. The pertinent clauses from Æthelberht's laws are as follows:[53]

> §36. If the outer [layer of the skull] becomes broken, let him pay with 10 shillings.
>
> > §36.1. If both [layers of the skull] should be [broken], let him pay with 20 shillings.
>
> §63. If a person becomes cured [after being wounded], let him [who caused the wound] pay with 30 shillings.
>
> > §63.1. If a person should be wounded such that he becomes bedridden, let him [who caused the wound] pay with 30 shillings.

Clause 36 regulates injury individually to the outer and inner *tabula* of the skull (as illustrated previously). Clause 63 requires the assaulter to pay medical fees, as well as a recompense of 30 shillings for work lost if the victim was bedridden as a result of the wound.

Presumably Francis would bring among his witnesses to the next hearing his wife and his doctor. Joseph would be wise to include in his group of supporters others (at least claiming to be) versed in medical practice who could support his contention that the original injury and the headaches were not necessarily related. Although it indeed seems unlikely that rural Kent would be teeming with doctors, it is important to remember that this was a society used to coping with medical emergencies, for livestock and for humans. Injuries, which in our own more professionalized days are promptly concealed within ambulances and whisked off to sanitized hospitals, were treated at home in full view of all members of the household.

53 I have emended the reading of both these clauses from Oliver, *BEL*. The update for 36 can be found in Lisi Oliver, "Æthelberht's and Alfred's Two Skulls," *Heroic Age* 13 (forthcoming September 2009); Oliver, "Sick-Maintenance," 63.

The permutations of the possible rulings for this case are laid out below. In all instances, the fine is in addition to the ten shillings Joseph paid following the first hearing. In calculating the size of these fines, it is important to keep in mind that Kentish wergild was 100 shillings.

A. Joseph must pay for damage to both tabula of the skull, since the trepanation of necessity pierced the inner tabulum as well. As he has already paid for the damage to the outer, he owes an additional 10 shillings for piercing of the inner (total: 20% wergild).
B. Joseph must pay the 30 shillings for Francis's cure. He need not pay additionally for the piercing of the inner tabulum, as this was part of the medical procedure, not of the injury (total: 40% wergild).
C. Joseph must pay the 30 shillings for the time Francis was confined to his bed (total: 40% wergild).
D. Combining A and B, Joseph must pay 10 shillings for piercing of the inner tabulum and 30 for the medical fee (total: 50% wergild).
E. Combining B and C, Joseph must pay 30 shillings for the medical fee and 30 for the work Francis was unable to perform while he was confined to his bed (total: 70% wergild).
F. Combining A, B, and C, Joseph must pay 10 shillings for the piercing of the inner tabulum, 30 for the medical fee, and 30 for the work lost while Francis was bedridden (total: 80% wergild).
G. An argument could even be made that since the trepanation caused a different break in the outer tabulum than the original blow, Joseph is responsible for the new piercing of the outer skull (and the inner as well), the doctor's fee, and the time Francis missed work: a total of 80 shillings (total: 90% wergild for a man who may already be back at work!).
H. Finally, it is also possible that the court could rule that there is insufficient evidence that Francis's headaches were caused by Joseph's original blow, and let Joseph off. Or it could present an alternative ruling that the quitclaim released Joseph from all responsibility not only for the original wound, but for any resulting damage.

The case is hypothetical, and there is no correct answer. Were I part of the deliberating body (which would not be possible as I am a woman), I would argue that Joseph should be assessed for the medical fee and at least part of the lost work (depending on how long Francis was actually incapacitated). My ruling would be a forty-five shilling fine for the second suit. The sum total amount Joseph would have to pay would be fifty-five shillings.

Yet even as I proclaim my judgement, I doubt its fairness on a wider scale. When Francis lost his hand, Joseph was fined a maximum of fifty shillings. But Francis's hand will never grow back, and his work will always be impaired. When Francis suffered a skull fracture and had to be trepanned as a result, I chose to fine Joseph fifty-five shillings. But the head wound should eventually heal, and it is perfectly possible that Francis will suffer no lasting damage. The two injuries are not commensurate in terms of their permanent impact. Is it, then, fair for Francis to receive less restitution for a lasting than for a temporary incapacitation? Although the laws themselves are perfectly clear, the process of arriving at a fair construal for any specific case must always rest on interpretation, both then and now.

Conclusion

The desire to ward off bloodfeud by requiring compensation in money or in kind for inflicting personal injury can be seen throughout the Germanic laws. Some tariffs are extremely detailed, such as Frisia's regulation of damage to the individual joints of the fingers, or Alamannia's differentiation between harming the upper and lower eyelid. Others concentrate only on more prominent limbs such as hands and feet. No matter what the degree of specificity, a reading of these laws might leave the reader with the impression that personal injury was regulated fairly unambiguously in early medieval Europe. As the hypothetical cases above demonstrate, this is not at all the case: law in practice must have been far more complex than its representation in writing. These (literally) bare-bones schematics for protecting the body still leave many possible interpretations open. Three crucial attributes, then, must have distinguished a good *iudex*: familiarity with the written law; knowledge of precedent; and the ability to choose wisely between conflicting options. Although the laws may have provided the blueprint for protection, only a good judge could properly interpret them to maintain peace.

HELEN LACEY
University of Oxford

Protection and Immunity in Later Medieval England

The concept of immunity was a familiar one in later medieval England; broadly defined it might be applied to a diverse range of places and people, from the sanctuary provided by certain ecclesiastical foundations, to the protection given to royal messengers on the business of the crown.[1] The association between place and immunity, in particular, has recently attracted much scholarly attention. Barbara Rosenwein has shed light on the charters of immunity granted to particular properties in the early Middle Ages. Similarly, Alan Cooper has demonstrated that by the late eleventh century all major highways were designated as places of immunity for travellers, so long as they did not wander far from the road.[2] Work on the later Middle Ages has demonstrated that the boundaries of lands designated as "franchises" and "liberties" in the post-Conquest period were still recognized to restrict, although not prohibit, the entry of royal officers. Similarly the privileges of sanctuary long associated with certain religious foundations were protected by secular authorities.[3] Such immunities were

1 I would like to thank T.B. Lambert and V. Clark for their helpful comments on this paper.

2 Barbara Rosenwein, *Negotiating Space: Power, Restraint and Privileges of Immunity in Early Medieval Europe* (Manchester: Manchester University Press, 1999); Susan Wood, *The Proprietary Church in the Medieval West* (Oxford: Oxford University Press, 2006), 251–59; Timothy Reuter, *Medieval Polities and Modern Mentalities*, ed. Janet L. Nelson (Cambridge: Cambridge University Press, 2006), 342–54; Alan Cooper, "The Rise and Fall of the Anglo-Saxon Law of the Highway," *Haskins Society Journal* 12 (2002): 39–69; Wendy Davies, "'Protected Space' in Britain and Ireland in the Middle Ages," in *Scotland in Dark Age Britain*, ed. Barbara E. Crawford (Aberdeen: Scottish Cultural Press, 1996), 1–19.

3 Maitland's idea that English franchises emerged in the Anglo-Saxon period has been effectively challenged by Patrick Wormald and others. The consensus of opinion now dates them to the post-Conquest period. Patrick Wormald, "Lordship and Justice in the Early English Kingdom: Oswaldslow Revisited," in *Property and Power in the Early Middle Ages*, ed. Wendy Davies and Paul Fouracre (Cambridge: Cambridge University Press, 1995), 114–36; Rosenwein, *Negotiating Space*, 192–95; Helen Castor, *The King, the Crown and the Duchy of Lancaster: Public*

defined by geographical location; they applied, of course, to the people who dwelt within them, but they were not applicable once the person stepped outside the boundaries of the liberty or sanctuary.[4] Less attention, however, has been given to the forms of immunity that were not spatially defined, but were instead granted to individuals, in order to protect them wherever they went. These grants were necessarily more transitory than the land-based designations; rarely were they granted for life, and usually only for long enough to carry out a specific task or journey (an exception to this might be the privilege known as "benefit of clergy," which allowed churchmen immunity from the king's courts, so long as their case was transferred to an ecclesiastical tribunal).[5] As far as laymen were concerned, however, personal immunity was usually only granted to those who demonstrated a particular need for it, for a limited period of time.[6]

This study seeks to examine more closely the forms of protection offered in these temporary personal immunities, and the ways in which they expressed royal power. In particular, it focuses on two related concepts of immunity which seem to have been common in England by the later medieval period. The first was the well-established notion of immunity from molestation (known as *grið* in tenth- and eleventh-century sources), a form of protection that would be actively policed by the officers of the crown. It is an idea that appears in late Anglo-Saxon law codes and in letters of safe-conduct from the eleventh century onwards. As Rosenwein notes, these documents expressed *active* royal jurisdiction, rather than the

---

Authority and Private Power, 1399–1461 (Oxford: Oxford University Press, 2000), *passim*. Cf. T.B. Lambert, "Spiritual Protection and Secular Power: The Evolution of Sanctuary and Legal Privilege in Ripon and Beverley, 900–1300," below, 121–40.

4 With the exception of those who left sanctuary in order to abjure the realm, who theoretically "travelled under the protection of both king and Church and under the watchful eye of bailiffs or constables." Jessica Freeman, "'And He Abjured the Realm of England, Never to Return,'" in *Freedom of Movement in the Middle Ages: Proceedings of the 2003 Harlaxton Symposium*, ed. Peregrine Horden (Donington: Shaun Tyas, 2007), 297.

5 The privilege was defined after the conflict between Henry II and Archbishop Becket. Originally clerics claimed the privilege at the onset of a trial and were handed over to a church official. By the mid-fourteenth century, offenders were usually tried first in the king's courts, and if found guilty, their goods would be seized until sentence had been passed by an ecclesiastical tribunal. John Bellamy, "Benefit of Clergy in the Fifteenth and Sixteenth Centuries," in *Criminal Law and Society in Late Medieval and Tudor England*, ed. John Bellamy (Gloucester: Alan Sutton, 1984), 115–72; Leona C. Gabel, *Benefit of Clergy in England in the Later Middle Ages* (Northampton, MA: Department of History of Smith College, 1929).

6 In addition to the spatial and personal immunities, Lambert has identified certain limited temporal immunities which applied on specific festival days (below, 134).

modern understanding of immunity as non-intervention.[7] In addition to this, another concept of immunity had also been established by the later Middle Ages: the more familiar idea of immunity from arrest. This form of protection emerged in the wake of the judicial initiatives taken by Angevin and Plantagenet rulers in the twelfth and thirteenth centuries. The network of royal courts they established throughout the realm sought to enforce standard judicial procedures, and in so doing made the royal legal system more pervasive than ever before.[8] In this new environment, immunity from arrest became a tangible and valued concession. Rather than guaranteeing the holder protection *by* royal officers, this form of immunity protected them *from* royal officers and their power to arrest or distrain those accused of wrongdoing. When Edward Coke came to survey the traditions surrounding immunity in the seventeenth century, he drew an important distinction between the two forms outlined above:

> Protection is of two sorts, one, to give a man an immunitie or freedome from actions or suits, the second, for the safety of his person, servants and goods, lands and tenements whereof he is lawfully possessed from violence, unlawfull molestation or wrong.[9]

The two ideas were not, of course, always clearly distinguished, but elements of the older notion of immunity from molestation did retain a certain currency in the later Middle Ages. Parliamentary petitions, for example, alluded to these privileges as "liberties and privileges as have been customary and used from of old" and "where of tyme that mannys mynde is not the contrarie."[10] Vestiges of these immunities still survived in legal

7 See, for example, the laws of Æthelberht which stipulate fines for anyone who attacks the people summoned by the king to attend the witenagemot (Abt 2; this is clause 8 in Oliver, *BEL*). Similarly, Cnut grants *grið* to all those travelling to and from the *gemot* (II Cn 82). Several scholars have engaged in a debate over whether letters of protection can be traced as far back as the sixth century; Rosenwein, *Negotiating Space*, 3–4, n. 3, gives the historiographical references. For letters of safe-conduct, see Karsten Plöger, *England and the Avignon Popes: The Practice of Diplomacy in Late Medieval Europe* (London: Legenda, 2005), 127.

8 John Hudson, *The Formation of English Common Law: Law and Society in England from the Norman Conquest to Magna Carta* (London: Longman, 1996), *passim*.

9 Edward Coke, *The First Part of the Institutes of the Laws of England, A Commentary on Littleton*, ed. Charles Butler, 19th ed. (London: J. and W.T. Clarke, 1832), II, ii.199 (103a).

10 "Edward IV: Parliament of January 1478, Text and Translation," in *PROME*, item 35; "Henry VI: Parliament of March 1453, Text and Translation," in *PROME*, item 25.

memory and, when adapted for new purposes, they lent the legitimizing authority of ancient custom.[11] This paper, then, aims to examine the forms of personal immunity granted by the crown in England in the later Middle Ages, and to elucidate the notions of peace and protection that lay behind them.

Personal Immunity from Molestation

a. Early Medieval Precedents

The concept of immunity from molestation featured prominently in the "communal peace-making policies" of the tenth-century West Saxon kings.[12] Alan Cooper argues that these policies were specifically designed to regulate feuding between enemies. Laws from the reigns of Æthelred II and Cnut stipulated that all people were to be immune from the attack of an enemy (without due warning) if they were in a house, or travelling on the highway, or if they held a grant of peace from the king. Breaches of any of these three immunities were deemed to be offences (known as *hamsocn*, *forsteal* and *griðbryce* respectively) for which fines were payable to the crown. Two of these immunities were therefore spatially defined; the individual had to be in a house or on the highway to be protected. The third, however, was a personal form of immunity, which applied to anyone who had been specifically granted protection (*grið*).[13] Additionally, the laws of Æthelred II and Cnut also referred to protected social groups.[14] The clergy were obviously set apart, but there were other groups, including foreigners and widows, who were also placed under the direct protection of the king.

11 Anthony Musson, "Appealing to the Past: Perceptions of Law in Late-Medieval England," in *Expectations of the Law in the Middle Ages*, ed. Anthony Musson (Woodbridge: Boydell, 2001), 165–79; Paul Brand, "'Time Out of Mind': The Knowledge and Use of the Eleventh- and Twelfth-Century Past in Thirteenth-Century Litigation," *Anglo-Norman Studies* 16 (1994): 37–54.

12 Cooper, "Law of the Highway," 58.

13 Cooper, "Law of the Highway," 54–55; R.V. Colman, "Hamsocn: Its Meaning and Significance in Early English Law," *American Journal of Legal History* 25 (1981): 95–110.

14 Stephanie Hollis, "'The Protection of God and the King': Wulfstan's Legislation on Widows," in *Wulfstan, Archbishop of York: the Proceedings of the Second Alcuin Conference*, ed. Matthew Townend, Studies in the Early Middle Ages 10 (Turnhout: Brepols, 2004), 443–60; T.J. Rivers, "Widows' Rights in Anglo-Saxon Law," *American Journal of Legal History* 19 (1975): 208–15; Keechang Kim, *Aliens in Medieval Law: The Origins of Modern Citizenship* (Cambridge: Cambridge University Press, 2001); Norbert Ohler, *The Medieval Traveller*, trans. Caroline Hillier (Woodbridge: Boydell, 1989); Cooper, "Law of the Highway," 47, 62.

Their immunity from molestation purportedly followed the Old Testament exhortation for a monarch to be protector of the defenceless: "Thou shall neither vex a foreigner, nor oppress him: for ye were foreigners in the land of Egypt. Ye shall not afflict any widow, or fatherless child."[15] Late Anglo-Saxon laws also gave special protection to those travelling to and from meetings of the king and his advisers, and fines were to be levied on anyone who attacked people en route to such a meeting.[16]

The question of whether or not these conceptions of immunity survived the arrival of the Common Law and remained, in any meaningful sense, part of the legal culture, is a pertinent one in light of recent revisionist work on the post-Conquest period. Until recently, legal historians continued to acknowledge the clear dividing line drawn by Pollock and Maitland between the old Anglo-Saxon legal order and the new ideas, procedures, and institutions that emerged in the late twelfth century. However, even this notion has been successfully challenged in recent work. Paul Hyams, for example, has demonstrated that ideas of feuding and vengeance survived into the eleventh and twelfth centuries, alongside the emerging Common Law, and Patrick Wormald has finally demolished the last vestiges of Maitland's argument that Henry II and his successors struggled to uproot ancient liberties that had been deeply embedded since well before the Conquest.[17] This scholarship has important implications for our understanding of immunities. Ideas of feuding, in particular, had been intimately connected with immunity since the earliest extant law codes. Hyams notes that, despite Henry I's attempts to impose a "firm peace" throughout his kingdom, "prudent men continued to buy from him and his successors special grants, in writing and so with lasting consequences. These converted violent acts against the grantees and *their* property into breaches of the king's special peace."[18] Evidence from the surviving thirteenth-century plea-rolls further suggests these grants of royal peace were actually becoming *more* frequent as time went on.[19]

15 Exodus 22:21–24.

16 II Cn 82.

17 Paul R. Hyams, *Rancor and Reconciliation in Medieval England* (Ithaca: Cornell University Press, 2003); Wormald, "Oswaldslow Revisited," 117.

18 Hyams, *Rancor and Reconciliation*, 134, 137–86. Hyams draws on the arguments of Garnett and O'Brien: George Garnett, "Coronation and Propaganda: Some Implications of the Norman Claim to the Throne of England in 1066," *Transactions of the Royal Historical Society*, 5th ser., 36 (1986): 91–116; Bruce R. O'Brien, *God's Peace and King's Peace: The Laws of Edward the Confessor* (Philadelphia: University of Pennsylvania Press, 1999).

19 Hyams, *Rancor and Reconciliation*, 133; Naomi D. Hurnard, "The Anglo-Norman Franchises," *English Historical Review* 64 (1949): 289–327, 433–60.

This being the case, it is easy to see why several historians have portrayed this concept of immunity as a forerunner to the general peace of the Common Law, which, by the thirteenth century, theoretically offered protection from molestation to all the king's subjects rather than just to select individuals. Frederick Pollock expressed such a view in his Oxford lectures of 1884: "Thus by the end of the thirteenth century, a time when so much else of our institutions was newly and strongly fashioned for larger uses, the king's peace had fully grown from an occasional privilege into a common right."[20] However, on closer inspection it does not seem that the older immunities were entirely subsumed into the general peace. Despite the emergence of the Common Law, and the introduction of "trespass" as a category of offence to cover crimes such as assault, the older ideas of specific immunities granted directly from the crown did survive into the later Middle Ages.[21] The survival and adaptation of these ideas were prompted by two factors in particular: the first, as Hyams indicates, was the persistence of cultural norms of vengeance and peace-making, which meant that personal immunities were still valued by recipients; the second was the conscious use and evocation of Anglo-Saxon precedents for contemporary purposes.

By the thirteenth century the emergence of the Common Law and particularly the concept of trespass had brought with it new legal remedies for the disputes and conflicts which arose at a local level. Individuals from a broad cross-section of the population increasingly looked to the royal courts for redress of their grievances. However, as Hyams argues, individ-

20 Frederick Pollock, "The King's Peace," in *Oxford Lectures and Other Discourses* (London; New York: Macmillan, 1890), 88. This interpretation has been endorsed by several other historians. See, for example: Alan Harding, "The Medieval Brieves of Protection and the Development of the Common Law," *Juridical Review*, n.s., 2 (1966): 115–49; David Feldman, "The King's Peace, the Royal Prerogative and Public Order: The Roots and Early Development of Binding Over Powers," *Cambridge Law Journal* 41 (1988), 101–128; Jack K. Weber, "The King's Peace: A Comparative Study," *Journal of Legal History* 10 (1989): 135–160. On the accession of Edward I and again when his grandson came to the throne, letters close ordered sheriffs to proclaim the king's general peace; the king was "the debtor" to his subjects "in the exhibition of justice and in the preservation of the peace" (*CCR, 1272–79*, 1; *CCR, 1327–30*, 1).

21 See Baker for the development of trespass writs: John Hamilton Baker, *An Introduction to English Legal History*, 2nd ed. (London: Butterworths, 1979), 56–59. Edward Coke noted that two forms of protection ran in parallel: "It is to be understood that there is a generall protection of the King ... and this extends generally to all the Kings loyall Subjects, Denizens and Aliens within the Realme, whose offences have not made them uncapable of it. ... And there is a particular protection By Writ" (Coke, *The First Part of the Institutes*, II, ii.199 (103a)).

uals learnt to adapt the new remedies toward their old goals. Direct vengeance, by taking the life of an enemy, might now be out of the question because of the risk of prosecution for homicide, but vendettas could still be pursued through the courts. Equally, the king's courts perpetuated long-standing local views and traditions; the jury system, for example, was staffed by local men with knowledge of neighbourhood reputation. Older methods of brokering concords were adapted but not supplanted: out-of-court peace settlements, arbitration, and reconciliation rituals still retained their place in local dispute-resolution.[22] This "underlying continuity of reception" meant that ideas of vengeance and personal immunity retained their significance alongside the innovations of the common law.[23]

b. Individual Grants of Peace

The concept of *grið*, as a personal immunity from molestation, continued to survive in the individual letters of peace, which were routinely issued by the crown's bureaucratic offices from the second half of the twelfth century. It seems that people were reluctant to give up these personal grants of peace because of the more immediate protection they offered in the face of direct threat from an enemy. The evidence for these grants of peace is somewhat sparse, but some archival references do survive. Hyams found several references to them in twelfth- and thirteenth-century case-records, and concluded that these individual grants represented a "common-law link with the older world of private-enterprise power-relations."[24] It is clear that individuals might petition the crown directly for a grant, if they perceived themselves to be under threat in some way, and a royal protection would be awarded in writing. A writ *de minis* (writ of threats) would

22 Hyams, *Rancor and Reconciliation*, 199–208; Thomas Andrew Green, *Verdict According to Conscience: Perspectives on the English Criminal Trial Jury, 1200–1800* (Chicago; London: University of Chicago Press, 1985), *passim;* Bernard William McLane, "Juror Attitudes toward Local Disorder: The Evidence of the 1328 Trailbaston Proceedings," in *Twelve Good Men and True: The Criminal Trial Jury in England, 1200–1800*, ed. James Swanston Cockburn and Thomas Andrew Green (Princeton, NJ: Princeton University Press, 1988), 36–64, at 51–52; Edward Powell, "Jury Trial at Gaol Delivery in the Late Middle Ages: The Midland Circuit, 1400–1429," in *Twelve Good Men*, ed. Cockburn and Green, 78–116, at 112; Edmund King, "Dispute Settlement in Anglo-Norman England," *Anglo-Norman Studies* 14 (1991): 115–30; Edward Powell, "Settlement of Disputes by Arbitration in Fifteenth-Century England," *Law and History Review* 2 (1984): 21–43; Edward Powell, "Arbitration and the Law in England in the Later Middle Ages," *Transactions of the Royal Historical Society*, 5th ser., 13 (1983): 49–67.

23 Hyams, *Rancor and Reconciliation*, 161–62.

24 Hyams, *Rancor and Reconciliation*, 197, nn. 30–33.

then authorize the local sheriff to award a recipient "firm peace." The wording of these writs, recorded in thirteenth- and fourteenth-century collections, suggested that this was a well-established practice:

> The king to the sheriff, greeting. Because A has complained to us grievously that B is threatening him openly as to his person, we command you to cause the aforesaid A to have our firm peace ... according to the custom of England, by taking security that the said A shall not suffer loss or peril ... from B.[25]

The use of the phrase "the custom of England" might have been no more than a vague attempt to lend the writ the authority of age, but the earlier medieval precedents do provide a more specific context for the wording of this writ.[26]

As an alternative to asking the crown directly for such protection, supplicants might instead ask the royal justices to grant letters of peace, in the face of an enemy who had been threatening them. Several such cases can be identified in the eyre rolls: in one example from the 1292 Shropshire eyre, two brothers, Henry and Piers, claimed to have been assaulted by one Thomas Pothelot of Shrewsbury, who had reportedly attacked them on several occasions, once with his knife drawn, intending to kill them. They asked the court "for God's sake that they may have the peace against Thomas." Interestingly, in this case the brothers alluded to a special period of peace, lasting as long as the eyre justices resided in their county: Thomas, they said, attempted to beat them "in the peace of your eyre."[27] Entries in the coroners' rolls also demonstrate that individuals with a par-

25 The earliest recorded writs date from the mid-1260s: Elsa de Haas and George D.G. Hall, ed. and trans., *Early Registers of Writs*, Selden Society 87 (London: Quaritch, 1970), CC. 107–107a. An early fourteenth century example can be found in the same volume: de Haas and Hall, *Early Registers of Writs*, R.253–54.

26 Bracton's law code, dating from the mid-thirteenth century, also includes a brief mention of this form of protection: "A. appeals B. for the death of C. his brother, that whereas the said A. and C. his brother were in the peace of God and of the king at such a place, doing such a thing (or 'crossing from such a place to such') on such a day in such a year and at such an hour, the said B. came with such persons (to be named) and wickedly, feloniously, in premeditated assault and against the king's peace given to him, dealt the aforesaid C. his brother a mortal wound" (Samuel E. Thorne, ed. and trans., *Bracton on the Laws and Customs of England* [Cambridge, MA: Harvard University Press, 1977], 2: 388).

27 William Craddock Bolland, ed. and trans., *Select Bills in Eyre, A.D. 1292–1333*, Selden Society 30 (London: Quaritch, 1914), 7; H.G. Richardson and G.O. Sayles, *Select Cases of Procedure without Writ under Henry III*, Selden Society 60 (London: Quaritch, 1941), xi.

ticular grievance against an enemy could force them to agree to peace in court, and to find sureties to that effect. In one case from November 1275, Richard Reaper came to court and "sought the king's peace" of Everard of Beeston and Richard Woodward, because they had made threats to his life, and had beaten and ill-treated him. It was therefore ordered that the two men were to be required "to come to the next county court to wage peace to him." Everard duly appeared before the court the following month, to wage peace to Richard, and to produce pledges who would stand surety for his future peaceful conduct.[28]

By the later fourteenth century this process was also being undertaken in the Court of Chancery; individuals were able to present their case against an enemy to the court, who would then demand that the defendant find "sureties for peace." In one such case from 1388, Robert Dane, citizen and mercer of London, complained that when he journeyed to Kent to survey certain lands and tenements, he found that a certain Thomas Holbein had laid an ambush for him with "twenty archers and many other people," who intended to kill him. Robert therefore asked the court to order Thomas to appear before them and find surety for the peace.[29] The final stage in such a process appears to have been the proclamation of the grant of peace in court (the county court was the usual venue, although another declaration might also be made by the royal justices in eyre, or at a session of *oyer et terminer* or gaol delivery).[30] In one case from Edward II's reign it was noted that final peace had been proclaimed (this time after a royal pardon had been read aloud), and that the marshal was to receive 2 shillings for carrying out the service:

> Solemn proclamation is now made that if any there be who will make suit against him for the aforesaid death, let him now come forward. And none there is to bring suit. So firm peace is granted to him. And note that every clerk shall have a pair of gloves, and the chief clerks 2 shillings and the marshalls 2 shillings for proclaiming his peace.[31]

28 Charles Gross, ed. and trans., *Select Cases from the Coroners' Rolls, A.D. 1265–1413*, Selden Society 9 (London: Quaritch, 1896): 33–34 (for further examples, see 35–38, 104).

29 William Paley Baildon, ed. and trans., *Select Cases in Chancery, A.D. 1364 to 1471*, Selden Society 10 (London: Quaritch, 1896), 8, no. 7 (see also nos. 5, 6, 22, 37, 52, 54, 59, 62, 65, 68, 69, 82, 84, 93, 139, 145).

30 Naomi D. Hurnard, *The King's Pardon for Homicide before A.D. 1307* (Oxford: Clarendon Press, 1969), 61, n. 4, 62; R.F. Hunnisett, *The Medieval Coroner* (Cambridge: Cambridge University Press, 1961), 78–79.

31 Frederick William Maitland, Leveson William Vernon Harcourt and William Craddock Bolland, ed. and trans., *The Eyre of Kent: 6 and 7 Edward II,*

Violations of these grants of peace also appear among the court records. In one such case from the mid-thirteenth century, William Bardolf brought a case against William of Kyme for burning down one of his houses, stealing his goods, and assaulting his men. Bardolf claimed that he had already demanded the protection of the King's Peace against Kyme, because of the large number of threats the latter had issued against him. Kyme had finally contravened the peace by sending 300 armed men to attack Bardolf's lands, men, and possessions. Bardolf estimated his losses amounted to £1,000.[32] In this case, and in the other extant examples, seeking the King's Peace against an individual seems to be one stage in a long-running feud. Contravention of this peace ultimately saw the case brought to court, and added to the gravity of the accusations levelled at the defendant. Clearly, the parties involved (or at least one of them) were willing to use the apparatus of the royal courts, but their grievances and their request for peace and protection harked back to a world of private bonds of protection.

c. Simple Protection

Letters of "simple protection" also provided immunity from molestation, but this time the protection applied to the servants and property of the bearer, whilst they themselves were away from home on royal business. Anyone who interfered with their lands, goods or servants in their absence was threatened with prosecution. Inquiries were made into alleged contraventions of these orders:

> Order to inquire ... which evildoers and disturbers of our peace with force and arms took and carried away goods and chattels to the value of £10 found at N. belonging to A., when we had taken into our special protection and defence his men, lands and rents, forbidding all and singular from causing them injury, annoyance, damage or loss ... the said A being on our business under our protection ... against our aforesaid protection and against our peace.[33]

Several cases concerning breaches of these protections reached the courts. From these records, it is clear that writs of simple protection were

---

A.D. 1313–1314, Selden Society 24 (London: Quaritch, 1910), 1: 139. See Hurnard, *King's Pardon*, 65.

32 Richardson and Sayles, *Procedure without Writ*, 31–32, no. 22.

33 De Haas and Hall, *Early Registers of Writs*, 269. See also: Elsie Shanks, ed. and trans., *Novae Narrationes*, Selden Society 80 (London: Quaritch, 1963), 15, 122, 237; Oxford, Bodleian Library, MS Additional C. 188, *fols.* 166r–v.

issued to a wide range of people; "royal service" was conceived in broad terms. Soldiers such as William de Goneville, on the king's service in Wales in 1282, might complain that their neighbours had entered their lands in their absence, violating a grant of protection (these complaints, it seems, were often lodged with the crown by the soldier's military commander, on their behalf).[34] Similarly, royal clerks enjoyed such protection; in one case from 1384, a writ was sent to the sheriff of Sussex, ordering him to inquire into a theft perpetrated against Thomas de Middelton, king's clerk and precentor of Chichester. It appeared that while Thomas had been "constantly employed in his [the king's] service," thieves had forced entry into his property at Oving in Sussex and stolen his goods, including three horses and the cart harnessed to them.[35]

Immunity from Arrest

a. Judicial Protections

By the mid-thirteenth century, letters of judicial protection were being issued to guarantee the safety of the recipient's servants and possessions for a limited period of time in their absence, and to protect them from a court summons or arrest.[36] Anyone going abroad in the service of the king, or for certain approved journeys such as pilgrimage, might collect such a letter from the royal writing-office of Chancery before departing.[37] The number of letters being issued varied considerably across the period, but certainly never exceeded one hundred in any given year, and figures were often far lower. As the graph below shows (p. 92) peaks occurred at times of political insecurity or particularly intense diplomatic activity. One such peak at the start of Edward II's reign (1307–13), for instance, highlights the range of diplomatic activity initiated by the new government. Envoys and diplomats were sent abroad in higher numbers than usual on missions to the French court to arrange Edward's marriage to Isabella and to discuss the

34 J. Goronwy Edwards, ed. and trans., *Calendar of Ancient Correspondence Concerning Wales*, History and Law Series 2 (Cardiff: University Press Board, 1935), 107; J.S. Critchley, "The Early History of the Writ of Judicial Protection," *Bulletin of the Institute of Historical Research* 45 (1972): 196, n. 6.

35 *CIM 1377–88*, vol. 4, 176–77.

36 Critchley explains the difference between simple protection and judicial protection in more detail in "Judicial Protection," 196–97. See also: Harding, "Medieval Brieves," 115–49; Pierre Chaplais, *English Medieval Diplomatic Practice*, part 1: *Documents and Interpretation* (London: H.M.S.O, 1982), 308–10.

37 George Peddy Cuttino, *English Diplomatic Administration, 1259–1339*, 2nd ed. (Oxford: Clarendon Press, 1971), 158.

Scottish truce. They were also dispatched to the papal curia to promote the canonization of Thomas Cantilupe, to persuade the pope to rescind the excommunication of Piers Gaveston, and to annul the Ordinances of 1311. Another peak in 1330–34 related to the heightened diplomatic activity at the time of Edward III's assumption of majority rule; while in 1385–89 the insecurity generated by the challenge of the Lords Appellant led to an increase in the number of protections being issued.[38]

Sometimes the fraudulent use of these protections generated inquiries which ultimately resulted in the grant being revoked. This abuse of letters of protection prompted critical comments about the ease with which supplicants seemed to secure them. Soldiers, in particular, were investigated for claiming protections fraudulently, on the basis that they were going overseas on the king's service, when in fact they remained at home.[39] The year books record examples of lawyers arguing against the validity of protections. In one example from Edward II's reign, the lawyer asked for the protection to be disallowed on the grounds that the recipient had not departed for royal service abroad. Possession of the letter alone did not prove that he had actually served, and its terms of protection were only valid if he did so:

> There is no reason for adjourning this cause without day by virtue of this protection for the king does not attest by his protection that he is in service; but he gives him leave to go beyond the sea, and there remain in his service for one year. And that is what the protection said. And "the new ordinances" state that the Great Charter is to be kept in all its points; and it says that "to no man will we sell or deny right or justice." But if this cause were awarded to be without day by virtue of this protection, it would be so awarded without reason, and against the Great Charter.[40]

Similarly there are references to "fraudulent transcripts of protection" being enrolled in the plea rolls, having first been written out in chancery

38. Figures used for this graph are based on the Patent Rolls, and should be viewed as approximations; duplications exist in the rolls, and some letters were intended to cover more than one person.

39 *CIM, 1348–1377*, vol. 3, 107, 291, 343, 401; *CIM, 1392–1399*, vol. 6, 78–79; *CIM, 1399–1422*, vol. 7, 254; *CCR 1313–18*, 555; de Haas and Hall, *Early Registers of Writs*, 172.

40 William Craddock Bolland, ed. and trans., *Year Books of Edward II: 5 Edward II, A.D. 1312*, Selden Society 33 (London: Quaritch, 1916): 6–8; A.J. Horwood, ed. and trans., *Year Books of the Reign of King Edward the Third, 20 Edward III*, Rolls Series 31a (London, 1883–1911), 1: 26.

and sealed by the chancellor.[41] In one case it was claimed before the chancellor that a "false" letter of protection was being used as a delaying tactic in court proceedings, to the detriment of the plaintiff. The implication was that the chancellor had the authority to repeal the protection, which had been purchased "by fraud and ill design."[42] Judicial protections might also be disallowed if the letter had not been properly drafted, or if the recipient was trying to claim full judicial protection, when in fact their letter only gave them "simple" protection.[43] The repeal of letters of protection could also force a court case to be reconvened; in one example from 1356, Thomas Mott, a draper, had been summoned to court on a charge of abducting Joan de Coggeshall.[44] However, on the day appointed, an associate of Thomas appeared in court and proffered the lord king's letters of protection, which excused Thomas from attending court for the duration of his service overseas (in the fortification at Calais). By virtue of this letter, the case was postponed. However, the court rolls then record that the king subsequently sent a letter to William de Shareshull, the chief justice, advising him that Thomas's letter of protection had been cancelled, because it had been proved before Chancery that Thomas had not in fact embarked for the Continent. The justices duly appointed a day for Thomas to appear before them, and when he defaulted again they awarded damages to Joan's guardian, Henry Galeys, and ordered that Thomas be arrested. Fraudulent use of these protections was treated by the crown with some seriousness; the ability to guarantee protection was an important manifestation of royal power, and any such abuse might bring this into question.

b. Letters of Safe-Conduct

The English chancery issued letters of safe-conduct to provide for the physical safety of recipients while they travelled within the king's realm. Letters patent of recommendation and credence might also be issued to Englishmen travelling abroad, to request protection from a foreign monarch.[45] Recipients of safe-conducts tended to be foreign merchants or envoys coming to

41 George Osborne Sayles, ed. and trans., *Select Cases in the Court of King's Bench Under Edward I*, Selden Society 57 (London: Quaritch, 1938), cxxxii, cxxxv.

42 Baildon, *Select Cases in Chancery*, 124.

43 M. Dominica Legge and William Holdsworth, ed. and trans., *Year Books of Edward II: 10 Edward II, A.D. 1316–1317*, Selden Society 52 (London: Quaritch, 1934), 15.

44 Morris S. Arnold, *Select Cases of Trespass from the King's Courts*, Selden Society 100 (London: Quaritch, 1985), 1: 94–96.

45 Chaplais, *Diplomatic Practice*, 311–19; Cuttino, *Diplomatic Administration*, 157–59; Plöger, *Avignon Popes*, 126–36.

England for a set period of time. In the reigns of Edward I and II they were also issued quite frequently to English subjects, often because they were travelling at the king's request from one part of his realm to another on royal business. However, far fewer safe-conducts were issued for this reason in the later fourteenth century and this seems to have contributed to an overall decline across the century (see graph below, p. 92). Why this decline in use occurred is uncertain – possibly it was felt that the peace of the common law was sufficient protection for native Englishmen, or perhaps kings like Richard II increasingly relied on a smaller clique of royal servants to carry out the business of the crown.

Envoys routinely carried standard letters of safe-conduct, but in a few examples, these letters contained an extra clause stipulating that the bearer had been granted immunity from arrest whilst they were in a foreign realm. Karsten Plöger refers to one case in which Edward III asked Pope Clement VI to issue letters of full immunity to his envoys in Avignon.[46] These letters were unusual, in that they granted immunity from arrest and from legal action relating to any acts or offences already committed by the envoys (but not for any new cases while in Avignon). As Plöger points out, Edward's request was intended to question the protection offered by the papacy, and, by implication, the power it exercised; one of Edward's previous envoys to the curia had been abducted from his home, and the king was not slow to use this incident as a delaying tactic to hold up the peace process between the English and the French, which had been instigated by the pope.[47]

By the later fourteenth century, cases of infringement of this form of protection were being heard before the court of chancery. In one such case, a merchant from Lucca, in Lombardy, described how he was staying in England under the protection of the king, when he was arrested on false accusations of theft and abduction.[48] His accuser failed to appear in court on the appointed day, but subsequently continued to sue "divers plaints before the sheriffs of London ... on which plaints the said supplicant hath been arrested and imprisoned and put to fine and ransom for his deliverance; and every time when the said supplicant appeared in court to answer, the said Richard [plaintiff] was non-suited." It seems that the real reason the merchant was being targeted through the courts in this way was that his accuser held him responsible for abducting his wife (the merchant finally claimed at the end of the hearing that she had left of her own accord, and was already divorced). Implicit in this case seems to be the suggestion that the king's letters of protection should allow the merchant full

46 Plöger, *Avignon Popes*, 131–33.
47 Plöger, *Avignon Popes*, 128–29.
48 Baildon, *Select Cases in Chancery*, 20.

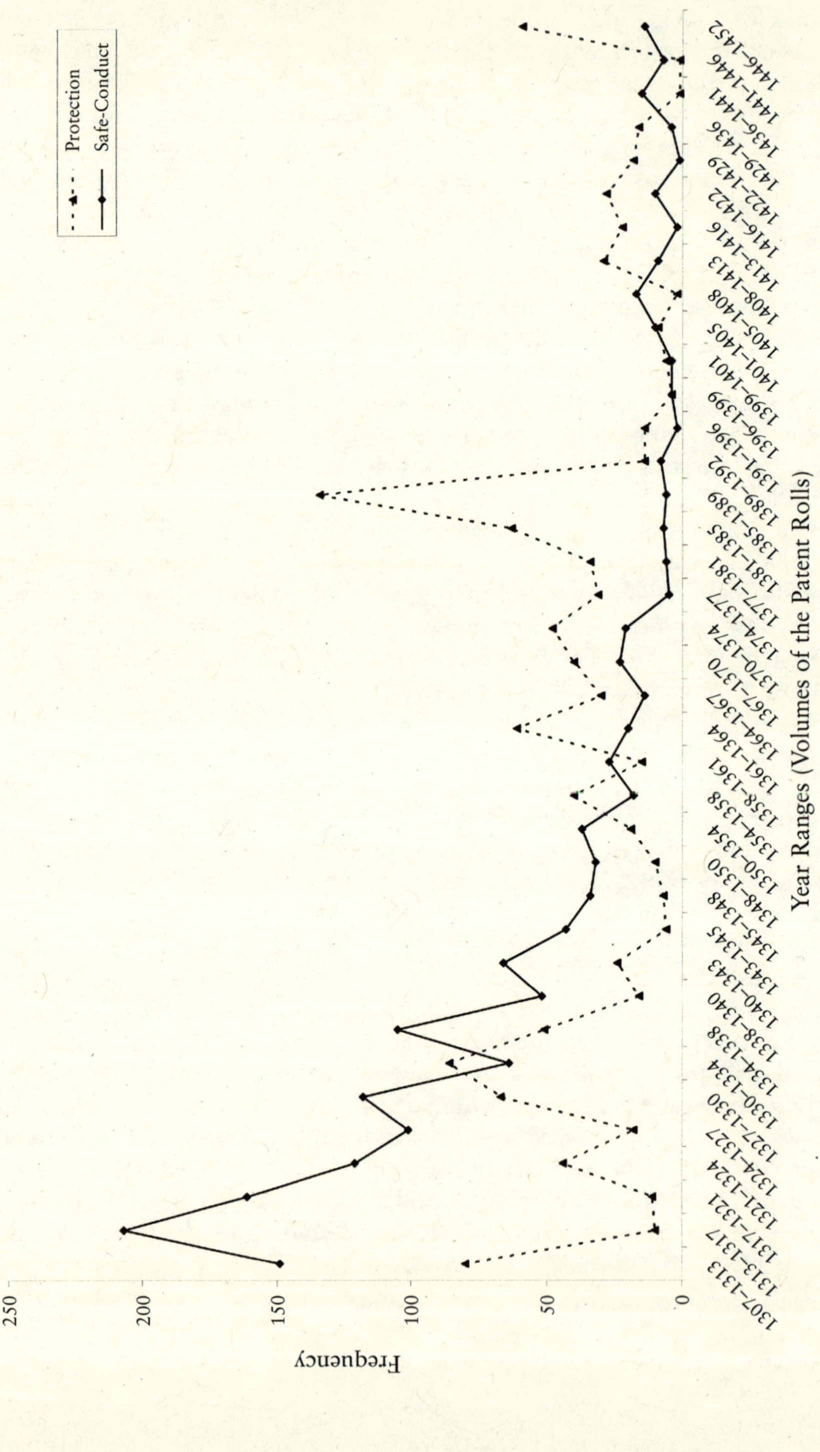

Letters of Judicial Protection and Safe-Conduct

immunity from the proceedings repeatedly initiated against him in the law courts.

Survival and Adaptation

a. Parliament

The idea that personal immunity had an ancient provenance gave it a certain currency in the later Middle Ages. Parliamentary representatives, for example, were, at particular times, keen to claim their long-standing privileges of immunity. In one petition submitted to parliament in the 1320s, for example, the supplicant complained that he had been attacked whilst attending parliament in London, despite being "in the king's protection." In response, the crown restated that the supplicant "should have protection for prosecuting the king's and his business for one year."[49] In another case from the end of Edward II's reign, Roger du Brok stated that "although all those who come to parliament should be under the king's protection, both as regards their lands and possessions and as regards their bodies, one of the Sheriffs of London has sued in time of parliament, by colour of his office, to have half his [du Brok's] lands and chattels, based on a recognizance made by him in Chancery, under coercion by Hugh le Despenser the son, John de Charleton, and Thomas de Sibethorp." Despite his invocation of the privilege, however, du Brok's petition was refused.[50]

In legislation of the early fifteenth century, the Commons referred to the privilege of parliament, suggesting that it should be regarded as a custom of long standing, rather than a new innovation. In 1404 they petitioned for special protection to cover those travelling to and from parliament, citing the recent case of Richard Chedder, a servant of a Member of Parliament, who had been attacked and maimed. Their suggested scale of punishment was particularly severe:

> If anyone kills or murders anyone who has come in this way under your protection to parliament, it should be adjudged to be treason, and if anyone seriously injures or disfigures any such person who has come in this way under protection, he should lose his hand. And if anyone

49 London, National Archives, SC 8/42/2094.

50 London, National Archives, SC 8/97/4815. See also W.N. Bryant, "Commons' Immunity from Arrest: The Earliest Known Case (1340)," *Bulletin of the Institute of Historical Research* 43 (1970): 214–15. From the beginning of Richard II's reign, the Commons claimed immunity from arrest for anything said during parliament. This was reaffirmed at the start of each parliamentary session: "Richard II: Parliament of October 1377, Text and Translation," in *PROME*, item 15.

> wounds or assaults any of those people who have come in this way, he should be put in prison for a year and pay a fine and redemption to the king.

However, the crown did not endorse this, stipulating instead that the offender would be liable to double damages if they did not appear for trial.[51] The issue arose again in 1453, when the arrest of the Commons' speaker, Thomas Thorpe, for trespass, provoked a dispute over the applicability of the privilege of immunity; the Commons claimed that their ancient liberties had been disregarded, but their stance was opposed by the Duke of York, who was joined by the Lords in calling upon judges to arbitrate in the matter. The judges concluded that Thorpe should be released, but their advice was subsequently ignored.[52] In another petition of January 1478, it was claimed that these parliamentary privileges had existed beyond living memory:

> where of tyme that mannys mynde is not the contrarie it hath been used that the knyghtes of the shires, citezeins of citees, burgies of burghes, and barons of .v. portes of this your reame, called to any of the parlementes of your noble progenitours or yours ... have had and used pryvylege that eny of theym shuld not be empleded in any action personell, nor be attached by their persone or goodes in their comyng to any such parlement, there abidyng, nor fro thens to their propre home resortyng.[53]

In other petitions dating from the fourteenth century, supplicants complaining of molestation and attack made a point of mentioning their link with parliament, perhaps in an attempt to invoke the privilege. In 1322, Reginald de Frome stated that he was on his way to parliament in York to represent the county of Somerset, when one William de la Beche came to the hall of the king at the church of the Friars Minor and attacked him, "against the dignity of the crown and the king of £1000." Reginald was

51 "Henry IV: Parliament of January 1404, Text and Translation," in *PROME*, item 78; *Statutes of the Realm*, 11 vols. (London: Record Commission, 1810–28), 2: 144. This case was again referred to by the Commons in the parliament of July 1433, and the penalty of double damages was confirmed. *PROME*, "Henry VI: Parliament of July 1433, Text and Translation," item 60; *Statutes of the Realm*, 2: 286; Carl Frederick Wittke, *The History of English Parliamentary Privilege* (Columbus, OH: Ohio State University, 1921), 32–49.

52 "Henry VI: Parliament of March 1453, Text and Translation," in *PROME*, item 25.

53 "Edward IV: Parliament of January 1478, Text and Translation," in *PROME*, item 35.

instructed to sue before the steward and marshal of the king.[54] In 1378, James de Pykeryng, Member of Parliament for Westmorland, accused Thomas de Roos of ambushing him with 300 armed men just as he had set out on the journey south to parliament, killing two of his men and wounding six.[55] The premeditated nature of the attack in this instance added to the culpability of the accused. In two other petitions, the proximity to parliament, and in particular the proximity to the king himself was noted: in the first case a petitioner asked for an order to be made that no one in the king's service "should thereafter be ruined, and that due remedy be made for certain wrongs and damages," after assailants had waited in ambush "near the door of the palace of Westminster and there (in the presence of the king), attacked William [the petitioner's brother] and struck him on the head such that he despaired of life."[56] In the second case, a Member of Parliament serving in Westminster was murdered by two of Richard II's notorious Cheshire archers. The two assassins had lain in wait for him "both on the River Thames and on the high roads from London to Westminster," before finally ambushing him and murdering him on Fleet Street. The petition made clear that they murdered him "in the presence of the king and the whole parliament."[57] It seems plausible to suggest that these petitions were invoking the status of parliament and the presence of the king in part at least to bring to mind the notions of special protection and immunity that went with them.

b. Legal Memory

This invocation of "ancient immunities" can be viewed in the wider context of scholarship on legal memory and knowledge of past legal custom. Paul Brand has demonstrated that defendants in thirteenth-century land-claims and in Edward I's *quo warranto* proceedings attempted to base their defence on Anglo-Saxon precedent. Some cited particular pre-Conquest charters, but for others the claim was based on oral tradition. However, by the beginning of the fourteenth century, the limit of general "legal memory" was increasingly taken to be the date of Richard I's accession on 3 September 1189; the period prior to this was "time out of mind."[58] Despite this development, the idea of "ancient" legal precedents still carried an air of authority, even if they were inadmissible in a court,

54 London, National Archives, SC 8/219/10927.

55 London, National Archives, SC 8/67/3308.

56 London, National Archives, SC 8/103/5108.

57 London, National Archives, SC 8/249/12437; Gwilym Dodd, "Getting Away with Murder: Sir John Haukeston and Richard II's Cheshire Archers," *Nottingham Mediaeval Studies* 46 (2002): 102–17.

58 Brand, "Time Out of Mind," 37–54.

and the claim that parliamentary privilege had existed "where of tyme that mannys mynde is not the contrarie" was intended to support, rather than to question its legitimacy. Anthony Musson argues that appeals to the legal past had three main functions: to legitimize the present; to inform or transform it; or to provide a sense of identity.[59] As far as the concept of immunity was concerned, letters of protection were said to accord with the "custom of England" and claims of ancient parliamentary privilege lent support to proposed legislation, thus transforming the legal present. The privilege of immunity perhaps also augmented the sense of a distinct identity among those who could claim an association with parliament.

Medieval chroniclers, too, were interested in ancient legal precedent and its potential to inform present legislation. Andrew Horn's legal collections of the early fourteenth century, for example, were attempts to compile law codes from the Anglo-Saxon period up to his own day, providing ancient provenance for contemporary liberties.[60] Invocation of these ancient law codes, then, provided a shorthand reference to a generalized sense of established principles, liberties, privileges, and immunities. Letters of protection, safe-conducts, and parliamentary immunity all granted the recipient the King's Peace, and with it, a clear sign of the monarch's ultimate power over the judicial system that operated in his name. In another sense, they also embodied a more general concept of ancient privilege and immunity, which, although perhaps never a reality, was certainly an influential and pervasive idea in the later Middle Ages.

59 Musson, "Appealing to the Past," 165.

60 Jeremy Catto, "Andrew Horn: Law and History in Fourteenth-Century England," in *The Writing of History in the Middle Ages: Essays Presented to Richard William Southern*, ed. R.H.C. Davis and J.M. Wallace-Hadrill (Oxford: Oxford University Press, 1981), 383.

PART II

The Peace of the Church

STEFAN JURASINSKI
SUNY Brockport

Madness and Responsibility in Anglo-Saxon England

This paper reconsiders the thesis, first proposed by Nigel Walker in 1968, that Anglo-Saxon law offered particular protection for insane offenders by urging "leniency" towards them.[1] Walker's arguments have been repeated approvingly in subsequent studies and never, as far as I can tell, disputed.[2] Yet, pioneering as they were, they face serious difficulties that have yet to be explored in published scholarship. The legislative evidence adduced by Walker often seems more equivocal than he suggests, and his arguments undoubtedly perpetuate misrepresentations of this evidence by earlier commentators. The range of evidence considered in the above-mentioned studies is also strikingly limited. Inexplicably absent from the discussion are the penitentials, Church councils and secular legislation promulgated on the Continent that address the liability of the insane. Saints' lives assuming a distinct position toward those so afflicted likewise go unremarked. The present paper both reevaluates the prescriptive texts Walker assumed were evidence of leniency and situates the discussion initiated by Walker within a broader range of evidence. My hope is that this inquiry will afford a clearer sense of the protections enjoyed by the insane in the era before the Conquest than has previously been possible.

Walker's thesis that Anglo-Saxon law urged "leniency" for insane offenders was based on early English legislative statements which he considered might refer to those who kill while insane. Now, in spite of formidable arguments to the contrary launched over a century ago by Heinrich Brunner, there can be little doubt that late Anglo-Saxon royal legislation unreservedly acknowledged a distinction between accidental and deliberate

1 For their comments on earlier versions of this paper, I am greatly indebted to R.D. Fulk, Bruce O'Brien, and Lisi Oliver, as well as to the editors of this volume. Any errors that remain are, of course, my own.

2 Nigel Walker, *Crime and Insanity in England*, vol. 1: *The Historical Perspective* (Edinburgh: Edinburgh University Press, 1968), 17; Simon Kemp, *Medieval Psychology*, Contributions in Psychology 14 (New York: Greenwood Press, 1994), 126; Don Grubin, *Fitness to Plead in England and Wales*, Maudsley Monographs 38 (East Sussex: Psychology Press, 1996), 6–7.

wrongs and regarded the absence of volition as a mitigating circumstance.[3] Such attitudes are especially evident in one clause adduced by Walker: a chapter of the code known as VI Æthelred that is one of the few directives in Anglo-Saxon legislation explicitly securing lighter penalties for those whose wrongs are unintentional:

> And if it happens that a man commits a misdeed, involuntarily or unintentionally (*unwilles oþþe ungewealdes*), the case is different from that of one who offends of his own freewill, voluntarily and intentionally; and likewise he who is an involuntary agent (*se þe nydwyrhta bið*) in his misdeeds should always be entitled to clemency and to better terms, owing to the fact that he acted as an involuntary agent (*þe he nydwyrhta wæs*).[4]

The usage of contemporaneous normative texts, however, suggests that this statement (which Wulfstan was to reiterate in II Cnut 68.2) refers to a set of unintended wrongs too limited to encompass the acts of the insane. The adverb *ungewealdes* is typically used to describe accidents, as is the case in Alfred's code and subsequent prescriptive writings in Old English.[5] As for the second clause, compounds in Old English legislation of which *nyd* is the first element designate cases of external compulsion, as in *nydhemede* ("rape") and *nidgild* ("tribute"); in the *Old English Penitential*, a man who "neadunga man ofslyhð" ("slays a man unwillingly") is assigned the same penance as one who accidentally suffocates his child in his sleep, and the editor of the penitential plausibly assumes that this provision refers

3 See Heinrich Brunner, "Über absichtslose Missethat im altdeutschen Strafrechte," in *Forschungen zur Geschichte des deutschen und französischen Rechtes* (Stuttgart: J.G. Cotta, 1890), 487–523; John H. Wigmore, "Responsibility for Tortious Acts: Its History," *Harvard Law Review* 7 (1894): 315–37; Frederick Pollock and Frederic William Maitland, *The History of English Law Before the Time of Edward I*, 2nd ed., 2 vols. (Cambridge: Cambridge University Press, 1898), 54–55. For criticisms of Brunner's views see Percy Winfield, "The Myth of Absolute Liability," *Law Quarterly Review* 42 (1926): 37–51.

4 VI Atr 52: "Gif hit geweorþeð, þæt man unwilles oþþe ungewealdes ænig þing misdeð, na bið þæt na gelic þam þe willes gewealdes sylfwilles misdeð; eac se þe nydwyrhta bið þæs þe he misdeð, se bið gebeorhges þy beteran domes symle wyrðe, þe he nydwyrhta wæs þæs þe he worhte." Trans. A.J. Robertson.

5 Af 13. Cf. also *Old English Penitential* II.1.d, "Gif hwa his cild ofslyhð to deaðe ungewealdes, fæste III ger ...," which refers to the accidental suffocation of a child in one's sleep and likely translates *Excarpsus Cummeani* VI.10: "Si quis infantem oppresserit, tres annos pœniteat ..." (Josef Raith, ed., *Die Altenglische Version des Halitgar'schen Bussbuches*, Bibliothek der Angelsachsischen Prosa 12 [Darmstadt: Wissenschaftliche Buchgesellschaft, 1964], 16).

to one who kills at the urging of his lord.[6] That the interest of VI Æthelred is confined to those who kill accidentally or under orders makes sense given that these are the two forms of unintentional wrongs with which penitentials and secular legislation routinely concern themselves.[7]

Let us now turn to the other texts routinely invoked in favour of the thesis that Anglo-Saxon legislation extended leniency towards the insane, as these continue to suffer under grave mischaracterizations inherited by Walker and his adherents from earlier scholarship. Foremost among them is chapter 78.7 of the *Leges Henrici Primi*, a twelfth-century recasting of pre-Conquest laws. Though the chapter is now seen as proof that early English law allowed "for persons to be not guilty on the grounds of their state of mind," the text itself says only (in L.J. Downer's translation) that "their relatives should compassionately care for insane persons and dangerous people of this kind (*insanos et eiusmodi maleficos*)."[8] Earlier scholarship had understood this chapter merely to imply that the insane, violent or otherwise, were committed to the care of their kin and kept under "considerate" conditions.[9] Walker was the first to suggest its relevance for the legal liability of the insane, and his remarks would appear to form the basis of all subsequent discussion:

> Succinct as this precept is, several inferences can be drawn from it. In the first place, the word "misericorditer" is probably more significant than it seems at first sight. *Misericordia* was the technical term for the king's mercy, and *misericorditer* probably means not merely "with pity," but "with leniency" or even "without punishment." Secondly, it seems clear that even when the insane person had been an "evildoer" (*maleficus*) it was for his parents to keep him in such a way that he could not do further harm, and probably – as in the case of the deaf and the dumb – to pay his forfeitures.[10]

In a broad sense, Walker is right about the legal connotations of *misericordia*. But it is hard to see why he dismisses so readily the notion that *misericordia* is best translated here as "pity," particularly since the small amount of evidence we have suggests that mercy was conspicuously lacking

6 Raith, *Altenglische Version*, 15; cf. Af 25, 29.

7 Cf. Bede IV.4–8, in F.W.H. Wasserschleben, ed., *Die Bußordnungen der abendländischen Kirche* (Halle: Verlag Graeger, 1851), 225.

8 Kemp, *Medieval Psychology*, 126; Hn 78: 7.

9 Wilfrid Bonser, *The Medical Background of Anglo-Saxon England: A Study in History, Psychology, and Folklore* (London: Wellcome Historical Medical Library, 1963), 259; cf. Liebermann, *Gesetze*, 2, s.v. "Wahnsinn."

10 Walker, *Crime and Insanity in England*, 17–18.

from the care of the insane. The medical treatise known as *Bald's Leechbook* suggests that a demoniac be forced to drink a vomit-inducing mix of herbs from a church bell, while *Leechbook III* prescribes lashings with the skin of a porpoise.[11] Even the less exotic remedies were far from kind. "In the earlier non-medical literature," Stanley Rubin observes, "the management of the lunatic or the mentally disturbed was often to bind their limbs until the acute phase had subsided."[12] The connotations of binding in this era presumably would have reinforced an impression of its cruelty: Alfred's code imposes a substantial tariff on forcible binding with language acknowledging its power to humiliate.[13]

That legislation would have urged the merciful application of these measures seems unsurprising, as their cruelty occasionally made them the objects of clerical denunciation. Walter Daniel's *Epistola ad Mauricium* shows St. Ailred of Rievaulx, upon being nearly slain by an insane monk, declining to have his assailant "beaten or bound or fettered as a madman."[14] Perhaps most relevant to the interpretation of this chapter is the case of a girl briefly mentioned in William of Malmesbury's *Vita Wulfstani* who is driven by her madness to wander uncontrollably (a conventional symptom in hagiography), whereupon her parents bind her with fetters. While acknowledging that some might say the parents' measures were unduly severe, the narrator reassures us that "on this harshness followed mercy (*misericordia*), and the more she suffered the greater the remedies they tried to hunt down."[15] None of these analogues is mentioned in any studies that touch on this portion of the *Leges Henrici Primi.* They show that the *Leges* cannot have been alone in their disdain for the cruelty to which the insane might be subjected, nor is it the only text to urge *misericordia* on their behalf. To translate *misericorditer* as "leniently" thus

11 Thomas Oswald Cockayne, ed., *Leechdoms, Wortcunning and Starcraft of Early England*, Rolls Series 35, 3 vols. (London: Longman, Green, Longman, Roberts, and Green, 1864–66; repr. Holland Press, 1961), 2: 137–39, 3: 335.

12 Stanley Rubin, *Medieval English Medicine* (New York: Barnes and Noble, 1974), 126–27. The laws of Hywel Dda define an insane person as someone "whom it has once been necessary to bind on account of his madness": see Basil Clarke, *Mental Disorder in Earlier Britain: Exploratory Studies* (Cardiff: University of Wales Press, 1975), 34.

13 Cf. Af 35.

14 *The Life of Ailred of Rievaulx*, ed. and trans. Sir Maurice Powicke (Oxford: Clarendon Press, 1978), 79: "Non iussit eum a monasterio expelli, non uerberari, non iussit quasi freneticum ligari uel compede constringi. ..." Cf. Rubin, *Medieval English Medicine*, 127.

15 *William of Malmesbury: Saints' Lives*, ed. and trans. M. Winterbottom and R.M. Thomson (Oxford: Clarendon Press, 2002), 68–69. "Sed enim seueritatem secuta est misericordia, et quo maior erat miseria maiora uenabantur remedia."

seems to overlook the less conjectural possibility that the text simply enjoins the relatives of a lunatic to employ a minimum of violence in pursuit of their obligation to restrain him.

In this way, an injunction that a lunatic's kin perform their obligations compassionately came to be seen, through a tendentious translation, as a statement on the liability of the insane. Similarly, rendering *maleficos* as "evildoers" converts the *misericordia* required for the insane into a normative response to their acts of violence. This translation is especially troublesome, for the suggestion that *maleficos* should be translated here as "evildoers" requires us to believe, as Downer observed, that the *Leges* here demand merciful treatment for a class of persons the text had earlier condemned to execution for their wrongs. In chapter 71 of the *Leges*, the term *malefici* designates sorcerers: should their spells result in death, they are to be abandoned to the vengeance of their victim's kin.[16] Accordingly, Downer suggests that "evildoer" might not be the best translation in the chapter concerned with insanity. Since the word *maleficus* "elsewhere means 'magician,' 'sorcerer' ... it is possible," Downer observes, "that 'victim of magic or sorcery' is the meaning here, though perhaps unlikely."[17] Downer's remarks seem needlessly dismissive of the possibility he suggests; it is a commonplace that the medical thought of the early Middle Ages made few apparent distinctions between insanity and possession, and so their collocation in this portion of the *Leges* is what one might expect. Inducing madness was also believed to be one of the occupations of sorcerers, as is attested by the ninth-century penitential of Halitgar of Cambrai: "If anyone is a wizard (*mathematicus*), that is, if he takes away the mind of a man by the invocation of demons, he shall do penance for five years, one year on bread and water."[18]

Given that some forms of sorcery were understood as requiring their practitioners to undergo demon possession, it seems likely that *maleficos* might designate in this instance demoniacs who suffer possession as a consequence of engagement in magic, yielding a translation of "insanos et eiusmodi maleficos" something like "insane people and sorcerers of that sort."[19] Though the belief has its origins in Rome, the assumption that some who engaged in auguries were possessed or otherwise under demonic

16 Hn 71. Walker does not mention this earlier attestation of the term in his discussion of chapter 78.7.

17 Downer, *LHP*, 395.

18 Wasserschleben, *Bußordnungen*, 368: "Si quis mathematicus, id est, per invocationem daemonum hominis mentem tulerit, quinque annos poeniteat, unum in pane et aqua." Translation from John T. McNeill and Helena M. Gamer, *Medieval Handbooks of Penance* (New York: Columbia University Press, 1938), 306.

19 I am indebted to the anonymous referee for this suggested translation.

influence gained Scriptural support from an episode in Acts in which Paul expels a demon from "a slave girl who had a spirit of divination and brought her owners a great deal of money by fortune-telling."[20] Accordingly, Isidore of Seville would include *phytonissae* ("pythonesses"), or women who engage in divination by yielding themselves to possession, in his influential typology of techniques of divination.[21] The semantic range of the term may well have undergone some broadening in Anglo-Saxon England, for Audrey Meaney notes its routine application in Old English sources "to anyone, female or male, who 'possessed a spirit of divination.'"[22] The wild woman who assaults St. Samson of Dol in his ninth-century *Vita* may well be a medieval descendant of the classical and biblical pythoness. Referred to by the narrator as both a *malefica* ("witch") and a *theomacha* ("sorceress" or "enemy of God"), she displays all the behaviours that were conventionally associated with madness or possession as she runs wildly through a forest and kills seemingly at random.[23] The necessity of restraining such people seems obvious.

The handling of the interpretive problems posed by *maleficos* highlights one of the major inadequacies of arguments in favour of the leniency of pre-Conquest law: their dependence on an ahistorical notion of insanity in spite of our sources' implicit recognition both of varieties (possession) and causes (divination, other proscribed conduct) of mental affliction that are unknown in the present era. The disadvantages of this approach become especially obvious when we turn to the second and somewhat less frequently mentioned item of evidence for the leniency of Anglo-Saxon law toward the insane, a chapter of a penitential collection erroneously attributed by all who have commented on it to Egbert, archbishop of York, but in reality an Old English penitential known as the *Canons of Theodore*

20 "... puellam quandam habentem spiritum pythonem" (Acts 16:16–18); this and subsequent quotations from the Vulgate Bible are drawn from *Biblia Sacra Iuxta Vulgatam Versionem*, ed. Roger Gryson et al. (Stuttgart: Deutsche Bibelgesellschaft, 1969, repr. 1994); trans. *The New Oxford Annotated Bible*, ed. Michael D. Coogan et al., 3rd ed. (New York: Oxford University Press, 2001), 217.

21 Pierre Bogliani, "L'Église et la divination au Moyen Âge, ou les avatars d'une pastorale ambiguë," *Théologiques* 8 (2000): 37–66, at 41.

22 Audrey Meaney, "Women, Witchcraft and Magic in Anglo-Saxon England," in *Superstition and Popular Medicine in Anglo-Saxon England*, ed. D.G. Scragg (Manchester: Manchester Centre for Anglo-Saxon Studies, 1989), 9–40, at 15.

23 *La vie de Saint Samson: Essai de critique hagiographique*, ed. Robert Fawtier (Paris: Honoré Champion, 1912), 124–25 (I.26–27); cf. J.S.P. Tatlock, "Geoffrey of Monmouth's Vita Merlini," *Speculum* 18 (1943): 265–87, at 269. Her depiction very much resembles that of the demoniac suicide in the *Penitential of Theodore* (see below).

which Benjamin Thorpe edited in 1840 as part of a collection to which he misleadingly gave the title *Pœnitentiale Egberti*.[24]

The *Canons of Theodore* were most likely compiled at some point in the ninth century.[25] Though there is evidence that the compiler consulted some of the non-Theodorean penitentials then issuing from Francia, most of its statements are derived either from the seventh-century penitential of Archbishop Theodore of Canterbury or from subsequent Frankish collections of Theodorean canons. It will be expedient, therefore, to consider at some length what Theodore's penitential had to say on the subject of insanity before dealing with the *Canons of Theodore*, particularly since provisions of the former would seem to be the most expansive remarks available from this period on the liability of the insane for their actions, something which makes their omission from Walker's study, and all subsequent published remarks on the liability of the insane, somewhat puzzling. Though the *Canons of Theodore* do not translate these specific provisions of Theodore's penitential on insanity, it seems likely that the compiler was acquainted with them, and it is possible that some traces appear in his own contribution to our small collection of pre- and post-Conquest discourses on the liability of the insane. The chapter in question is entitled "De vexatis a diabulo" (or in some manuscripts, "De his qui vexati sunt a demoniacis"):

> II.X.1: If a man is vexed by the devil (*vexatus est a diabulo*) and can do nothing but run about everywhere, and [if he] slays himself, there may be some reason to pray for him if he was formerly religious.
> 2. If it was on account of despair, or of some fear (*pro desperatione aut pro timore*), or for unknown reasons, we ought to leave to God the decision of this matter, and we dare not pray for him.

24 Benjamin Thorpe, *Ancient Laws and Institutes of England* (London: Eyre and Spottiswoode, 1840), 232–39. Walker's study describes this penitential as "existing in both a Latin and an Anglo-Saxon version." The "Latin version" to which Walker and all subsequent commentators refer is, however, no older than 1840, as it is the work of Thorpe himself. Neither Walker nor those who have repeated his claims are necessarily to blame for this error: in subsequent editions, Thorpe's authorship of the Latin version of the *Penitential* was so little discussed that virtually all later commentary would ignore his role in its composition. Cf. Walker, *Crime and Insanity in England*, 15; Walker, "The Insanity Defense before 1800," *Annals of the American Academy of Political and Social Science* 477 (1985): 25–30, at 27.

25 See Allen Frantzen, "Penitentials," in Michael Lapidge et al., eds., *The Blackwell Encyclopaedia of Anglo-Saxon England* (Oxford: Blackwell, 1999), 362–63. A complete edition of the *Canons of Theodore* has yet to appear in print. See F.J. Mone, *Quellen und Forschungen zur Geschichte der teutschen Literatur und Sprache* (Aachen and Leipzig: J.A. Meyer, 1930), 514–28; Thorpe, *Ancient Laws*, 232–39. An edition by R.D. Fulk and Stefan Jurasinski is forthcoming.

> 3. In the case of one who of his own will (*propria voluntate*) slays himself, masses may not be said for him; but we may only pray and dispense alms.
> 4. If any Christian goes insane through a sudden seizure (*subita temptatione*), or as a result of insanity slays himself – there are some who celebrate masses for such an one.
> 5. One who is possessed of a demon (*demonium sustinenti*) may have stones and herbs, without [the use of] incantation.[26]

Alexander Murray has recently pointed out that these provisions "fail to agree on a defining boundary for responsible suicide, since they imply different answers to the question, 'What excuses a suicide?'"[27] Ultimately, Murray holds that the chapter may offer more to textual criticism of the *Penitential* than it does to legal history, as its incoherence suggests the circumstances under which it took shape. That the statements fail to make sense when read as a group reveals the hand of "[an] emendator [who], wishing to add provisions about suicide to a penitential book that said next to nothing about it, saw his opportunity in clause 1 and squeezed in his entire contribution behind it, regardless of the anomalies the emendation imparted to the chapter as a whole."[28] Murray's description of the interpretive problems posed by the chapter is worth repeating here:

> Where inconsistencies enter is over the question what it is, precisely, that the priests did not "dare" to do. For in clause 2, it is that they dare not pray (*orare*) for the suicides. But we are not told what sort of prayer they mean. Clause 3, which affects to state the law, says expressly that while *Mass* is forbidden for culpable suicides, prayer and almsgiving are not. Does the ban refer, then, only to private prayer, and just fail to say how private it has to be? Meanwhile, clause 4, after

26 *Die Canones Theodori Cantuariensis und ihre Überlieferungsformen*, ed. Paul Willem Finsterwalder (Weimar: Hermann Böhlaus, 1929), 324: "II.X.1: Si homo vexatus est a diabulo et nescit aliquid nisi ubique discurrere et occidit semetipsum quacumque causa potest ut oretur pro eo si ante religiosus erat. 2. Si pro desperatione aut pro timore aliquo aut pro causis incognitis [se occiderit] Deo relinquimus hoc iudicium et non ausi sumus orare pro eo. 3. Qui se ipsum occiderit propria voluntate missas pro eo facere non licet, sed tantum orare et elemosinas largire. 4. Si quis Christianus subita temptatione mente sua exciderit, vel per insaniam se ipsum occiderit, quidam pro eo missas faciunt. 5. Demonium sustinenti licet petras et holera habere sine incantatione." Translation from McNeill and Gamer, *Handbooks*, 207.

27 Alexander Murray, *Suicide in the Middle Ages*, vol. 2: *The Curse on Self-Murder* (Oxford: Oxford University Press, 2000), 255.

28 Murray, *Suicide*, 254.

defining non-culpable suicide with masterful imprecision ("through sudden temptation ... or insanity") surpasses even *that* exemplar of vague drafting when it turns to describe current practice, for all it says on this topic is that "*some* priests say masses for them." A fine lot of use, that, in a law-book.[29]

Murray's arguments for the text's essential incoherence focus on the seeming anomaly that a voluntary suicide – presumably the most culpable given his consent – receives prayers and alms (but no Mass) without conditions, whereas the demoniac suicide of chapter one receives prayers only if he was previously pious (though *religiosus* here may simply refer to the regular clergy). Similar concerns were earlier expressed by Ludwig Bieler in his edition of the Irish penitentials, where he discusses not the *Penitential of Theodore* itself but its nearly verbatim reiteration in the ninth-century "Bigotian" penitential. "It seems strange," Bieler writes, "that one may pray for one who has killed himself in cold blood but not for one who has done so with a mind disturbed by fear or despair."[30] So strange, in fact, that Bieler suggests the *Penitential of Theodore* be emended: "Should we not read in the second instance, here as well as in Theodore, *inuoluntarie* 'unintentionally'?"[31]

What troubles modern commentators about these provisions may also have vexed the compilers of early medieval penitentials. The relatively lenient treatment of those who kill themselves *propria voluntate* is eliminated from subsequent collections of Theodorean materials, the *Capitula Dacheriana* and the *Canones Gregorii*, while the penitential of Halitgar of Cambrai ignores Theodore's discussion of suicide entirely. But dissatisfaction with the chapter was not sufficiently widespread to prevent its reappearance in the Bigotian penitential. Moreover, it must have seemed satisfactory to those who copied the multitude of surviving manuscripts of the two-book Theodorean collection without engaging in corrective emendation, as was not the case with other provisions of Theodore's penitential.

Murray's hypothesis is a suggestive response to the difficulties Theodore's provisions pose. But Theodore's discussion of suicide assumes a kind of orderliness that seems uncharacteristic of statements that accumulated arbitrarily.[32] There is some evidence of an attempt to classify

29 Murray, *Suicide*, 256.

30 Ludwig Bieler, ed., *The Irish Penitentials*, Scriptores Latini Hiberniae V (Dublin: Institute for Advanced Studies, 1975), 257, n. 25.

31 Ibid.

32 Murray translates "subita temptatione mente sua exciderit" as "sudden temptation and mental 'excess'" (Murray, *Suicide*, 255). McNeill and Gamer's translation renders this passage as "goes insane through a sudden seizure." The situation in this

mental disturbances in ways that roughly correspond to the taxonomies of contemporaneous medical literature. The text seems concerned with the liabilities of those suffering from three distinct types of disorders: demonic possession (definitely clause five, possibly clause one), insanity (clause four), and sudden madness (the person induced "subita temptatione" to commit suicide in clause four). The same tripartite organization of maladies occurs in *Bald's Leechbook*, something that suggests that the process of accretion Murray holds responsible for the formation of this chapter may not have been wholly capricious.[33] Additionally, the *Penitential* may admit of a distinction between one who harbours a demon within himself (*demonium sustinenti*) and one who is merely "vexed" externally by a demon. That allowances would have been made for formerly pious members of the latter group is to be expected, as SS. Benedict and Guthlac were harassed by demons while never suffering possession.[34]

That the organization of these afflictions is unlikely to be arbitrary suggests that the chapter as a whole may evince the compiler's view of the moral responsibility of the insane. The mental disturbances are listed in a descending scale of severity that appears also to be a descending scale of liability. Those who suffered from the most intense derangement prior to their suicides receive the least care after their deaths, while those affected merely by strong emotions receive more than the insane but less than those who showed no distress prior to their deaths. Such a pattern suggests the reluctance of the compiler to commemorate the deceased in any fashion

---

chapter may, however, resemble that of the following statement in Finnian's penitential: "Si autem subito occiderit et non ex odio, et amici fuerunt ante, sed instincto diaboli per obreptione, tres annos peniteat cum pane et aqua per mensura et .iii. alios abstineat se a uino et a carnibus, et non in sua patria" ("But if he kills him suddenly and not from hatred – the two having formerly been friends – but by the prompting of the devil ensnaring him, he shall do penance for three years on an allowance of bread and water, and for three more years he shall abstain from wine and meat, and not [stay] in his own country"). *Bußordnungen*, ed. Wasserschleben, 113 (ch. 24); trans. Bieler, *The Irish Penitentials*, 83. Murray insists that only clauses 1 and 5 formed part of the original section, and that the rest are unrelated to the question of one who has been harassed by the devil. Seeing clause 4 in light of Finnian's provision, however, would seem to suggest that we have in this clause another variety of harassment by the devil, perhaps adding a new significance to the text's use of the word *temptatione*.

33 Ch. lxiii of the *Leechbook* considers, in the following order, "demoniac[s]" ("feond seocum men þonne deofol þone monnan fede oððe hine innan gewealde mid adle"), "lunatic[s]" ("bræcseocum men"), and "the phrenzied" ("weden heorte"): *Leechdoms*, ed. and trans. Cockayne, 137–38.

34 Such an interpretation suggests the possibility that chapter 10 in fact contains no instance of demoniac suicide, though I am inclined to doubt this.

unless it is known to his priest that his suicide is not the result of possession or harassment by demons. Perhaps the text does not so much condone the suicide who slays himself *propria voluntate* as abhor particularly those suicides whose deaths issue either from emotions proscribed by pastoral manuals (fear, despair) or from more severe mental afflictions – an abhorrence which makes the treatment of the suicide *propria voluntate* seem lenient by comparison.[35]

The refusal of Theodore's penitential to excuse the mentally afflicted for their actions – encapsulated, perhaps, in its reservation of care only to demoniacs who were previously pious – suggests the reliance of the compiler on a tradition widely attested in legislative and narrative sources alike wherein the insane were viewed as responsible for their afflictions.[36] Of the canonical statements on madness that survive from this era the most important is the Council of Worms (868), which stipulated that one who kills in a state of temporary insanity is nonetheless obliged to do penance upon regaining his senses as his affliction is itself an outcome of sin.[37] While his penance is to be less severe than that of one who kills with a sound mind, the text plainly adheres to the view that the insane bear some moral responsibility for violent acts given their presumptive role in bringing about their own afflictions.[38] Gratian in his *Decretum* would ultimately decide

35 On the sinfulness of sorrow (*tristitia*), see Walter W. Skeat, ed. and trans., *Ælfric's Lives of Saints*, E.E.T.S. o.s. 94 and 114, 2 vols. (London: Oxford University Press, 1966), II: 357; *Irish Penitentials*, ed. Bieler, 85 (*Finnian*, ch. 29).

36 See Penelope B.R. Doob, *Nebuchadnezzar's Children: Conventions of Madness in Middle English Literature* (New Haven: Yale University Press, 1974), ch. 1 and *passim*. The *Penitential of Theodore* shows no traces of statements by SS. Ambrose and Augustine holding the insane to be innocent of their actions, some of which are discussed in R. Colin Pickett, *Mental Affliction and Church Law* (Ottawa: University of Ottawa Press, 1952), 43–44.

37 Pickett, *Mental Affliction*, 45.

38 "Si quis insaniens aliquem occiderit, si ad sanam mentem pervenerit, levior ei pœnitentia imponenda est, quam ei, qui sana mente tale quid commiserit. Cui quamvis pœnitentia sit imponenda, quia ipsa infirmitas causa peccati, licet fortassis occulta, contigisse creditur, tantum tamen levior, quam ei qui sanus aliquem occiderit, quantum inter insanum & sanum, irrationabile & rationabile, constat esse discriminis" ("If someone slays someone while insane, should [the slayer] be restored to sanity, the penance to be applied is to be lighter than that of one who did such a thing with a healthy mind. To him [i.e., the insane person] a penance is, however, to be applied, because this infirmity is believed to have come about through sin, even if it is hidden; however [the penance] should be lighter than that applied to the sane person, because there should be a distinction between the sane and the insane, the rational and the irrational"). *Sacrorum Conciliorum Nova et Amplissima Collectio*, ed. J.D. Mansi (Florence, 1759–1798; repr. Graz: Akademische Druck- u. Verlagsanstalt, 1960), 15: 874 (ch. 28).

against the liability of the insane *per se*, but he did not dispute the Council's argument that those who cause their own madness should be held liable.[39]

The few remarks we possess from the legislation of the Continental Germanic-speaking peoples seem more vehemently to reject the innocence of the insane. A code routinely described as the most authentically Germanic of the *Leges Barbarorum*, the seventh-century edict of Rothair, views sin as the pre-eminent cause of mental affliction and, accordingly, allows the wrongs of the insane to be avenged on them with impunity.[40] Though this is its only statement on the violent offences of the insane, Rothair's edict voids betrothals to women who are discovered to be insane or leprous with similar language concerning the causes of madness. Whether these provisions reflect ecclesiastical or popular belief is probably impossible to determine.

In Anglo-Saxon England, the view that madness was a consequence of sin appears likewise to have been widely held, though the evidence issues primarily from chronicles and hagiography.[41] Theodore's penitential can often be observed negotiating a "middle ground" between Church doctrine and secular tradition. Its concessions to local customs regarding the feud are acknowledged by Thomas Charles-Edwards, and the acquaintance of its compilers with Frankish legislation has also been plausibly suggested.[42]

39 Pickett, *Mental Affliction*, 45.

40 *Edictus ceteraeque langobardorum leges*, ed. F. Bluhme (Hannover: Hahnsche Buchhandlung, 1869), 61 (ch. 323). On the "Germanic" character of Rothair's laws, see Pollock and Maitland, *History*, I: 12; Patrick Wormald, *The Making of English Law: King Alfred to the Twelfth Century* (London: Blackwell, 1999), 39.

41 In saying so, I am mindful of the critique to which this view is subjected in Jerome Kroll and Bernard Bachrach, "Sin and mental illness in the Middle Ages," *Psychological Medicine* 14 (1984): 507–14. Their study is right to point out the deleterious effects of historians' long dependence upon G. Zilboorg's *History of Medical Psychology* (New York: Norton, 1941), which oversimplifies the demonological element in medieval thought on mental disorder. But as the present essay is concerned with the handling of mental illness in secular and canon law, wherein the moral responsibility of the insane is often taken for granted, I see no reason to qualify this statement. For Anglo-Saxon representations of madness as a divine punishment, see particularly *Bede's Ecclesiastical History of the English People*, ed. Bertram Colgrave and R.A.B. Mynors (Oxford: Clarendon, 1969), 150–51; *Lives of Three English Saints*, ed. G.I. Needham (Exeter: University of Exeter Press, 1972), 56; trans. Skeat, *Ælfric's Lives of Saints*, II: 331.

42 Thomas Charles-Edwards, "The Penitential of Theodore and the *Iudicia Theodori*," in *Archbishop Theodore: Commemorative Studies on His Life and Influence*, Cambridge Studies in Anglo-Saxon England 11, ed. Michael Lapidge (Cambridge: Cambridge University Press, 1995), 141–74, at 170; L.L. McReavy, "The Sunday Repose from Labour: An Historico-Theological Examination of Servile Work," *Ephemirides Theologicae Lovanienses* 12 (1935): 291–323, at 322.

Given the attestation elsewhere of attitudes resembling those of the *Penitential*'s discussion of insanity, it can safely be assumed that this discussion reiterates, however awkwardly, the conventionally sceptical view of the innocence of the insane for their actions, and in doing so is perhaps indebted more to custom than to established doctrine.

Do the *Canons of Theodore* share the attitude toward the insane of their most frequently consulted source? The scarcity of evidence naturally makes a firm conclusion elusive. But should we accept the received opinion that the *Canons* prescribe leniency for the wrongs of the insane, we would be required also to assume that their compiler resisted a durable tradition in both secular and canon law holding the insane at least somewhat culpable for their actions, an unlikely event in the conservative environment described by Gatch in his important study of eleventh-century pastoral theology.[43] And indeed, a consideration of the Old English version of this passage, which has yet to occur in any of the scholarly literature of which I am aware, yields a sense of its significance that is substantially at odds with all that has been said so far about the text. The Old English version of the canon is as follows:

> If any man falls from his thoughts or from his mind (*on his geðohtum oððe of his gewitte feole*), and it happens to him, that he kills a man, let [the slayer's] kin pay compensation, and keep him from other such [harm]. If one should slay him in a state of *ungewitte* (being out of [one's] senses), before one knows whether his kin are willing to pursue a settlement, let the men who killed him compensate his kin.[44]

It has already been said that this passage is among the few provisions of the *Canons of Theodore* for which no source can be identified. Nonetheless, its dependence on a Latin idiom for a portion of its language is suggested by the unusual phrase with which it describes the descent into madness. According to the *Dictionary of Old English* corpus, the only other instance of the collocation "feol(lan) fram geþohtum" occurs in the

43 Milton McC. Gatch, *Preaching and Theology in Anglo-Saxon England: Ælfric and Wulfstan* (Toronto: University of Toronto Press, 1977), ch. 1.

44 The text is drawn from Fulk and Jurasinski, *The Old English Canons of Theodore* (forthcoming): "Gyf hwylc man on his geðohtum oððe of his gewitte feole, and him gelimpe, þæt he man ofslea, forgeldon þonne man his magas, and hine wið oðær swylc gescyldan. Gyf man hine ofslea on ðam ungewitte, ær man wite hwæþer his magas him fore ðingian willon, forgeldon ðone man his magum þa men ðe hine ofslean." The most recent edition is that of Thorpe, *Ancient Laws and Institutes*, 236–37, where the canon appears as ch. 29 of the *Pœnitentiale Ecgberti* ("Additamenta").

Arundel Psalter's gloss of Psalm 5:10, in which the Psalmist enjoins God to abandon the unrighteous to confusion: "Judge them, God; let them fall by their own thoughts (*decidant a cogitationibus suis*); expel them inasmuch as they afflicted you."[45] That the author of this canon describes madness in language similar to that employed by the Psalmist in the latter's request that God condemn the wicked to confusion may reflect the tendency of his era to view madness as a consequence of sin and impiety. The evident ubiquity of these attitudes, along with their likely presence in the *Canons of Theodore* (the text on which his argument principally depended), suggests the weaknesses of Basil Clarke's assertion that Anglo-Saxon legislators and clerics would have held insanity to be an instance in which "intention was innocent."[46] So steadfast was the inclination to hold lunatics responsible for their affliction that the rule might even be held to apply where the moral laxity of the victim was not obvious. Such is the case with an unfortunate messenger whose cure is related in the *Vita Wulfstani:* "[A]fter he had gone some way, an unquiet spirit took hold of him and sorely disturbed him; such was the judgement of God, which may sometimes be hidden but is never unjust."[47]

Walker's contention that this canon shows the English Church "enjoin[ing] forbearance toward the insane long before the Norman Conquest imported Roman laws" rests heavily on the portion of the canon

45 The translation from the Vulgate is my own: the Latin reads "iudica illos deus decidant a cogitationibus suis secundum multitudinem impietatum eorum expelle eos quoniam irritauerunt te domine." For the Old English text, see Guido Oess, *Der altenglische Arundel-Psalter*, Anglistische Forschungen 30 (Heidelberg: C. Winter, 1910), 30: "dem þu hig god hi feollan fra*m* geþohtum heora æft*er* micelnesse arleasnesse heora utadrif ðu hig forðon hig gremedon þe driht*en*." Psalms such as the one discussed here may underlie Augustine's remark, in his discussion of divination and consequent madness in *De Doctrina Christiana*, that "it happens that, by some inscrutable divine plan, those who have a desire for evil things are handed over to be deluded and deceived according to what their own wills deserve. They are deluded and deceived by corrupt angels, to whom in God's most excellent scheme of things this lowest part of the world has been subjected by the decree of divine providence" ("Hinc enim fiet ut occulto quodam iudicio divino cupidi malarum rerum homines tradantur illudendi et decipiendi pro meritis voluntatum suarum, illudentibus eos atque decipientibus praevaricatoribus angelis, quibus ista mundi pars infima secundum pulcherrimum ordinem rerum divinae providentiae lege subiecta est"). *De Doctrina Christiana*, ed. and trans. R.P.H. Green (Oxford: Clarendon Press, 1995), 97.

46 Clarke, *Mental Disorder*, 59.

47 *William of Malmesbury: Saints' Lives*, ed. and trans. Winterbottom and Thomson, 72–73: "Iam enim aliquantum progressum spiritus inquietus arripiens dire inquietabat, Dei iuditio nonnumquam occulto, numquam iniusto."

requiring payment of compensation by the party who slays the violent lunatic.[48] In spite of its occurrence in a collection of penitentials, Walker holds this clause to be a statement of secular law. "The Church," Walker writes, "was concerned not with liability for restitution but with culpability for sin"; accordingly,

> [t]he passage in the Burgundian Library manuscript sounds more like a description of secular law than a passage from a penitential. ... There is nothing here about penance: simply a straightforward rule for ensuring that compensation was paid for an insane killer's victim, and that the insane man did not become in turn the victim of the spear.[49]

With his contention that the text contains "nothing about penance" because of its concern with compensation, Walker seems to assume that it is uncharacteristic of penitentials to enjoin the pursuit of monetary settlements as a specifically penitential remedy. This assertion does not square with claims made by John T. McNeill in a classic article of 1932 contending that the payment of compensation was central to the penitentials' objective of "recover[ing] to the offender a balanced state of mind," a means of curing deadly passions with their opposites.[50] "In the case of acts of violence or other crimes against persons," McNeill argues, "the penance involved payments in satisfaction to the injured or to the relatives of the slain. Thus the offender made his peace with society and was protected against private punishment and freed from social censure. He could once more function as a normal person, and his sense of personality was restored."[51] That this chapter recommends the payment of compensation without specifying an amount further indicates its conformity to the conventions of penitential literature rather than those of secular legislation, as is the case in an influential portion of the *Penitential of Theodore* discussing homicide: "If one slays in revenge for a relative, he shall do penance as a murderer for seven or ten years. However, if he will render to the relatives the legal price, the penance shall be lighter, that is, [it shall be shortened] by half the time."[52]

48 Walker, "The Insanity Defense before 1800," 27.

49 Walker, *Crime and Insanity in England*, 16.

50 John T. McNeill, "Medicine for Sin as Prescribed in the Penitentials," *Church History* 1 (1932): 14–26, at 21.

51 McNeill, "Medicine for Sin," 21.

52 *Die Canones Theodori Cantuariensis und ihre Überlieferungsformen*, ed. Finsterwalder, 294: "Si quis pro ultione propinqui hominem occiderit peniteat sicut homicida VII vel X annos. Si tamen reddere vult propinquis pecuniam aestimationis levior erit penitentia id est dimidio spatio." Translation in McNeill and Gamer, *Handbooks*, 187 (*Penitential of Theodore* I.4.1).

While it is reasonable to assume that the canon aims to preserve the lunatic from the spear, it is somewhat harder to establish that it is his madness that entitles him to this protection. It may be of some relevance that Ailred in the *Epistola ad Mauricium* seems to acknowledge an entitlement to pursue vengeance against the insane monk who attempts to slay him, but ultimately forswears revenge in imitation of Christ: "It was," he said, "against my person that he sinned, I, when I wish, will revenge myself, but I never shall; for the charity of your father is not to be destroyed but rather perfected continuously until the end by such happenings as these, and it is in this way that we shall be saved."[53] An entitlement to slay the insane may also be suggested by the description of the cure of Hwætred in the Old English prose life of Guthlac. In Felix's *Life*, the basis of the Old English translation, a crowd of men gathers and attempts to bind Hwætred, three of whom he slays with an axe.[54] No vengeance or settlement is sought by the kin of the slain, and it is probably to explain this seeming anomaly that the Old English life supplements the account with a statement that the crowd was made up of his kinsmen and his near-kinsmen.[55]

Significantly, the condition for which the *Canons* require compensation is that the avenging party kills the lunatic before a settlement can be reached, not that they kill him while insane, something which suggests that the canon means to protect not the insane killer but the option of monetary settlement of which the literature of penance was typically supportive.[56] It

53 *Life of Ailred of Rievaulx*, ed. and trans. Powicke, 80: "Quia, inquit, in persona mea peccauit, ego, cum uoluero, uindicabo, set ego nunquam quia caritas in patre uestro non est destruenda, set per talia pocius perfecienda iugiter usque in finem, et sic salui erimus."

54 "Nam quodam tempore, congregata multitudine, cum alii illum legare temptarent, arrepto limali bipenne tria virorum corpora letabundis ictibis humo sternens mori coegit" ("On one occasion, indeed, a great number gathered together while some attempted to bind him, but he seized a well-filed double-winged axe and with deadly blows he felled three men to the ground and slew them"). *Felix's Life of St. Guthlac*, ed. and trans. Bertram Colgrave (Cambridge: Cambridge University Press, 1956), 128–29.

55 "Ða gelamp sum síþe, þæt þær wæs mycel menigo manna gegaderod his maga and eac oþra his nehfreonda, þæt hi hine woldon gebindan ..." ("Then it happened that there were a great many men gathered of his kinsmen and also other of his near-kinsmen, that they wanted to bind him ..."). See *Das angelsächsische Prosa-Leben des hl. Guthlac*, Anglistische Forschungen 27, ed. Paul Gonser (Heidelberg: Carl Winter, 1909), 146.

56 Like the *Penitential of Theodore*, the *Old Irish Penitential* (trans. McNeill and Gamer, *Handbooks*, 166) reduces periods of penance for those who pay compensation to the kin of their victims.

is true that *ungewitt* can mean "insanity," though such a gloss in this instance might impute to the text an unattractive suggestion that the men would be more justified in killing the lunatic after his illness has subsided. A more acceptable possibility is that this canon takes the circumstances under which the retaliatory slaying occurs as evidence for the spiritual condition of its perpetrators. A likely parallel is a provision of the *Old English Penitential* imposing a two-year penance upon a man who kills his slave without first pursuing a formal judgment against him. Here the text asserts plainly that neglect of this formality afforded evidence that the slave had been killed in anger, which rendered the act sinful.[57]

Admittedly, the text offers little ground for certainty about the meaning of *ungewitt*: while the term appears with some consistency to have had the meaning "insanity," it might also mean "idiocy, simple-mindedness." It is probably on the basis of the latter meaning that Thorpe translates this phrase as "inscienter," i.e., the avenging party kills the insane man before it is known whether his kin will offer a settlement for the first slaying.[58] An equally plausible gloss is suggested by Alfred's translation of Gregory's *Regula pastoralis* given the concern of penitentials with the emotional and spiritual condition of the penitent(s), who would in this instance be not the lunatic but those who pursue vengeance against him. Alfred's text refers to "those who, when they fall into such anger (*weamodnesse*), are the more cautiously to be avoided the more out of their senses (*ungewitte*) they are seen to be."[59] Here Alfred seems to regard madness and anger as scarcely distinguishable, perhaps expressing a view of madness whose presence is an acknowledged feature of texts from the later Middle

57 "Be þam men þe his þeowan ofslyhð for þyfðe butan his hundredes gewitnesse. – Gif hwylc man his æht ofslehð, 7 he nane gewitnesse næbbe *þæt* he forworht sy, butan he hine for his hatheortnesse 7 for his gymeleaste ofslyhð, fæste II ger" ("Concerning one who kills his slave for theft without the observance of the hundred. – If a man slays his slave [lit. 'property'], and he has no witness that [the slave] is guilty, but slays him because of his [the owner's] anger and his thoughtlessness, let [the owner] fast two years"). The situation (*for þyfðe*) and the rationale concerning anger are not present in the source (Halitgar IV.4). See Raith, ed., *Altenglische Version*, 17.

58 Thorpe, *Ancient Laws and Institutes*, 237: "Si homo quis animo suo vel mente sua exciderit, et ei aliquem occidere evenerit, solvant pro homine propinqui ejus, et eum contra simile quid servent. Si quis inscienter eum occiderit, antequam cognitum erat, num amici ejus pro eo intervenire vellent, solvant pro homine propinquis ejus, homines qui eum occiderint."

59 *King Alfred's West-Saxon Version of Gregory's Pastoral Care*, ed. and trans. Henry Sweet, EETS o.s. 45 and 50 (London: Oxford University Press, 1871), II: 295: "Ða ðonne hie beræsað on suelce weamodnesse hie sindon sua micle wærlicor to oferbuganne sua mon ongiet ðæt hie on maran ungewitte beoð."

Ages.[60] Should such a meaning obtain within the *Canons of Theodore*, its compiler may be suggesting a parallel between the spiritual condition of the insane offender and that of the men who hastily take vengeance before the remedy of settlement has been ventured.

Parallelisms between rage and madness are attested elsewhere with sufficient frequency to have been conventional. Their identity is suggested by Ælfric: "The fourth vice is *ira*, that is in English *weamodnyss*, which causes a man to lose control over his mind, and makes slayings and great evils."[61] Idiosyncrasies of late Anglo-Saxon attitudes toward the mind would only have reinforced such a view of mental disorder. As M.R. Godden demonstrated in an essay of 1985, both Alcuin's *De animae ratione* and Alfred's translation of Boethius's *De consolatione philosophiae* have a peculiar tendency to identify the mind and the soul.[62] Given such conditions, it is possible that standard pastoral admonitions against indulging in anger such as those of Finnian's penitential, which warns that *iracundia* "kill[s] the soul and cast[s] it down to the depth of hell," might have assumed a particular significance for pre-Conquest clerics and legislators in their attempts to understand madness and its implications.[63]

The foregoing suggests that the act of slaying the lunatic is penanced because the haste with which it has been performed furnishes proof of the anger that motivated it. It is characteristic of penitentials to look to the circumstances of an offence for evidence of the spiritual condition that engendered it, the ultimate target of penance.[64] Significantly, it was accepted in

60 Doob argues that in a number of late medieval texts "anger *is* madness; it is not simply *like* madness"; such is the case in the fourteenth-century *Speculum Christiani*, which states flatly that anger is "pure wodnes or madness." See Doob, *Nebuchadnezzar's Children*, 28–29.

61 *Ælfric's Lives of the Saints*, ed. and trans. Skeat, I: 356–57 (XVI.285–87): "Se feorða leahtor is ira, þæt is on englisc weamodnyss, seo deð þæt se man nah his modes geweald, and macað manslihtas and mycele yfelu."

62 M.R. Godden, "Anglo-Saxons on the Mind," in *Learning and Literature in Anglo-Saxon England: Studies Presented to Peter Clemoes on the Occasion of His Sixty-Fifth Birthday*, ed. Michael Lapidge and Helmut Gneuss (Cambridge: Cambridge University Press, 1985), 271–98.

63 See *Irish Penitentials*, ed. and trans. Bieler: "Si quis clericus iracundus aut inuidus aut detractor aut tristis aut cupidus, magna sunt peccata haec et capitalia et occident animam et demergunt eam in profundum inferni," 85 (ch. 29). The causal relationship between anger and madness is narrativized in the account of Wulfstan's efforts on behalf of William Bald, who was guilty of an accidental slaying. One of the brothers who refuses a monetary settlement is so consumed with rage that he goes insane. See *William of Malmesbury: Saints' Lives*, eds. and trans. Winterbottom and Thomson, 90–93.

64 See, for example, chs. 25–29 of *Paenitantiale Oxoniense II* (ed. Raymund Kottje,

this era that motives of passion might taint otherwise praiseworthy actions. According to the *Libellus Responsionum* attributed to Gregory the Great, a text partially reiterated in several penitentials and reflective of the pastoral theology behind them, anger potentially renders even just punishments sinful.[65] While the slaying of the violent lunatic may well have been permissible, as the comments attributed to Ailred suggest, the rage evident in the fact of his being slain before settlement has been ventured would seem to have merited some sort of penitential remedy. Indeed, it might be said that the concern of the *Canons of Theodore* is less for the violent lunatic (whose soul, as Theodore's penitential seems to suggest, may already be beyond the help of pastoral care) than for the spiritual condition of those who deal with him, as this latter group, in contending with the lunatic, must also contend with the kinds of violent emotions that were seen as the conduits to madness.

It has so far been suggested that the evidence most frequently adduced in favour of the leniency of Anglo-Saxon institutions toward the insane probably indicates little about the nature of their liability. Moreover, the *Canons of Theodore*, with their faint allusion to the language of biblical punishment, seem to indicate that the innocence of the mentally afflicted was not a feature of canon law. While pity for the mentally afflicted is evident in many narrative accounts of madness that are conventional in Latin and vernacular hagiography, a willingness to excuse them for their wrongs is less apparent.[66] It is perhaps the omission both of this narrative evidence, and of the provisions of the *Penitential of Theodore*, from the principal legal-historical discussions that has allowed for wrongs performed by the insane to retain their status in scholarship as a surprising exception to the rule of "absolute liability" for involuntary wrongs that is

---

Paenitanentialia Minora Franciae et Italiae Saeculi VIII–IX [Turnhout: Brepols, 1994], 195–96).

65 *Bede's Ecclesiastical History of the English People*, ed. and trans. Bertram Colgrave and R.A.B. Mynors (Oxford: Clarendon Press, 1969), 82–83. On the transmission of the *Libellus* see Paul Meyvaert, "Bede's Text of the *Libellus Responsionum* of Gregory the Great to Augustine of Canterbury," in *England Before the Conquest: Studies in Primary Sources Presented to Dorothy Whitelock*, ed. Peter Clemoes and Kathleen Hughes (Cambridge: Cambridge University Press, 1971), 15–34.

66 See, e.g., *Orderic Vitalis. The Ecclesiastical History*, 6 vols., ed. Marjorie Chibnall (Oxford: Clarendon Press, 1969–80), II: 330–31; IV: 274–76. The latter is an *exemplum* concerning David of Scotland's mistaken pity for a Norwegian lunatic subjected to judicial mutilation after murdering a priest; though he takes him into his home and attempts to care for him, the lunatic murders David's infant child, and David ultimately orders him to be torn apart by horses.

routinely (and problematically) imputed to Anglo-Saxon law.[67] We receive from the *Canons of Theodore* and the *Leges Henrici Primi* only an insistence that the insane be forcibly bound by their relatives, along with suggestions from both that some insane offenders are responsible for their illness, an attitude attested in most normative statements of this period. The understanding of madness characteristic of the penitentials and other pastoral literature is one that acknowledges its status as a "medical" problem while ascribing to it a spiritual and moral causation: yielding to the passions that penitential discipline aimed to subdue threatened one not only with damnation but with illness.

Perhaps the simplest explanation for the tendency to deny the innocence of the insane is afforded by a peculiarity of pre-Conquest medical thought. Some texts from this era indicate no meaningful distinction between madness and what we would consider mere temptation. This can be seen most plainly in the episode concerning the cleric Beccel in Felix's *Vita Sancti Guthlaci*:

> But an evil spirit entered his heart and began to puff him up with pestiferous arrogance and vainglory; then after his swollen and empty pride had seduced him with its vanity, he also began to urge him to take a death-dealing sword and slay the master under whose teaching he had begun to live in the service of God. The devil suggested to him that if he could slay him, he would afterwards live in Guthlac's dwelling and also enjoy the great veneration of kings and princes. So on a certain day when this same cleric had come to tonsure Guthlac the man of God, as he was accustomed to do every twenty days, he was seized with a violent madness (*ingenti dementia vexatus*), and thirsting with an overwhelming lust for the blood of the man of God, without hesitation he approached to slay him.[68]

67 See, for example, Winfield, "The Myth of Absolute Liability," 42; also Stefan Jurasinski, *Ancient Privileges: "Beowulf," Law, and the Making of Germanic Antiquity*, Medieval European Studies 6 (Morgantown: West Virginia University Press, 2006), ch. 4.

68 *Felix's Life of Saint Guthlac*, ed. and trans. Colgrave, 112–13: "Cuius praecordia malignus spiritus ingressus, pestiferis vanae gloriae fastibus illum inflare coepit ac seduxit, admonere ipsum quoque exorsus est, ut dominum suum, sub cuius disciplinis Deo vivere initiavit, arrepta letali machera necaret, hoc ipsius animo proponens, ut, et, si ipsum interimere potuisset, locum ipsius postea, cum maxima regum principumque venerantia, habiturus foret. Quadam ergo die, cum praefatus clericus virum Dei Guthlacum, ut adsolebat, post bis denos dierum cursus tonderare devenisset, isdem, ingenti dementia vexatus, viri Dei inmenso desiderio sanguinem sitiens, indubius illum occidere successit."

Though Beccel is here described as "ingenti dementia vexatus" (glossed as "witleas" in London, British Library, MS Royal 13 A.XV), Guthlac nonetheless advises confession. The intent of the author that "dementia" be understood as a literal descriptor of Beccel's condition is suggested by the usage of *Leechbook III*, which prescribes in the same chapter drinks that will ward off "dementedness" ("ungemynde") and "temptations of the devil" ("deofles costunga") as if both constituted species of mental affliction.[69] Should these statements reflect prevailing views toward the insane in this era, it seems likely that the assumed absence of consent, which removed culpability from insane offenders in Rome, may not have been an element of pre-Conquest legal reasoning.[70]

It seems probable that the role demons were thought to play in mental affliction was responsible for the reluctance of pre-Conquest normative texts to exculpate the afflicted for their wrongs, and not merely because demoniacs were held to suffer as a result of their sins. Such a tendency furnishes a ready explanation for the curious refusal of the Old English life of Guthlac to translate the statement of his source that Beccel is "ingenti dementia vexatus," and the translator's reluctance elsewhere in the text to employ terms that designated medicalized notions of mental affliction. In an environment in which being insane meant being under the sway of demonic spirits, and in which demons were also held responsible for the temptations to engage in most misdeeds, the distinctions that canonists and homilists made when considering the insane alongside other wrongdoers seem not to have been of kind but of degree. The consequences of this development may manifest themselves in the discussion of suicide in the *Old English Penitential*, wherein the cases of those who commit suicide out of possession, insanity, despair or no discernible motive are all subsumed under the category of those who act under the compulsion of demons.[71]

69 *Leechdoms*, ed. Cockayne, 335 (ch. xli), 353 (ch. lxiv).

70 On the attitudes of Greek and Roman law toward the insane, see Daniel N. Robinson, *Wild Beasts and Idle Humours: The Insanity Defense from Antiquity to the Present* (Cambridge, MA: Harvard University Press, 1996), 43.

71 "Se man [se] hine sylfne ofslyhð mid wæpne oððe for hwylcum mislicum deofles onbringe, nis hit na alyfed þæt man <for> swylcum men mæssan singe oððe mid ænigum sealmsange þæt lic mid eorðan befæste" (*Altenglische Version*, ed. Raith, 18). The same passage is lightly revised by the compiler of the *Old English Handbook*: "Gif man hine sylfne gewealdes ofslihð mid wæpne oððe mid hwilcum deofles onbrincge, nis na alifed þæt man for swilcne man mæssan synge, ne mid ænigum sealmsange þæt lic eorðan befæste, ne on clænan legere ne licge bebirged" ("A Late Old English Handbook for the Use of a Confessor," ed. Roger Fowler, *Anglia* 83 [1965]: 1–34, at 23). The latter adds "gewealdes" ("intentionally") in spite of the insistence both of the Latin source (Halitgar IV.6) and the rubric of the

Given the weight of both popular and ecclesiastical tradition, and the reluctance of some sources even to recognize insanity as a valid category, it is nearly impossible to see how the normative statements of Anglo-Saxon England, in so far as the few examples we have should be seen as at all representative, can be understood as offering protection to the mentally afflicted.

Old English Penitential (*Altenglische Version*, ed. Raith, 17) that this chapter is to refer specifically to those who slay themselves unintentionally ("Be þam men þe hine sylfne ofslyhð for hwylcere gymeleaste" = "De his qui sibi quacumque negligentia mortem inferunt"). That the compiler of the *Penitential* subsequently attributes the suicide to "the instigation of the [or a] devil" (*deofles onbringe*) seems to have permitted the *Handbook*'s elimination of the conditions set forth in the rubric. The chapter of the *Handbook* considered here is translated by Murray: "If a man slay himself of his own will with a weapon or with any means the devil offers, it is not allowed that Mass be sung for such a man, or that psalms be chanted when the corpse is committed to the earth, or that it should lie in an unpolluted tomb"; Murray conjectures that the reference to the devil in this chapter and its source "could be an echo of the Theodorean suicide chapter," possibly "the sole vestige of it to survive in its native land." See Murray, *Suicide*, 265.

T.B. LAMBERT
Durham University

Spiritual Protection and Secular Power: The Evolution of Sanctuary and Legal Privilege in Ripon and Beverley, 900–1300

Sanctuary in the Middle Ages was based on two fundamental ideas: that churches ought to be places of peace and non-violence, and that people in fear of violence ought to be able to take advantage of this.[1] The forms taken by sanctuaries, the functions that they fulfilled in practice, and even the ways that they were understood could vary greatly, not only between churches but also in stages of development. In England alone we find Anglo-Saxon sanctuaries proudly displaying extended periods of protection – York claimed thirty days and Durham thirty-seven – which by the later Middle Ages, when every church could offer forty days and privileged ones could protect permanently, were obsolete and had been replaced.[2] Most sanctuaries were of the standard size, limited to the church and churchyard, but the more privileged could cover sizeable monastic precincts or sometimes large circular areas of a mile or more radius (known in the lit-

I would like to thank David Rollason, Cynthia Neville, and Clare Stancliffe for their helpful comments and suggestions on several earlier versions of this paper. Additionally, I gratefully acknowledge the support of the Arts and Humanities Research Council, the University of Durham, and the Royal Historical Society through the various phases of this project.

1 Richard H. Helmholz, *The* Ius Commune *in England: Four Studies* (Oxford: Oxford University Press, 2001), 25–30.

2 David W. Rollason with Derek Gore and Gillian Fellows-Jensen, eds., *Sources for York History to A.D. 1100*, The Archaeology of York 1 (York: York Archaeological Trust, 1998), 223; Symeon of Durham, *Libellus de exordio atque procursu istius hoc est Dunhelmensis, ecclesie: Tract on the Origins and Progress of this Church of Durham*, ed. David W. Rollason (Oxford: Clarendon Press, 2000), II.13; Ted Johnson South, ed., *Historia de Sancto Cuthberto: A History of Saint Cuthbert and a Record of His Patrimony* (Woodbridge: D.S. Brewer, 2002), ch. 13; David Hall, "The Sanctuary of St Cuthbert," in *St Cuthbert, His Cult and His Community to A.D. 1200*, ed. Gerald Bonner, Clare Stancliffe, and David W. Rollason (Woodbridge: Boydell, 1989), 425–36, at 426; R.H. Forster, "Notes on Durham and Other North Country Sanctuaries," *Journal of the British Archaeological Association* 61 (1905): 118–139, at 128–34; Roy F. Hunnisett, *The Medieval Coroner* (Cambridge: Cambridge University Press, 1961), 37.

erature as "banleucas").[3] It was even possible, as in the truly exceptional case of late medieval Durham, for a sanctuary to span an entire county.[4]

In terms of role, sanctuaries could act as providers of clemency in an Augustinian mould, saving sinners from execution so that they could do penance and attain salvation.[5] This seems to have been part of the thought-process behind the later medieval English custom of allowing sanctuary-seekers to "abjure the realm" and go into exile.[6] But sanctuaries could also play a role in the working of feud, providing an enforced pause in the violence during which negotiation could take place, as we see most clearly in Alfred's law code; or they could serve simply as refuges from ravaging armies or bandits for use by the local peasantry.[7] They could even, according to late medieval complaints from London, act as havens from which criminals could prey on their sanctuaries' neighbours.[8] If we look beyond England we can find sanctuaries functioning as population hubs, with lay people living within and benefiting from their protected zones. These include, most strikingly, the *sagreres* of Catalonia – tiny villages crammed into the thirty-pace-radius circle within which all churches could offer sanctuary – and their equivalents in Languedoc, and also much larger sanctuary zones such as the Irish *termonn* and, possibly, the Welsh *noddfa* which typically took the form of a sizeable banleuca around the church.[9]

3 Hunnisett, *Medieval Coroner*, 37; André Réville, "L'abjuratio regni: Histoire d'une institution anglaise," *Revue Historique* 50 (1892): 1–42, at 2; J. Charles Cox, *The Sanctuaries and Sanctuary-Seekers of England* (London: G. Allen and Sons, 1911), 3, 50, 124. For a detailed discussion of the term "banleuca" see M.D. Lobel, "The Ecclesiastical Banleuca in England," in *Oxford Essays in Medieval History: Presented to Herbert Edward Salter*, ed. F.M. Powicke (Oxford: Clarendon Press, 1934), 122–40, at 122–25.

4 Forster, "Notes on Durham," 139.

5 Karl Blaine Shoemaker, "Sanctuary Law: Changing Conceptions of Wrongdoing and Punishment in Medieval European Law" (Ph.D. thesis, University of California, Berkeley, 2001), 43–57.

6 Réville, "L'abjuratio regni," 17–18.

7 Af 5, 42; Charles H. Riggs, *Criminal Asylum in Anglo-Saxon Law* (Gainesville, FL: University of Florida Press, 1963), 33–36; Paul R. Hyams, *Rancor and Reconciliation in Medieval England* (Ithaca: Cornell University Press, 2003), 95–98; Cox, *Sanctuaries*, 156–57; James Raine, ed., *Reginaldi monachi Dunelmensis libellus de admirandis beati Cuthberti virtutibus quae novellis patratae sunt temporibus*, Surtees Society 1 (London: J.B. Nichols and Son, 1835), chs. 90, 129.

8 Isobel D. Thornley, "Sanctuary in Medieval London," *Journal of the British Archaeological Association*, 2nd ser., 38 (1933): 293–315, at 312–15.

9 Pierre Bonnassie, "Les 'sagreres' catalanes: La concentration de l'habitat dans le 'cercle de paix' des églises (XIe s.)," in *L'environnement des églises et la topographie religieuse des campagnes médiévales*, ed. M. Fixot and E. Zadora-Rio (Paris: Maison des Sciences de l'Homme, 1994), 68–79; Dominique Baudreu and Jean-

The possible implications of the term "sanctuary" can seem quite bewildering, but in general it means "a church able to offer some level of protection to those in fear," that is, to sanctuary-seekers.

The purpose of this paper is to explore the implications of sanctuary for the secular world and, in particular, to ask whether sanctuary rights should be understood as a type of secular legal privilege. It is an investigation of how far early sanctuary privileges had a place in the development of later legal privileges that may, at first sight, appear to be unrelated. The paper aims to do this through a case-study of a particular type of sanctuary found in the north of England, as exemplified in the relatively well-documented, and probably most ancient, examples of Ripon (Yorkshire North Riding) and Beverley (Yorkshire East Riding). Both were seventh-century ecclesiastical foundations in the ancient Kingdom of Northumbria, but there is no evidence for their sanctuary-privileges until much later (see below). The key feature of this Northumbrian sanctuary model – there are similar examples in Hexham (Northumberland), Wetheral (Cumberland), and possibly Tynemouth (Northumberland)[10] – is the mile-radius banleuca that defined the sanctuary-area, and was an unchanging aspect of the sanctuary-privileges at both Beverley and Ripon.

This paper's aim to consider unusually strong ecclesiastical sanctuary rights in the context of secular legal privileges is justifiable because the two are frequently found together. Indeed, the correlation is so pronounced that in some cases a causal relationship has been suggested; the following is Isobel Thornley's assessment of the situation in late medieval England:

> There were some places which, unlike ordinary parish churches, could give permanent protection to criminals fleeing to them. ... [This right's] basis was no sanctuary charter in express words but an independence of royal justice. ... The privilege was thus purely secular and jurisdic-

---

Paul Cazes, "Les villages ecclésiaux dans le bassin de l'Aude," in *L'environnement des églises*, ed. Fixot and Zadora-Rio, 80–97; Charles Doherty, "The Monastic Town in Early Medieval Ireland," in *The Comparative History of Urban Origins in Non-Roman Europe*, British Archaeological Reports, Brit. Ser., 255, ed. H.B. Clarke and A. Simms (Oxford: B.A.R., 1985), 45–76; L.A.S. Butler, "The 'Monastic City' in Wales: Myth or Reality?" *Bulletin of the Board of Celtic Studies* 28 (1979): 458–67.

10 James Raine, ed., *The Priory of Hexham its Chroniclers, Endowments and Annals*, vol. 1, Surtees Society 44 (Durham: Surtees Society, 1864), 61–62; J.E. Prescott, ed., *The Register of the Priory of Wetherhal*, Cumberland and Westmorland Antiquarian and Archaeological Society, Record Series (Kendal: T. Wilson, 1897), 490–91; Cox, *Sanctuaries*, 166–74.

tional; but long before the Tudor period opened, circumstances had given it a false ecclesiastical colour.[11]

From Thornley's late medieval viewpoint the intermingling of jurisdictional and sanctuarial privilege was clear, and it was plain that the former underlay the latter. In earlier periods, however, the reverse may have been the case, as Wendy Davies argued for the Welsh *noddfa*. These large banleuca sanctuaries had functions beyond the provision of a refuge: any violent offence within the *noddfa* was deemed a breach of protection and understood as an insult that legally required compensation. Davies found evidence of these compensations in penitential grants of land to such churches and has shown that, in at least one case, a tenth-century *noddfa* developed into an eleventh-century "full territorial immunity."[12] Once again, the coexistence of sanctuary rights and secular privilege is clear but here the picture is the opposite of Thornley's: the sanctuarial privileges form the root of later jurisdictional ones. In essence, this paper investigates the possibility that something similar happened in Northumbria.

In Anglo-Saxon England, the right to offer protection was not limited to the Church; indeed, it came, in royal hands, to be a key element of criminal law. The offences of *hamsocn* and *forsteal* were, respectively, the breach of the royal protection over houses and over roads; if we add to these the offence of *griðbryce*, breach of the king's *grið* (literally, "peace" or "protection") as given by a sheriff or other royal officer, we have the main elements of royal jurisdiction over violence.[13] Despite valiant attempts to argue otherwise, there is no compelling evidence that homicide, in itself, was a royal plea in this period; killings and other violent offences thus usually became a matter for royal justice only if they breached such protections.[14]

11 Isobel D. Thornley, "The Destruction of Sanctuary," in *Tudor Studies Presented ... to Albert Frederick Pollard*, ed. R.W. Seton-Watson (London: Longmans, Green & Co., 1924), 182–207, at 183–84.

12 Wendy Davies, "Adding Insult to Injury: Power, Property and Immunities in Early Medieval Wales," in *Property and Power in the Early Middle Ages*, ed. Wendy Davies and Paul Fouracre (Cambridge: Cambridge University Press, 1995), 137–64, at 144–49; Wendy Davies and Paul Fouracre, "Conclusion: Property and Power in Early Medieval Europe," in *Property and Power in the Early Middle Ages*, ed. Davies and Fouracre, 245–71, at 256.

13 Hn 79: 4, 80: 2, 80: 10–80: 11c; II Cn 12. The traditional view of these offences is that they were of much lesser significance: see Naomi Hurnard, "The Anglo-Norman Franchises," *English Historical Review* 64 (1949): 289–327, 433–60, at 310.

14 Hurnard, "The Anglo-Norman Franchises," 299–300; Patrick Wormald, "Giving God and King their Due: Conflict and its Regulation in the Early English State," in

These protective powers were so similar to sanctuary that this paper will consider it as one of the same group of legal protections, and will analyze it as a type of legal privilege. The neutral term "privilege" is important because it allows us to look at sanctuary rights, jurisdictional rights (that is, rights involving both the administration and profits of justice) and rights to only the profits of justice, without over-emphasizing the distinctions. This paper is interested in relationships that cross these divides and it seems wisest to acknowledge their presence without becoming subject to them. It is well-known, for example, that rights to receive fines could over time "ripen" into rights to hold the courts imposing them; thinking in terms of evolving privilege seems a good way of dealing with such phenomena.[15]

Sanctuary, as noted at the start, was a combination of two distinct but related ideas: the church as a sanctified and therefore non-violent space and the sanctuary-seeker as someone in need of the church's charitable protection. This comes through in sanctuary's practical operation: it can be the space that is protected, shielding not only the fugitive but everyone else who enters it, or it can be the fugitive's person that acquires the protection through his supplication. We can, therefore, speak of "spatial protection" and "personal protection." This distinction, though not unique to sanctuary (*hamsocn* and *forsteal* are clearly spatial protections whilst *griðbryce* seems primarily personal), is vital to our understanding it. In Davies's analysis of the *noddfa* it was spatial protection, not personal, that developed into jurisdictional privilege. If we now turn to Ripon and Beverley, what sort of protection could they offer and what impact did it have upon the evolution of these communities' privileges?

Wulfstan, Ciricgrið, *and Protected Space*

The first step in answering these questions must be an analysis of the late Anglo-Saxon conception of sanctuary. Fortunately it is a subject Archbishop Wulfstan II of York, Anglo-Saxon England's last major law-maker, treated in depth. The term he used when discussing sanctuary was *ciricgrið* ("church-peace" or "church-protection"); anyone violating this by committing homicide within church walls forfeited his life. This, however, was

Legal Culture in the Early Medieval West (London: Hambledon, 1999), 333–57, at 340–42. I argue this case in detail in my thesis, "Protection, Feud and Royal Power: Violence and Its Regulation in English Law, *c.*850–*c.*1250" (PhD thesis, Durham University, forthcoming) and in my forthcoming article, "Royal Protections and Private Justice: A Reassessment of Cnut's 'Reserved Pleas.'"

15 Julius Goebel, *Felony and Misdemeanor: A Study in the History of English Criminal Procedure* (New York: The Commonwealth Fund, 1937), 397.

not all; as Æthelred's 1014 code makes clear, *ciricgrið* was a much more general concept:

> And if *ciricgrið* is violated in some other respect, without the taking of life, amends shall diligently be made in accordance with the nature of the offence, whether it be fighting or robbery or illicit intercourse or whatever it may be. And always first the church is to be compensated for the breach of its protection, in accordance with the nature of the offence and also in proportion to the status of the church.[16]

At first glance, then, *ciricgrið* emerges as a strong but non-specific protection that could be breached by any offence. Such a breach would result either in a killer's life being forfeited to the king or a lesser offender paying compensation to the church. However, on careful inspection it is evident this is not the whole story. What is being discussed is clearly a spatial protection: the non-lethal offences described have nothing to do with a refuge-function and, crucially, Wulfstan never refers to anyone actually claiming *ciricgrið*. Indeed, the term he employs for the sanctuary which wrongdoers could seek is *friðsocne* – a strong indication that he was deliberately keeping the concepts of personal and spatial protection separate.[17]

This being the case, we must surely ask what Wulfstan meant by his use of the phrase "within church walls" (*binnan ciricwagum*) when specifying the offence of homicide for which the killer's life was forfeit. This appears with such consistency throughout his legal writings that it is impossible to regard it as a mere stylistic flourish, yet he never explains it.[18] Its implication, however, must surely be that it was possible to breach *ciricgrið* through homicide both inside and outside church walls, with only the former being deemed unforgivable. There is evidence to support this interpretation in an unofficial Wulfstanian compilation on protection known as *Grið*. Firstly, it is stated that in "South English" law if anyone fought within a minster but outside the church (*on mynstre butan cyrcean*), that is presumably within the precincts of the minster, they were to make full compensation to the minster according to its rank.[19] There is also a

16 VIII Atr 4–4: 1. Cf. I Cn 3–3a. The reference to *unriht hæmed* – illicit intercourse – appears only in the A manuscript of VIII Atr.

17 VIII Atr 1: 1; I Cn 2: 3.

18 EGu 1; *Grið* 2, 13; VI Atr 14; VIII Atr 1: 1; I Cn 2: 2. Also, perhaps, *Nor Grið* 1. See Richard J.E. Dammery, "Editing the Anglo-Saxon Laws: Felix Liebermann and Beyond," in *The Editing of Old English*, ed. Donald G. Scragg and Paul E. Szarmach (Woodbridge: D.S. Brewer, 1994), 251–61, at 257.

19 *Grið* 10.

rather odd passage, supposedly stating "North English" law, that draws a distinction between killing within church walls (*binnan cyricwagum*) and within church doors (*binnan cyricderum*).[20] This could, conceivably, be a reference to the churchyard – the "doors" in question being the cemetery gates – or it could, as Felix Liebermann suggested, mean *Vorhalle* ("entrance hall," "porch").[21] Neither explanation is particularly satisfactory,[22] but regardless of the finer points both these passages do show the existence of an area outside the main church building covered by *ciricgrið*.

The picture of *ciricgrið* that emerges is thus a complex one. The king has some jurisdiction, but only when *ciricgrið* is breached through homicide within the church itself. For homicides outside the church and for lesser offences, wherever committed, the church has the right to compensation payments – providing, of course, that they fall within its zone of *ciricgrið*, whose precise extent probably varied but may frequently have included the churchyard or monastic precincts. What we have, in theory, is spatial protection not only operating as a refuge but also justifying the imposition of fines for every conceivable misdeed. This was a powerful legal privilege, albeit rather limited spatially. However, these rights take on an added significance when it is considered that churchyards and monastic precincts were often venues for markets throughout the period in ques-

20 *Grið* 13–13: 2.

21 Liebermann, *Gesetze*, 1: 471.

22 Liebermann's explanation is problematic in that the porch could very easily have been regarded as *binnan cyricwagum*, and even if this is disregarded we would surely expect to find the singular, *cyricdere*, rather than the plural, *cyricderum*, if a porch were being referred to. My suggested alternative explanation, on the other hand, does rely on translating *duru* or *dor* as "gate" rather than "door." Some support for this can be found in the *Dictionary of Old English*, which defines *duru* as "a barrier, door or gate of an entrance" and *dor* as simply "door, gate," though it does, of course, translate *cyric-dor, cyric-duru* as "church-door, outer door of a church," with two occurrences where this appears clearly to be the correct translation (Angus Cameron, Ashley Crandell Amos, and Antonette diPaolo Healey, eds., *Dictionary of Old English: A to G Online*, http://www.doe.utoronto.ca [accessed 2 October 2008], s.vv. "dor," "duru," "cyric-dor, cyric-duru"). Though linguistically uncertain this interpretation is supported by the reasonable parallel with southern law and the fact that, according to a long tradition of church councils, sanctuary could be claimed in the churchyard. See Elisabeth Zadora-Rio, "La topographie des lieux d'asile dans les campagnes médiévales," in *L'église, la campagne, le terroir*, ed. Michel Fixot and Elisabeth Zadora-Rio (Paris: Éditions du CNRS, 1989), 11–16; Pierre Timbal Duclaux de Martin, *Le droit d'asile* (Paris: Librairie du Recueil Sirey, 1939), 134–35; Anne Ducloux, *Ad ecclesiam confugere: Naissance du droit d'asile dans les églises* (Paris: De Boccard, 1994), 207–20, 284–85.

tion.[23] If eleventh-century churchyards were places that could bustle with mercantile activity, it is possible to think of *ciricgrið* as being of value both to churches as a source of revenue, and to traders as a deterrent to theft and general disorder.

One text, however, proves that spatial protection could operate on a much larger scale. The law fragment known as *Pax*, possibly of a late tenth-century Danelaw origin, describes the king's *grið* extending for over three miles from his residence.[24] The only plausible interpretation is that, as *ciricgrið* did for churches, this *grið* allowed the king to impose fines for any offences committed within this zone. It is easy to imagine that sanctuary banleucas, such as Ripon's and Beverley's, could operate in a similar way. If they did – if they could in effect impose fines for breach of *ciricgrið* on anyone committing an offence within their banleucas – then it would be reasonable to follow Davies's example and see such spatial protection as the root from which later jurisdictional privileges evolved. But is there evidence that this happened in practice?

Ripon and Beverley: Dating

Fortunately, Ripon and Beverley are exceptions to the general rule that we have little evidence of Anglo-Saxon sanctuary practices outside the laws. However, our information, though relatively plentiful, is also problematic. One source, known as *The Customs of York Minster* (henceforth *Customs*), goes into some detail on the operation of Ripon's and Beverley's sanctuaries, but in its current form it dates from the fourteenth century.[25] Therefore, before we can address the central issues of spatial protection and the evolution of these houses' privileges, it is essential to have a solid assessment of the dates for which the information in *Customs* is valid. The key passage is as follows:

> The church of St. John in Beverley has one mile around it free and quit of all claim to any royal custom or to any monetary renders or to any

23 Richard Morris, *Churches in the Landscape* (London: J.M. Dent & Sons, 1989), 212–13; Tim Pestell, "Using Material Culture to Define Holy Space: The Bromholm Project," in *Defining the Holy: Sacred Space in Medieval and Early Modern Europe*, ed. Andrew Spicer and Sarah Hamilton (Aldershot: Ashgate, 2006), 161–86, at 180.

24 *Pax*; Patrick Wormald, *The Making of English Law: King Alfred to the Twelfth Century* (Oxford: Blackwell, 1999), 371–72.

25 R.C. Van Caenegem, ed., *English Lawsuits from William I to Richard I*, vol. 1, Selden Society 106 (London: Selden Society, 1990), no. 172. Also, in a slightly truncated form, Rollason, *Sources for York History*, 220–25.

> geld which is paid to the king throughout England. From the beginning of this mile up to the cross of King Æthelstan, if anyone breaks the peace, the penalty will be one hundred (*hundreth*) [that is, eight pounds]; from the cross of Æthelstan to the churchyard, three hundred; inside the churchyard, six hundred; inside the church twelve hundred; inside the choir, whoever breaks the peace shall forfeit all his possessions and shall submit his body to the peril, without any possibility of rendering satisfaction by a nominated sum of money. In a similar way the church of St. Wilfrid in Ripon has around it a mile with a similar liberty, from the beginning of which up to the churchyard a violator of the peace must pay three hundred; in the churchyard six; in the choir, as has previously been specified.[26]

According to *Customs*, then, we have two sanctuary banleucas within which a 'peace' – presumably a Latin form of *grið* – offered a degree of protection defined by location. Over these banleucas, it is emphasized, the king had no rights whatsoever. For current purposes, however, the most important element is the *Customs* scheme's strong association with King Æthelstan (d. 939). Some have taken this at face-value, or even assumed a seventh-century origin for the sanctuaries, in line with the churches' foundations, but can such views survive close examination?[27]

Customs is a copy of a fourteenth-century letter from the Chapter of York Minster to the Chapter of Southwell Minster, purporting to contain the record of an 1106 inquest into the privileges of the Archbishopric of York. In spite of its late date, commentators on *Customs* have been positive about the authenticity of its information.[28] Possibly they have been too kind; certainly A.G. Dickens's conclusion that it is an "authentic account" of this inquest cannot be justified.[29] Though the lists of inquisitors and jurors testify strongly that the inquest took place, was recorded, and that this record was used in preparing *Customs*, there is also clear evidence of later interpolation into the text. Shortly after the introductory matter, we

26 Rollason, *Sources for York History*, 224. The absence of a fine in Ripon for breaches of the peace taking place in the church but outside the choir is almost certainly a scribal error. Earlier in the text it is explained that "in hundreth sex libre continentur"; the usual figure, however, is eight pounds.

27 Lobel, "Ecclesiastical Banleuca," 123; Hurnard, "Anglo-Norman Franchises," 315.

28 Rollason, *Sources for York History*, 30–31; Van Caenegem, *English Lawsuits*, vol. 1, n. 138; Arthur G. Dickens, "The 'Shire' and Privileges of the Archbishop in Eleventh-Century York," *Yorkshire Archaeological Journal* 38 (1952–55): 131–47, at 139.

29 Dickens, "'Shire' and Privileges," 139.

find most of the text of a rather suspicious charter of Henry I.[30] Wherever this text originally came from, it was not *Customs*. Its presence disrupts the document's structure, leading to a two-part discussion of sanctuary, and its emphasis on the canons' rights over the archbishop – who is credited with calling the inquest – seems out of place. The text following the charter, however, has few suspicious signs, makes reasonably modest claims, and its information is partially confirmed by less problematic late-eleventh-century texts.[31] This section, which contains the material on Ripon and Beverley, may well represent the text of the original inquest. It must, at any rate, have been in existence in the early twelfth century as it was used in Richard of Hexham's description of his own church's privileges.[32]

The Ripon and Beverley sanctuary schemes given in *Customs*, therefore, are at least as old as the early twelfth century, and we do have earlier evidence that supports an Anglo-Saxon origin for them: Ripon's banleuca, for example, appears in *Domesday Book*.[33] Yet, the pre-Conquest evidence is contradictory. An archiepiscopal estate-survey, dated by W.H. Stevenson to about 1030,[34] whose section on Ripon begins "at Ripon first the space of one mile on each side"[35] confirms the early existence of the banleuca, but the similarly early-eleventh-century text that Liebermann called *Norðhymbra Ciricgrið* offers a very different sanctuary scheme. It states that York, Ripon, and Beverley had sanctuaries of the highest rank, killings

30 James Raine, ed., *The Historians of the Church of York and its Archbishops*, 3 vols., Rolls Series 71 (London: Longman, 1879–94), 3: 34–36; Charles Johnson and H.A. Cronne, *Regesta Regum Anglo-Normannorum*, vol. 2, *Regesta Henrici Primi 1100–1135* (Oxford: Clarendon Press, 1956), no. 1083.

31 Rollason, *Sources for York History*, 210–13, 218. The only grounds for suspicion is a reference to Hexham in a list of churches offering a similar sanctuary to York Minster. Hexham was not refounded until 1113. The church, however, had been in use beforehand, its possessions administered by provosts from Durham (see Raine, *Priory of Hexham*, vol. 1, l–lxii). It is, therefore, possible that it was a long-standing sanctuary. It is, however, equally possible that it was not and that the Hexham reference was a later addition. The structure of the list, "ad ecclesiam beati Iohannis in Beverlaco, ad ecclesiam beati Wilfridi in Ripun, *et* beati Cuthberti in Dunelmo, *et ad* ecclesiam sancti Andree in Hestoldesham," is awkward, perhaps signifying some tampering (Rollason, *Sources for York History*, 223–24; emphasis added).

32 Raine, *Priory of Hexham*, vol. 1, 61–62.

33 *DB* 303d (Yorkshire). The distance of a league (1½ miles), a common banleuca measurement in Normandy, is given here in error; see Lobel, "Ecclesiastical Banleuca," 124.

34 W.H. Stevenson, "Yorkshire Surveys and Other Eleventh-Century Documents in the York Gospels," *English Historical Review* 27 (1912): 1–25, at 14.

35 Ibid., 18.

within church walls being *botleas* (unemendable) and breaches short of killing being compensated by three hundred. It adds that churches of lesser rank were entitled to lesser sums, and bans women and weapons from churches, but there is no mention of any banleuca.[36]

How can these two documents be reconciled? Patrick Wormald's view that *Norðhymbra Ciricgrið* was "obviously ... a local application of Wulfstan principles" suggests a solution.[37] His argument is a solid one: the text gives northern churches a ranking similar to that found in Wulfstan's work and displays identical spatial principles, using exactly the same phrase, *binnan cyricwagum*, to describe where homicide was unforgivable.[38] If, then, we see this as part of an attempt to recast Northumbrian institutions in a Wulfstanian mould, should we not see it as an attempt that failed? There is, after all, no later sign of this Wulfstanian scheme and the official character of *Norðhymbra Ciricgrið* is far from certain.[39] This seems, to my mind, the most sensible view and its implications are interesting: rather than casting doubt on the antiquity of the scheme in *Customs*, *Norðhymbra Ciricgrið* serves to strengthen the case. To be able to survive this early-eleventh-century assault, the banleuca scheme would probably need to have been regarded as a long-standing custom. If we add that the structure of fines in "hundreds" is extremely close to that in III Æthelred, a late-tenth-century code for the Danelaw, a tenth-century origin for the *Customs* scheme seems most probable.[40] It is, of course, possible that these Scandinavian fines were added to a pre-existing sanctuary scheme. Its similarity to the sanctuary banleuca with concentric subdivisions described in the eighth-century *Collectio Canonum Hibernensis* could be an indication of this, but it would also be consistent with a tenth-century origin as the *Hibernensis* is known to have been circulating in England at that time.[41]

Ripon and Beverley: Interpretation

With the probable antiquity of the *Customs* scheme thus established, it is possible to move on to the key issue: what did it mean? What sort of special privileges should we imagine inhering in Ripon's and Beverley's banleucas in the period before the Norman Conquest? For sanctuary itself we at least have ample evidence to interpret, but what should be made of *Customs*'

36 *Nor Grið* 1–4.

37 Wormald, *Making of English Law*, 395.

38 *Nor Grið* 1.

39 Dammery, "Editing the Anglo-Saxon Laws," 259.

40 III Atr 1–1: 2.

41 F.W.H. Wasserschleben, ed., *Die Irische Kanonensammlung*, 2nd ed. (Leipzig: Bernhard Tauchnitz, 1885), XLIV: 5, 8. For discussions of this text see Kathleen Hughes,

statements on the banleucas' other privileges, specifically the opening statement that "the church of St. John in Beverley has one mile around it free and quit of all claim to any royal custom" and the one stating that Ripon "has around it a mile with a similar liberty."[42] *Customs* represents this privilege of being free of all customs as restricted to the banleucas, yet *Domesday Book* shows that both churches enjoyed the same privilege for lands outside them.[43] Furthermore, King Stephen's confirmation-charters do not mention anything solid other than sake and soke and the tantalizing statement that each church had *pacem suam infra leucam suam* (its peace within its banleuca).[44] It is possible, therefore, that this is merely a high-flown way of referring to common privileges like sake and soke, toll and team, and *infangþeof*, combined with the wider right, mentioned later in *Customs*, to have the archbishop's reeve represent his tenants in shire, riding, and wapentake courts.[45]

The other option is to take the claim literally and accept that it meant that under no circumstances would any payment to the king be made from these territories. This would not mean, of course, that the population would be freed from their liability to all the royal exactions that their less privileged neighbours were subject to; the payments would still be levied but the churches holding this liberty would receive them instead of the king.[46] At

---

The Church in Early Irish Society (London: Methuen, 1966), 148; Doherty, "The Monastic Town in Early Medieval Ireland," 55–57. On early Hiberno-Northumbrian contacts, see Kathleen Hughes, "Evidence for Contacts between the Churches of the Irish and English from the Synod of Whitby to the Viking Age," in *England Before the Conquest: Studies in Primary Sources Presented to Dorothy Whitelock*, ed. Peter Clemoes and Kathleen Hughes (Cambridge: Cambridge University Press, 1971), 49–67. On the *Hibernensis* in England, see Patrick Wormald, "Archbishop Wulfstan and the Holiness of Society," in his *Legal Culture in the Early Medieval West*, 225–51, at 238 n.; Denis L.T. Bethell, "English Monks and Irish Reform in the Eleventh and Twelfth Centuries," *Historical Studies* 8 (1971): 111–35, at 116–18. Cf. Mary Bateson, "A Worcester Cathedral Book of Ecclesiastical Collections, made *c.*1000 A.D.," *English Historical Review* 10 (1895): 712–31, at 721–22.

42 Rollason, *Sources for York History*, 224: "Ecclesia uero beati Iohannis in Beuerlaco miliare unum habet circa se liberum et quietum ab omni regali consuetudine"; "Simili modo cum eadem libertate miliare suum habet circa se ecclesia beati Wilfridi in Ripum."

43 Rollason, *Sources for York History*, 218; *DB* 298c (Yorkshire).

44 R.H.C. Davis and H.A. Cronne, *Regesta Regum Anglo-Normannorum*, vol. 3, *Regesta regis Stephani ac Mathildis imperatricis ac Gaufridi et Henrici Ducum Normannorum, 1135–1154* (Oxford: Clarendon Press, 1968), nos. 99, 717.

45 Van Caenegem, *English Lawsuits*, vol. 1, no. 172.

46 The basic logic of this interpretation is well outlined in F.W. Maitland, *Domesday Book and Beyond: Three Essays in the Early History of England* (Cambridge: Cambridge University Press, 1897), 274–75.

face-value, then, this is the highest possible form of financial privilege, with these churches possessing the right to receive all legal fines and forfeitures originating within their banleucas, in addition to a full tax exemption.[47] However, to insist that this privilege included forfeitures from even *botleas* offences would be historiographically controversial, as there is no established precedent for such rights. Naomi Hurnard, in an article later hailed by Wormald as "masterly," argued that *botleas* offences were so quintessentially royal that the idea the king could grant them out for others' benefit was unthinkable.[48] If we follow the orthodox approach, therefore, we must limit our understanding of Ripon's and Beverley's non-sanctuarial privileges to the highest royal rights that we do know to have been exercised by ecclesiastical institutions: *hamsocn*, *griðbryce*, and *forsteal*.[49]

A potential problem with such an interpretation is that these rights are not mentioned by name in Stephen's confirmation-charters. Therefore, if they did exist at all, they must have been encompassed by the phrase *pacem suam infra leucam suam*. This is not, in fact, that far-fetched. All three were, as noted above, protections very similar to sanctuary: *griðbryce*, being personal protection usually given by a sheriff, when offered by a church would effectively be sanctuary. Similarly, it is easy to imagine that, exercised within the banleucas, *hamsocn* and *forsteal* (the protection of houses and roads) could be seen as part of the same "peace" that covered sanctuary-seekers. This, in fact, is the crucial point: we cannot know precisely what rights Ripon and Beverley possessed above sake and soke but we do know that, as far as Stephen's charters were concerned, everything worthy of note was part of the same "peace" within the banleucas that underpinned the sanctuaries.

It is, therefore, vital to examine the evidence for these sanctuary rights in detail: it is the only solid evidence by which we can understand what was meant by this "peace." Given Wulfstan's spatial understanding of *ciricgrið*,

47 In fact, we know from *Domesday Book* that while Beverley had a *geld* exemption, Ripon did not (*DB* 303d, 304a [Yorkshire]).

48 Hurnard, "The Anglo-Norman Franchises," 291–95; Patrick Wormald, "Lordship and Justice in the Early English Kingdom: Oswaldslow Revisited," in *Legal Culture in the Early Medieval West*, 313–32, at 317.

49 My own view on this is that though Hurnard may have been partially right about the exclusively royal nature of *botleas* offences, she was mistaken in affording them so much more significance than contemporary sources such as *Domesday Book*, in which they do not loom anywhere near as large as *hamsocn*, *griðbryce* and *forsteal*. This view is explored in more detail in my forthcoming thesis, "Protection, Feud and Royal Power," and article, "Royal Protections and Private Justice: A Reassessment of Cnut's 'Reserved Pleas.'" The offence of *forsteal* seems to have been unknown in northern law at the time of Cnut (see II Cn 12, 15), so its presence here is somewhat less likely than *hamsocn* or *griðbryce*.

the notion that the banleucas were zones of spatial protection is an extremely tempting one. However, close examination of *Customs* reveals a problem. The key passage follows on from the sanctuary regulations quoted earlier:

> Moreover, at the three feasts and at Pentecost, all coming and going from their homes have peace; fine for breach of the peace, one hundred. Likewise on the feast of St. John the Baptist and John the Confessor, and similarly on the feast of the dedication of the church of Beverley. All those coming to or going from the two feasts of St. Wilfrid shall have peace, and whosoever infringes this peace, within one mile on the inward journey and one mile on the outward journey, shall be liable to a fine of one hundred for peace-breaking.[50]

The clear implication is that on these particular feast-days the protection was broadened from its usual scope into something more general. This could be interpreted to mean that on every other day the protection of the banleuca applied only to those officially in sanctuary; people simply going about their daily business would not be covered. According to this interpretation, what we have here is not a spatial protection at all, but an essentially personal one, albeit qualified by location.

There are, however, problems with this view. How do you define who qualifies for such personal protection? The only workable solution would be to insist that the sanctuary-seeker come to the church and officially register his status, after which he could roam the banleuca with the church's protection. Any looser system would lead to a situation where the status of every victim of violence within the banleuca was at issue – had he or had he not claimed the peace? In the case of a dead victim, we might imagine that this would lead to his being presumed a sanctuary-seeker unless the killer managed to prove him otherwise, just as in cases of *murdrum* (the offence of murdering a Norman) corpses were presumed French until Englishry was proven.[51] The more stringent definition, however, does create the problematic possibility of genuine sanctuary-seekers being pursued into the banleuca and killed with impunity before they reached the churchyard (where all churches were entitled to offer sanctuary). This is not necessarily an improbable state of affairs but it is important to note that, if this was the custom, it would have seemed less than ideal to churchmen concerned with the potential dishonour to their saints. They would, surely, have preferred a wider spatial interpretation of

50 Rollason, *Sources for York History*, 224–25; Van Caenegem, *English Lawsuits*, vol. 1, no. 172.

51 Hn 92: 6.

the peace of the banleucas, which would eliminate this possibility (and, of course, be significantly more lucrative).

Another possible interpretation, retaining the idea of spatial protection, involves drawing a distinction between voluntary and compulsory peace. We could imagine that the banleuca outside the churchyard operated in a way analogous to the king's highway as described in the account of *forsteal* in the *Leges Henrici Primi*. There, any man had the right to take advantage of the peace of the road but he was equally entitled to answer his enemy's challenge and fight – thereby taking himself out of royal protection.[52] We could, perhaps, suggest that a similar system operated in Ripon and Beverley: men who wished to fight could do so, whilst those who wanted to be left in peace were protected from attack. According to this view the special protection of the feast-day had a compulsory quality: people had to remain peaceful whether they wanted to or not. This would be consistent with *ciricgrið* as described by Wulfstan as well as with the general eight-day peaces at major feasts and royal coronations described by the *Leges Edwardi Confessoris*, and Cnut's offence of *lencgtenbryce* which required double compensation for any fighting during Lent, as at high festivals.[53]

We have, then, two possible interpretations of the *Customs* scheme, a minimalist one based on personal protection, and a maximalist one based on spatial protection. On balance, the minimalist interpretation probably provides the best fit, since the large fines are appropriate to the enormous crime of killing a sanctuary-seeker, and its explanation of the feast-day peaces is more straightforward. The idea of a sanctuary-zone that expands to cover a large area once the central point is reached also accords with later sanctuary-practices in Durham, Wetheral, and even Brittany. In all these it seems that the larger sanctuary area was only officially available after the sanctuary-seeker had made a confession and rung a bell in the church.[54] The maximalist interpretation, however, does have some virtues. It fits rather better with the possibly high-level privileges conveyed by *Customs*' claim that there was freedom from all royal exactions, and with the laconic phrase *pacem suam infra leucam suam* of King Stephen's charters.[55] Both interpretations could even be correct, for there may have been a personal sanctuary scheme, with its vast fines, overlaying a more moderately conceived spatial peace.

52 Hn 80: 4a.

53 ECf 12a; II Cn 47.

54 Forster, "Notes on Durham," 127–30; Prescott, ed., *The Register of the Priory of Wetherhal*, 491; Timbal Duclaux de Martin, *Le droit d'asile*, n. 177. In practice, however, it is clear that the right to exclude sheriffs and other officers would have prevented official pursuit within all these sanctuaries.

55 Davis and Cronne, *Regesta*, vol. 3, nos. 99, 717.

However, these are not points that need to be pushed too strongly. A more important aspect of this analysis is that it highlights just how simply a personal protection scheme could be reinterpreted as a spatial one. A determined archbishop, we might imagine, would have been sufficiently powerful to impose such a shift, reforming a spatially-limited scheme of personal protection (with all the impracticalities and imperfections just outlined) into a spatial one that combined the virtues of simplicity, practicality, and greater honour for the respective saints, with the temptations of increased power and wealth. Our maximalist view, then, could be simply a reformed version of the minimalist one that seems the most likely interpretation of *Customs*. Indeed, it seems more productive to view our two interpretations not as mutually exclusive, but as possible stages in an evolutionary process.

An Evolutionary Process?

If, as the preceding analysis argued, the minimalist interpretation of *Customs* is the more credible for 1106, what reason do we have to believe that it was later reformed into something akin to our maximalist interpretation? Why should we accept that the proposed evolution from personal to spatial protection took place at all? There are two good reasons. First, twelfth-century legal changes show precisely this sort of conversion from personal to spatial protection. An extremely close parallel development can be seen, for example, in the evolution of royal powers, specifically the King's Peace. In the early twelfth century the basic approach of Anglo-Saxon justice to violent offences remained current. With the probable addition of *murdrum* (effectively a group protection for the Normans),[56] the same powers of spatial protection on roads (*forsteal*) and in houses (*hamsocn*), and personal protection given by his officers (*griðbryce*), were the mechanisms that allowed kings to punish violence. All these protections were specific; in theory they only applied in the particular conditions they described.

In the *Leges Henrici Primi* (completed by 1118), however, we see signs of a shift. The author complains that litigants were making false allegations of *hamsocn* or *griðbryce* in order to expose their opponents to harsher penalties. He also hints at official encouragement of this practice which,

56 Probable because there is no solid evidence for it before the Conquest. Frederick Pollock and F.W. Maitland, *The History of English Law before the Time of Edward I*, 2nd ed., 2 vols., (Cambridge: Cambridge University Press, 1968), 1: 89, 2: 487. For an alternative argument, see Bruce R. O'Brien, "From *Morðor* to *Murdrum*: The Preconquest Origin and Norman Revival of the Murder Fine," *Speculum* 71 (1996): 321–57.

apparently, was particularly rife in London.[57] At this point, it seems, this was still generally thought to be an abuse; the author of the *Leges Henrici*, at least, links it to the offence of erroneous pleading (*miskenning*), something which both King Henry I and King Stephen were keen to be seen prohibiting.[58] Yet by the end of the century the situation had changed so much that what used to be an offence had become institutionalized; now anyone alleging homicide was compelled to claim that there had occurred both breach of the peace and felony. This fundamental change was not effected by any royal edict, but rather through complicity between plaintiffs and court-holders in making, and accepting as valid, what would previously have been regarded as false allegations. Legally speaking, the situation had not changed in any extreme way. Homicide was still prosecuted through other offences; it was just that these offences were now regarded as integral to every killing. Without it ever being declared as such, the personal protection of *griðbryce* had become a spatial protection covering the entire kingdom – precisely the sort of process suggested for the banleucas of Ripon and Beverley.[59]

The second argument in favour of this evolutionary process rests on what emerges in the thirteenth century. For Ripon we have the record of a 1228 inquest into the secular privileges of the chapter, as distinct from those of either the archbishop or the sheriff. Here we find, once again, that sanctuary takes pride of place in the chapter's list of privileges. The discussion of Ripon's immense jurisdictional privileges – at the core of which is the right to try appeals in all cases, hang felons on its own gallows, and receive all the profits associated with doing so – follows directly on from this, without even a break in the sentence, giving the distinct impression that the two are related.[60] This is confirmed in a later document, a *Quo Warranto* inquiry of 1292 directed at the Archbishop of York's possessions generally but paying particular attention to Ripon and Beverley. Here we find a picture that attributes to the archbishop privileges similar to those Ripon's chapter claimed in 1228. The specific connection with sanctuary is not so strong here but, crucially, there is a greater attention to the details of jurisdiction, including the spatial dimensions of both houses' liberties. In

57 Hn 22.

58 William Stubbs and H.W.C. Davis, eds., *Select Charters and Other Illustrations of English Constitutional History*, 9th ed. (Oxford: Clarendon Press, 1921), 130, 144.

59 Pollock and Maitland, *The History of English Law*, 2: 462–68. Cf. Frederick Pollock, "The King's Peace," in *Oxford Lectures and Other Discourses* (London: Macmillan, 1890), 65–90. Again, I argue this case in more detail in my thesis, "Protection, Feud and Royal Power."

60 J.T. Fowler, ed., *Memorials of the Church of Saints Peter and Wilfrid, Ripon*, vol. 1, Surtees Society 74 (Durham: Surtees Society, 1882), 51–52.

both cases it is perfectly clear that the highest levels of jurisdiction pertained specifically to the banleuca.[61]

Why should this have been? If the *pacem suam infra leucam suam* of King Stephen's charters referred only to personal protection, there is no reason to think that the banleuca would have been the obvious zone in which to claim these entirely new jurisdictional privileges. If, on the other hand, we believe that both banleucas had evolved into zones of spatial protection over the course of the twelfth century, the thirteenth-century situation is readily comprehensible. If the early peace had become one breached by all violent offences committed within the banleucas, then the later development of a zone of formalized jurisdiction makes perfect sense. The thirteenth-century privileges were thus not entirely new, but were an updated version of the same "peace" we find in *Customs*, a peace whose roots go back at least as far as the late tenth century.

Conclusions

The development postulated here is, therefore, a three-stage one. First, we have a stage of purely personal protection, where each banleuca serves as a zone of safety for people who have specifically claimed the protection of sanctuary. Next, we have the stage of spatial protection in which, through what amounts to a legal fiction, everyone within each banleuca was regarded as under protection. Whether ultimately benefiting the respective chapters or the archbishop, the churches claimed the right to fines for violent offences in their banleucas. In the final stage, this spatial protection is formalized to create a zone endowed with the highest level of jurisdiction. These stages are, of course, rather idealized – reality was no doubt somewhat messier, particularly with regard to wrangling between the archbishop and the chapters – but the evidence we have does suggest that a development along these lines was what occurred. The issue of *Customs*' claim to freedom from all royal exactions muddies the waters slightly but King Stephen's charters make it clear that whatever rights were involved were either so insignificant they did not need to be mentioned, or were so intimately linked with the sanctuary-scheme that they could be discussed as the same thing. Either way the effect is the same: we have a limited, mainly personal form of protection evolving into a general and largely spatial one, which in turn becomes the keystone of later high jurisdiction. Impossible though it may be to prove the existence of the second stage, there is enough, I believe, for us to make the modest leap of faith required. The impeccable pedigree of Wulfstan's ideas of spatial protection, the close par-

61 Ibid., 70.

allels in the twelfth-century development of royal law and, above all, the continuity of the banleucas as the primary zones of privilege, all speak in favour of the evolution suggested.

We might, then, view Ripon and Beverley as a pair of Anglo-Saxon banleuca sanctuaries that evolved into Angevin jurisdictional immunities. This would turn Thornley's interpretation neatly onto its head and place Ripon and Beverley's development on a trajectory similar to that of the Welsh *noddfa*. It is an interesting enough conclusion, perfectly valid in most respects, but it remains somewhat misleading. We would do better to envisage two highly privileged Anglo-Saxon churches evolving into two similarly highly privileged thirteenth-century churches. Though in absolute terms the value of the liberties they enjoyed clearly did increase, this is because the privileges of 1292 would have been, quite literally, inconceivable in the 1030s. At that point the right to offer such a huge sanctuary with such large fines protecting it would have been a major privilege; it did on a grandiose scale what royal laws attempted to do in a more piecemeal fashion: that is, it provided a secure safe haven for those involved in feuds.

This was, at our most conservative estimate, combined with all the common legal privileges of the time: sake and soke, toll and team, and *infangþeof*. Though these sometimes seem to be derided in the literature, it is hard to see why. Sake and soke alone comprised the right to fines for the vast majority of amendable offences (excepting only *hamsocn*, *griðbryce* and *forsteal*), whilst *infangþeof* added the forfeits of executed hand-having thieves – easily the most common and, therefore, lucrative capital offence.[62] Even the lack of court-holding rights at this point need not reflect a relative lack of judicial influence. Indeed, if *Customs* provides us with a true picture of the archbishop's eleventh-century privileges, his officers stood between his tenants and royal justice at every turn, attending shire, riding and wapentake courts on their behalf, and thus affording him ample opportunity for profitable interference.[63] These were institutions with important secular privileges even before the evolutionary process described here started. What we see at first as a process of fraudulent self-aggrandizement may well, in fact, have been little more than a struggle to keep up with rapidly changing times. Without such an updating process, by the end of the twelfth century these impressive privileges would have been meaningless.

Ripon and Beverley, then, can be seen evolving as privileged institutions from the tenth to the thirteenth centuries. The argument presented here is that the tenth-century personal protections visible in *Customs*

62 Hurnard, "Anglo-Norman Franchises," 310, 322; Wormald, "Oswaldslow Revisited," 317. Cf. Goebel, *Felony and Misdemeanor*, 371–73.

63 Van Caenegem, *English Lawsuits*, vol. 1, no. 172.

proved to be important not only as a legal privilege in their own right but also as fertile ground for later growth. It seems unlikely that these two were alone in this type of evolution. Other Northumbrian sanctuaries may offer direct parallels for all or part of this process, but more important is the general point that post-Conquest secular legal privileges, even jurisdictional immunities, may owe something to their Anglo-Saxon predecessors. The debate about the presence or absence of the immunity has often pushed native forms of privilege into obscurity. The conclusion that immunities, as understood in a Frankish context, were absent from pre-Conquest England has left us with something of a void. Further analysis that focuses on what Anglo-Saxon privileges were – rather than what they were not – may well give greater support to the sort of evolutionary model suggested by Ripon and Beverley.[64]

64 For an example of this being done successfully, see Julia Crick, "Liberty and Fraternity: Creating and Defending the Liberty of St Albans," in *Expectations of the Law in the Middle Ages*, ed. Anthony Musson (Woodbridge: Boydell, 2001), 91–103.

DANIEL E. THIERY
Iona College

Charitable Constraint: The Sacred Obligation of Charity as a Protective Force in Late Medieval England

> Let those who have been fighting against their brothers and relatives now fight in a proper way against the barbarians.[1]

At the Council of Clermont in 1095, Pope Urban II allegedly employed the above words to goad "those who fight" to recognize the spiritual brotherhood that bound them, cease fighting each other, and instead take up arms against "the infidel." Such a solicitation illumines an important characteristic of medieval Christianity and many other religions: their astounding ability both to foster peace and to promote violence, a duality whose potency derives from the grounding of their tenets in the demands of an omnipotent, often suprarational deity.[2] A great deal of scholarly as well as popular attention has been paid to violence that has been inspired or influenced by the major monotheistic religions of the West.[3] Scholars have wrangled time and again over whether acts of violence by believers are products of a fundamental aspect of a religion[4] or are perversions of a

1 O.J. Thatcher and E.H. McNeal, trans., *A Source Book for Medieval History* (New York: Charles Scribner's, 1905), 513–17.

2 Parts of this essay are derived from or further explored in my forthcoming work. See, Daniel E. Thiery, *Polluting the Sacred: Violence, Faith and the "Civilizing" of Parishioners in Late Medieval England* (Leiden: Brill, 2009).

3 See, for example, Richard Dawkins, *The God Delusion* (Boston: Houghton Mifflin, 2006). Hector Avalos's work provides both a comprehensive and critical overview of theories about human violence and also theories about religious violence. See, Hector Avalos, *Fighting Words: The Origins of Religious Violence* (Amherst, NY: Prometheus, 2005), 17–92.

4 For studies that argue for the inherently violent nature of the major religions of the world, see: Avalos, *Fighting Words*; Jack Nelson-Pallmeyer, *Is Religion Killing Us? Violence in the Bible and Quran* (Harrisburg, PA: Trinity Press, 2003); Regina M. Schwartz, *The Curse of Cain: The Violent Legacy of Monotheism* (Chicago: University of Chicago Press, 1997); Timothy Gorringe, *God's Just Vengeance: Crime, Violence and the Rhetoric of Salvation*, Cambridge Studies in Ideology and Religion 9 (Cambridge: Cambridge University Press, 1996); Richard Dawkins, *The God Delusion*. For an earlier critique of religion, see Arthur Schopenhauer, *Parerga and Paralipomena: Short Philosophical Essays*, trans. E.F.J. Payne, 2 vols. (Oxford: Clarendon Press, 1974).

peaceful essence.[5] Having examined the arguments of both sides, I have become increasingly fascinated by one enduring axiom: in general, religions promote concord among believers long before they ever, if at all, promote notions of brotherhood and acceptance of those of a different creed. One could argue that religions create a new form of tribalism, often far more encompassing than familial, ethnic, social, or national bonds, but still limited and thus still prone to legitimizing violence against an "other."

The history of Christianity in the West certainly exemplifies this axiom. In the high and late Middle Ages, as clerical leaders called for crusade and others sanctioned the right of the state and individuals to punish the wicked,[6] the Church also developed a profound set of teachings concerning sacraments and salvation that promoted forgiveness and fellowship. As scholars such as Jean Delumeau and John Bossy have shown, late medieval parishioners were products of centuries of Christian teachings mainly from clerical sources, which both promoted and demanded the vigilant maintenance of one's personal state of charity, roughly defined as both a state of accord with, and an absence of animosity toward, one's fellow Christians.[7]

5 The following studies produce notable arguments for the "peaceful essence" of Christianity: René Girard, *Job: The Victim of His People*, trans. Yvonne Freccero (Stanford: Stanford University Press, 1987); idem, *La violence et le sacré* (Paris: Bernard Grasset, 1972); idem, "Violence Renounced: Response by René Girard," in *Violence Renounced: René Girard, Biblical Studies and Peacemaking*, ed. W.M. Swartley (Telford, PA: Pandora Press, 2000); J. Harold Ellens, ed., *The Destructive Power of Religion: Violence in Judaism, Christianity and Islam*, 4 vols. (Westport, CT: Praeger, 2004); Jessica Stern, *Terror in the Name of God: Why Religious Militants Kill* (New York: HarperCollins, 2003); Martin E. Marty and R. Scott Appleby, *The Fundamentalism Project*, 5 vols. (Chicago: University of Chicago Press, 1991–95); Charles Y. Glock and Rodney Stark, *Christian Beliefs and Anti-semitism* (New York: Harper and Row, 1966); Rodney Stark, *One True God: Historical Consequences of Monotheism* (Princeton: Princeton University Press, 2001); Marc Gopin, *Holy War, Holy Peace: How Religion Can Bring Peace to the Middle East* (Oxford: Oxford University Press, 2002); Charles Kimball, *When Religion Becomes Evil* (San Francisco: HarperSanFrancisco, 2002).

6 See, for instance, *Dives et Pauper*, ed. P.H. Barnum, 2 vols., EETS, o.s. 280 (Oxford: Oxford University Press, 1976–80), 1: 13.

7 Jean Delumeau, *Sin and Fear: The Emergence of a Western Guilt Culture, 13th–18th Centuries*, trans. Eric Nicholson (New York: St. Martin's Press, 1990). Time and time again, John Bossy's studies have inspired my own research; see John Bossy, *Christianity in the West, 1400–1700* (Oxford: Oxford University Press, 1985); "Blood and Baptism: Kinship, Community and Christianity in Western Europe from the Fourteenth to the Seventeenth Centuries," *Studies in Church History* 19 (1973): 129–143; "The Mass as a Social Institution 1200–1700," *Past and Present* 100 (1983): 29–61. Also see Eamon Duffy, *The Stripping of the Altars* (New Haven: Yale University Press, 1992).

For example, parishioners learned through sermons, didactic texts, and even verbal admonition during the mass that the most cherished connection to God's grace, the Eucharist, could not be worthily gazed upon at the moment of elevation, let alone received at communion, unless they had embraced charity in both thought and deed. Those who failed to foster a humble and charitable spirit in the presence of their Lord and Saviour, and to manifest it through their comportment such as a bent knee and a bowed head, blackened their souls as well as their reputations as upright parishioners.[8] Reminded through a wide variety of media to think on death and dread God's might, late medieval parishioners and clerics alike understood that a state of charity was integral to their worthy reception of the sacraments and divine blessing, and consequently their welcome into paradise.

Yet what constitutes the core concern of this study, and what seems most fascinating about late medieval culture, is that this burgeoning of anxious introspection and self-restraint existed side by side with a seemingly antithetical attitude toward interpersonal violence and honour. While late medieval spirituality stressed personal scrutiny of one's conscience and restrained comportment as a sign of reverence, the contemporary culture demanded obsessive attention to the behaviour of one's peers because personal reputation hinged upon the public evaluation of one's words and actions – for most medieval folk, "Never mind what they think. I know I'm good" just would not work as a personal mantra. Violence and aggression were part of the fabric of normative social relations, for late medieval and early modern society valued violence as a way to resolve disputes, compete for status, and preserve the social order.[9] The everyday conduct of parish-

8 Daniel E. Thiery, "Welcome to the Parish. Remove Your Cap and Stop Assaulting Your Neighbour," in *Reputation and Representation in Fifteenth-Century Europe*, ed. Douglas L. Biggs, Sharon D. Michalove, and A. Compton Reeves (Leiden: Brill, 2004), 235–66.

9 Also see Johann Huizinga, *The Waning of the Middle Ages* (New York: Doubleday, 1989); Lawrence Stone, *Family, Sex and Marriage in England, 1500–1800* (New York: Harper and Row, 1979); idem, "Interpersonal Violence in English Society, 1300–1980," *Past and Present* 101 (1983): 22–33; John G. Bellamy, *Crime and Public Order in England in the Later Middle Ages* (Toronto: University of Toronto Press, 1973); James B. Given, *Society and Homicide in Thirteenth-Century England* (Stanford: Stanford University Press, 1977); Barbara Hanawalt, "Violent Death in Fourteenth- and Early Fifteenth-Century England," *Comparative Studies in Society and History* 18 (1976): 297–320; idem, *Of Good and Ill Repute: Gender and Social Control in Medieval England* (Oxford: Oxford University Press, 1998); Margery K. McIntosh, *Controlling Misbehaviour in England, 1300–1600* (Cambridge: Cambridge University Press, 1998); Roger B. Manning, "Violence and Social Conflict in Mid-Tudor Rebellions," *Journal of British Studies* 17 (1977): 18–40; Charles Phythian-Adams, "Rituals of Personal Confrontation in

ioners was guided by a notion of *fama* that legitimized the use of both physical and verbal violence for the defence of status. Even when matters did not directly concern their reputation, late medieval parishioners believed that physical violence could be employed licitly in three other situations: to enforce the God-given social hierarchy, to fulfil one's duties as a servant, or to execute one's obligations as an officer of the courts. Indeed, violent conduct was not seen as pathological behaviour and only rarely did it result in the ostracism of an individual from his or her community. Both clergy and laity alike believed that society needed violence – enacted not only by royal authorities, like constables and sheriffs, but also "average individuals" – lest it fall into chaos. Social order, social status and even social relations sometimes required preservation through force.[10]

So now, having finally set this incongruous scene where charity and belligerency were both prized by parishioners, I would like to explore, as best as one can explore the motivations of mankind, a hitherto neglected topic: the capacity for a spiritual ideal, in this case the ideal of charity, to serve as a protective force and in particular as a restraining influence on the aggressive impulses of late medieval English parishioners. Though Bossy broached this subject decades ago, little has been done to follow up on his initial exploration of the influence of notions of charity on conflict. Some scholars of early modern culture, such as James Sharpe, have noted a ten-

---

Late Medieval England," *Bulletin of the John Rylands Library* 73 (1991): 65–90; James A. Sharpe, *Crime in Early Modern England, 1550–1750* (New York: Longman, 1999); idem, "Such Disagreement betwyxt neighbours: Litigation and Human Relations in Early Modern England," in *Disputes and Settlements: Law and Human Relations in the West*, ed. John Bossy (Cambridge: Cambridge University Press, 1984), 167–87; Susann D. Amussen, "Punishment, Discipline and Power: The Social Meanings of Violence in Early Modern England," *Journal of British Studies* 34 (1995): 1–34; Mervyn E. James, *English Politics and the Concepts of Honour: Past and Present Supplement no. 3* (1978); Philippa C. Maddern, "Honour among the Pastons: Gender and Integrity in Fifteenth-Century English Provincial Society," *Journal of Medieval History* 14 (1988): 357–71; idem, *Violence and Social Order in East Anglia, 1422–1442* (Oxford, 1992); William Ian Miller, *Humiliation, and Other Essays on Honor, Social Discomfort and Violence* (Ithaca: Cornell University Press, 1993); Julius R. Ruff, *Violence in Early Modern Europe* (Cambridge: Cambridge University Press, 2001); Richard Kaeuper, ed., *Violence in Medieval Society* (Woodbridge: Boydell Press, 2000); Mark D. Meyerson, Daniel E. Thiery, and Oren Falk, eds., *'A Great Effusion of Blood'? Interpreting Medieval Violence* (Toronto: University of Toronto Press, 2004); Guy Halsall, ed., *Violence and Society in the Early Medieval West* (Rochester: Boydell Press, 1998).

10 See Maddern, *Violence and Social Order*.

dency for parishioners to link sin with crime and disorder.[11] However, most of these references have been made in passing and, due to the chronological focus of some studies, one could all too easily regard the influence of religion on attitudes toward violent conduct as a product of the Reformation.[12] This essay will show that, at least in England, there is evidence for the influence of religious beliefs on violent sentiment and action long before reformers ruminated over the morality of the godly. The most glaring omission on the part of scholars has been a lack of study of court records in conjunction with proscriptive and didactic sources to discern the prevailing attitudes of late medieval parishioners. Therefore, this study will provide an overview of select court cases in order to gain some perspective on how strongly parishioners considered the ideal of charity to be a protective force, as well as how effectively this ideal of spiritual fellowship actually prevented violence. I have chosen most of my examples from cases brought before the court of King's Bench or Star Chamber. These records tend to contain more detailed material than other court rolls. Moreover, the simple fact that these two courts are not part of the ecclesiastical system provides us with more remarkable evidence because we will not have to fret as much that references to charity or Christian fellowship are entirely a product of catering to the concerns of clerical officials. Afterward, I will

11 Much more than their medievalist peers, early modern scholars have explored the formation of methods of social control and social discipline. See, for example, Herman Roodenburg and Pieter Spierenburg, eds., *Social Control in Europe*, vol. 1: *1500–1800* (Columbus: Ohio State University Press, 2004); Jean Delumeau, *Le Peur en Occident* (Paris: Fayard, 1978); idem, *Le Catholicisme entre Luther et Voltaire* (Paris: Presses Universitaires de France, 1996); Ruff, *Violence in Early Modern Europe*; Sharpe, *Crime in Early Modern England*; idem, "Social Control in Early Modern England: The Need for a Broad Perspective," in *Social Control in Europe*, 37–55; Leo Braudy, *From Chivalry to Terrorism: War and the Changing Nature of Masculinity* (New York: Random House, 2005); Bossy, *Christianity in the West*; Martin Ingram, *The Church Courts, Sex and Marriage in England, 1570–1642* (Cambridge: Cambridge University Press, 1987); idem, "The Reformation of Manners," in *The Experience of Authority in Early Modern England*, ed. Paul Griffiths, Adam Fox and Steve Hindle (New York: Macmillan, 1996), 54–78.

12 See, for example, Philip Benedict, "New Calvinist Men and Women?" in *Christ's Churches Purely Reformed: A Social History of Calvinism* (New Haven: Yale University Press, 2002), 429–544. Benedict argues that a new concern among Dutch parishioners for "Christian gentleness" and the violation of such "gentleness" by violence does not appear until the late seventeenth century. While Benedict's evidence certainly supports such an assertion, as we shall see, late medieval English records reveal a much earlier connection by parishioners between violence and a lack of Christian fellowship.

turn to a few other sources in order to gain a more rounded perspective on the evidence gleaned from the two royal courts.

The first point of note is that, judging from my examination of thousands of indictments and complaints from the Court of King's Bench and Star Chamber rolls between 1400 and 1536, explicit references to charity rarely appear in complaints about acts of violence. As Susan Brigden has remarked, it can be a difficult, though not vain, task to find instances where spiritual concerns palpably affect social relations.[13] Indeed, legal narratives of violence are far from devoid of religious sentiment. Violent individuals, especially those whose aggression took place in sacred space or during holy rituals, were often censured by plaintiffs and witnesses as impious offenders who lacked a fitting fear of God.[14] For example, in his legal recollection of a familial feud from Yorkshire in 1530, Thomas Savell pedantically noted that Henry Savell and an armed gang had assembled on Palm Sunday, a day "when every true Christian man shuld have been in parfite love and charite."[15] Likewise, in a bill before a special inquisition of the King's Bench in the mid-fifteenth century, the belligerence of John Roche within and outside of the parish church of Whixley was castigated as "holding God with little regard," while the record of the assaults committed by Richard Vaughan in the parish church of Bredwardine (Herefordshire) characterized the assailant as "a son and tyrant of the devil who had no fear of God or the church."[16]

Jean Delumeau asserts that fear, conveyed through art, sermons, the liturgy, and didactic texts, was the prime factor in the formation of a guilt culture, and its accompanying anxiety about the effect of customarily condoned aggression upon one's standing with God.[17] According to clerical sources, this emphasis on dread of the divine should entail, in theory, a concern for one's state of charity, since God's wrath would surely fall upon those who stood beyond its bounds.[18] Yet, in the cases themselves, such

13 Susan Brigden, "Religion and Social Obligation in Sixteenth-Century London," in *Past and Present* 103 (May 1984): 67–112, at 68.

14 Thiery, "Welcome to the Parish."

15 London, National Archives, Court of Star Chamber, Proceedings, STAC 2/29/158; J. Lister, ed., *Yorkshire Star Chamber Proceedings*, Yorkshire Archaeological Society Record Series 70 (1927), 44–46.

16 London, National Archives, Court of King's Bench, KB 9/349/94; KB 9/35/60.

17 Delumeau, *Sin and Fear*.

18 See, for example, *Middle English Sermons*, ed. W.O. Ross, EETS, o.s. 209 (1940), 62; W. Maskell, ed., *Monumenta Ritualia Ecclesiae Anglicanae* (London, 1846–47),

nuance tends to be buried beneath a more general notion of respect for God. This tendency suggests a conclusion that parishioners, when they did refrain from violence, did not primarily do so out of a positive sentiment, such as an idea of Christian fellowship, but rather out of a more negative and visceral fear of divine punishment, either on earth by clerical authorities or upon death by God himself.

Whether the underlying motivation was a dread of the divine and/or preservation of charity, in numerous cases the diction of litigants or description of events does reveal a shared expectation of restrained comportment within sacred spaces and during sacred rituals. By employing phrases such as "standing in the peace of God," "reverently kneeling before God" or "attending mass in a peaceable manner as they ought to do," plaintiffs or defendants tried to accentuate their pious, proper, and charitable demeanour before an assault took place.[19] As I have explored in more detail in previous studies,[20] other cases reveal that when in churches or churchyards, or in the presence of the host, many parishioners were both reluctant to engage in violence and quick to censure in courts of law or the court of public opinion those who did not show self-restraint. Indeed, this reluctance was so well-known and expected that constables and sheriffs, hoping to avoid a confrontation, often tried to serve writs before, after, or in between services.[21] Notably, violence during the sacring, the moment when the priest elevated the host after the words *hoc est enim corpus meum*, was specifically referenced in multiple cases.[22] Yet, even though these cases contain specific references to a sacred moment in order to heap greater opprobrium on the offender – whereas most cases involving violence provide little or no specific details concerning timing or location – there are still no explicit references made to uncharitable or sinful behav-

3: 348–49; John Mirk, *Festial*, ed. T. Erbe, EETS, e.s. 96 (1905), 130–31; idem, *Instructions for Parish Priests*, ed. E. Peacock and F.J. Furnivall, EETS, o.s. 31 (1969), 35–36; *Lay Folks Catechism*, ed. T.F. Simmons and H.E. Nolloth, EETS, o.s. 118 (1901), 90; *Speculum Christiani*, ed. G. Holmstedt, EETS, o.s. 182 (1933), 62–63; *Speculum Laicorum*, ed. J.T. Welter (Paris, 1914), 68–69; *The Book of Vices and Virtues*, ed. W.N. Francis, EETS, o.s. 217 (1942), 3, 25; *Jacob's Well: An English Treatise on the Cleansing of Man's Conscience*, ed. A. Brandeis, EETS, o.s. 115 (1900), 89–103; Robert of Brune, *Handlyng of Synne*, ed. F.J. Furnival, EETS, o.s. 119 (1901), 47–49, 127–130. See also Duffy, *Stripping of the Altars*, 92–94.

19 London, National Archives, KB 9/149/34; KB 9/84/1/3; STAC 2/8/153, 2/10/135–36, 2/12/224–26, 2/23/95; STAC 2/26/336; STAC 2/19/319; STAC 2/15/233–37, 2/19/248.

20 Thiery, *Polluting the Sacred*; idem, "Welcome to the Parish."

21 See, for example, London, National Archives, STAC 2/26/336.

22 See, for instance, London, National Archives, KB 9/12/2/182, 9/85/131, 9/149/34; STAC 2/8/78–94, 2/14/113–15, 2/15/151, 2/30/54.

iour. So, even if a shared expectation of restraint is evident, the specific reason why such an expectation exists is hard to conceptualize beyond a contextual understanding of common teachings about fearing God and preserving charity among the sacred.

Furthermore, references to dread of the divine or any other spiritual notion appear to be missing from narratives of violence that do not involve sacred spaces, persons, or rituals. Assaults in streets, homes, and unspecified locations usually entail classic legal topoi, such as references to violation of the King's Peace. This absence of religiously-tinged diction in cases concerning violence outside of sacred places and moments intimates that the promotion of introspection, as well as charitable, restrained comportment, was still in the first stage of Christianity's slow but successful influence on the "Civilizing Process."[23] As teachings and commands that called for parishioners to maintain a state of charity mounted, both laity and clergy grew more introspective and anxious about the state of their souls and the impact of their actions during sacred rituals or within sacred space. As evinced by the frequency of descriptive terms like "godly conduct" in the sixteenth-century court rolls, one could argue that a second stage, emphasizing restrained comportment in mundane fora as a sign of one's honour and piety, would bloom in the late Reformation.

Now, rather than rashly conclude that the ideal of charity was not an effective source of protection against violence, we must set the apparent absence of references in royal court rolls alongside quite clear manifestations of parishioners' anxiety about the discordance between their need for charity and their acceptance of aggression. In letter collections and some ecclesiastical court cases, there are both implied or direct references to states of charity, as well as anxiety over the damage which ongoing feuds or aggressive behaviour may have upon it. Since most parishioners understood well that charity was a prerequisite for participation in the sacrifice of the mass, they sometimes sought to redress their own and others' grievances by either gentle persuasion or aggressive clamour so that they might maintain their public reputation, the spiritual efficacy of communion, and, most importantly, their personal state of charity. When he recounted a violent affray in church to Agnes Paston, the vicar, Sir Robert Williamson, implicitly revealed the consensus between clergy and laity on the need for personal restraint and maintenance of charity; he decried the aggressors who "stood out of peril of soul," in other words, whose violence placed them beyond charity and

23 Norbert Elias first argued for a "Civilizing Process" in the West in which society slowly became emotionally and physically restrained. However, Elias did not think that religious beliefs promoted the "Civilizing Process." See Norbert Elias, *The Civilizing Process*, trans. Edmund Jephcott (Oxford: Blackwell, 2000).

thus beyond salvation.[24] As recounted before ecclesiastical authorities, after service on Easter Sunday in 1530, Nicolas Tyting came weeping into the churchyard of Little Plumstead in Norfolk because he had not received communion, "his rightes," because "the parson and he could not agree." Despite the parishioners' hasty attempts to make amends between the two, the parson refused to "meddill with him."[25] Tyting was perhaps as upset over his loss of honour as he was over his spiritual loss but the parishioners themselves appear to have been more concerned with Tyting's and the parson's state of charity. The presence of conflict in the parish was a serious threat to salvation because it disallowed communion to any parishioners who were involved; therefore, the community of the parish sought to redress grievances as quickly as possible lest the contagion of conflict place more of them beyond charity and consequently beyond salvation.[26] Reflecting a similar, if somewhat more belligerent, concern for charity, Johanna Carpenter grabbed Margaret Chamber by the arm as she was heading to communion and said, "I pray you let me speke a worde with you, for you have nede to axe me forgyuness, before you reseyve your rights."[27] Despite the aggressive aspects of these examples, the infiltration of ideas about purging wrath and embracing charity for a worthy communion is readily apparent. Gradually but discernibly, notions of sin and salvation were pushing parishioners' anxieties toward greater concern for their private standing with God. This potent push toward greater introspection is best seen in one last case from the depositions found in the records of the Consistory Court of Norwich.

In the early hours on Easter Sunday, 1512, Walter Southgate and his wife hustled off to attend mass at the parish church of Great Worlingham Magna (Suffolk). While the Paschal candle flickered against the shadowy interior, Walter and his wife joined their fellow parishioners in prayer and celebration of the most hallowed day of the liturgical year. For a precious

24 *Paston Letters and Papers of the Fifteenth Century*, ed. Norman Davis (Oxford: Clarendon Press, 1976), 18. Furthermore, in the mid-sixteenth century, the vicar and parishioners of Hayes, Middlesex, were angered and shocked when Henry Kyng and his friends threatened an approaching apparitor right out of the church with the cry, "It would be well done to make the sayd apparitor to eate the sayd citation." See London, National Archives, STAC 2/8/78–80.

25 *Norwich Consistory Court Depositions, 1499–1512, 1518–1530*, ed. E.D. Stone and B.C. Hardy, Norfolk Record Society, 10 (1938): case 428. Duffy also discusses this case in some detail. See Duffy, *Stripping of the Altars*, 94.

26 For an exploration of notions of violence and conflict as a contagious threat to society, see René Girard, *Violence and the Sacred*, trans. Patrick Gregory (Baltimore: Johns Hopkins University Press, 1972).

27 William H. Hale, ed., *A Series of Precedents and Proceedings in Criminal Causes, extending from the year 1475 to 1640* (London, 1847), 109.

few hours, the Southgates were encouraged to experience a wide array of emotions. They bowed their heads amidst the clouds of incense while the joyous rhythm of the *exultet* echoed through the nave. During the reading of the Gospel proclaiming the power of God over Sin and Death, they perhaps shifted restlessly and glanced curiously around at their neighbours, like Thomas Betlynton. Then, as the liturgy of the Eucharist began, they fell upon their knees, anxiously anticipating the two most important moments of the entire mass. First, as bells chimed, Walter and his wife sought blessing by snatching a glimpse of the sacring. Then, shortly after, the vicar moved to the edge of the chancel and admonished the attendant parishioners with words such as these found in a late medieval handbook:

> Good men and women, y charge yow by the Auctoryte of the holy churche, that no man nother woman that this day proposyth here to be comenyd [communicated] that he go note to Godds bord ... lase he be of ys synns clen confessyd, and for hem contryte. ... Furthermore, I charge yow yf ther be eny man or woman, that beryth yn his herte eny wrothe or rancor to eny of his evencristen [fellow christians] that he be not ther howselyd, ther to the tyme that he with hym yn perfyte love and cheryte, for ho so [whoso] beryth wrethe or evyll wyll in herte, to eny of hys evencristen [fellow christians], he ys note worthy hys God to receyve; and yf he do, he reseyvythe his dampnacyon, where he schuld receyve his salvacion.[28]

After this warning, Walter and his wife, like most of their fellow parishioners, knelt before their parish priest and, as obliged by canon law, waited to receive communion. For most parishioners, this reception was a joyous moment: a one-time opportunity when, having confessed their sins in days prior, they *dared* to receive the body of Christ. It was also a moment when parochial harmony displaced the norm of agonistic and aggressive social relations – what John Bossy dubbed decades ago "the social miracle."[29] But for the Southgates, this moment was far from a miraculous time of conciliation and concord. As they knelt before the body of Christ, they fretted over what seemed to be a most sinister situation. Indeed, just as the vicar had warned, what should have been one small step toward salvation appeared to them, as well as to others in the know, to be a giant leap toward the gaping maw of hell. For the couple knew well that they were not fit to receive their Lord and Saviour. Yet, they still took communion – possibly out a mixture of desires, ranging from a sublime longing

28 Maskell, *Monumenta*, iii, 348–49. A similar admonition occurs in Mirk, *Festial*, 130–31. Also see Duffy, *Stripping of the Altars*, 94.

29 Bossy, "The Mass as a Social Institution."

for a sense of salvation to a commonplace concern for their worldly reputation. As the mass drew to a close, Walter wondered and worried about his actions. Was his soul blackened by his reception? Was he to blame for his unworthiness? Did any others actually *know* of his existent grudge and thus regard him as a sacrilegious hypocrite?

Three days later, Walter could no longer contain his anger and anxiety. Having encountered the alleged source of his sacrilege, the parson of the church, one Sir Hugh Witterans, he lashed out, slandering him with these words: "Sir Hugh yo arte the cause that I and my wife receyved ye sacrament of ye autr at Easter even in synne without love and charyte."[30] Now, as anyone who has had the chance to peruse court rolls can attest, late medieval slander does not typically entail such theological nuance. Usually it involves less subtle and more sexual diction, like whoreson, knave, false thief, etc. Indeed, in a conversation that he had with Betlynton sometime prior to Holy Week, Walter, who was disgruntled over tithes and other perceived slights, *did* call both Witterans as well as the vicar "whoreson priests who use his goods to keep their brothels." However, along with this earlier castigation, Walter's irate words to Witterans himself were weighed as slander in the consistory court of the Bishop of Norwich, and it is those words that place into stark relief the burgeoning potency of the late medieval guilt culture, outlined so well by Jean Delumeau in *Sin and Fear*. Southgate was so shamed by internal strife, as well as the potential for disrepute, that he openly tried to transfer the culpability for a seemingly private sin onto his rival. Ironically, his concern for his state of charity had not restrained, but rather, spurred further aggression – though, to give him his due, Southgate, failing to notice the beam in his own eye, certainly considered his action to be the just correction of an unrepentant sinner. The concern of late medieval parishioners for their own and others' self-restraint and charitable state, so that they might receive communion or observe the host aptly, reflects the movement toward a guilt culture identified by Delumeau and, consequently, the "Civilizing Process" at work: such anxiety for internal state emphasized introspection, self-restraint and pious sentiment as much as, if not more than, extroversion, bravado, and belligerency.

So, besides a merely Machiavellian conclusion that fear of an authority, whether worldly or divine, is a greater catalyst of self-restraint than love, what else may we tentatively conclude from this brief study? First, while

30 *Norwich Consistory Court Depositions*, case 166. My use of a third person narrative is based upon both the court case itself as well as an understanding of the religious and cultural context of the age.

late medieval parishioners did understand, care about, and even promote the maintenance of charity, the discourse of charity that flowed through so many rituals and aspects of parochial life did not make its way into most narratives of conflict – despite its relevance to such situations. Such absence is worth extra consideration since litigants were obviously motivated to heap as much opprobrium as possible on their opponents. Does this then suggest that the ideal of charity was altogether lacking in potency as a source of protection? Of course not. Charity was part and parcel of a more general, but certainly strong, concern for personal standing with God, and thus it forms part of the context of parishioners' castigation of their violent and aggressive peers, especially those who used aggression among the sacred.

For, in truth, this study has only explored a single type of protection – one that is an immediate defence against violence and aggression, a search for charity as an ideological Taser, "the stun gun of God" so to speak. Parishioners' notion of charity served as a subtle source of protection whose effectiveness can only be traced over the *longue durée*. An idea of Christian fellowship was one element in a mixture of elements, such as humanist codes of courtesy, greater policing powers, and standing armies. This mixture ever so slowly blended together and, as it did, it helped to devalue the use of violence as a means of interpersonal conflict resolution and, concurrently, inflate the value of personal restraint as a sign of good repute. In short, what would first be castigated as "sacrilegious," "sinful," and "ungodly" conduct would later be primarily considered "criminal" and "nefarious," and now, "pathological" and "uncivilized." The path of the "Civilizing Process" is a rough and crooked one, but a notion of charity helped to pave some of it and thus provided protection for the majority of men and women who tried to tread upon it. Therefore, to borrow from the methodology of Aquinas, this study has provided one distinction of a much larger question – can a notion of charity affect attitudes toward violence? – for a far greater *summa* – the influence of Christianity on attitudes toward violence. As a scholar, I hope to continue penning this *summa* but, for now, in order to preserve the bond of charity between reader and writer, I shall show some restraint.

PART III

Feud and Protection

STEPHEN D. WHITE
Emory University

Protection, Warranty, and Vengeance in *La Chanson de Roland*

For a poem that is supposedly "studded with the terminology of feudal law," "impregnated with the feudal spirit," and embroidered "on the warp" of "feudal juridical concepts," *La chanson de Roland* includes few references to fiefs.[1] Moreover, although *Roland* is supposedly "a song that glorifies a perfect, ideal, absolute relationship between vassal and lord," it says little about vassals or vassalage, as historians of feudalism commonly use these terms. Instead, as Susan Reynolds points out, it usually employs *vassal* "to mean something like 'man of valour'" and *vasselage* for "the qualities appropriate to a vassal, like courage and loyalty."[2] Moreover, the poem's famous lines about what a "man" (not a "vassal") should do for "his lord" do not add up to the "feudal credo" that one literary scholar finds in them;[3] nor is an oblique reference to an oath that the traitor Ganelon is assumed to have sworn to Charlemagne strong evidence of the poem's "feudal" character.[4]

Nevertheless, if *Roland* is not the "feudal" epic that literary scholars have commonly taken it to be, it still illuminates an important obligation

1 Paul Aebischer, "Pour la défense et l'illustration de l'épisode de Baligant," in *Rolandiana et Oliveriana* (Geneva: Droz, 1967), 211–20 (at 213–18); extract translated and cited in Robert Francis Cook, *The Sense of the* Song of Roland (Ithaca: Cornell University Press, 1987), 197–98. For the text, see *La chanson de Roland*, ed. Ian Short, 2nd ed., Lettres Gothiques, ed. Michel Zink (Paris: Livre de Poche, 1990), abbreviated henceforth as R, followed by line numbers to Short's edition, which are occasionally followed, in those places where his line numbers differ from the ones in other editions, by alternative line numbers. English translations largely follow those in *The Song of Roland*, trans. Glyn Burgess (Harmondsworth: Penguin Books, 1990).

2 Susan Reynolds, *Fiefs and Vassals: The Medieval Evidence Reinterpreted* (Oxford: Clarendon Press, 2001), 22, 24, 126.

3 Cook, *Roland*, 64. See R 1010–12: "Pur sun seignor deit hom susfrir destreiz / E endurer e granz chaiz e granz freiz, / Si'n deit hom perdre e del quir e del peil"; and R 1117–19: "Pur sun seigneur deit hom susfrir granz mals, / E endurer e forz freiz e granz chalz, / Si'n deit hom perdre del sanc e de la char."

4 See R 3830, where Thierry's charge that Ganelon was a perjurer implies that he had violated an oath he had taken to Charlemagne.

of political leaders to their followers and thus an aspect of lordship by invoking the expectation that a king, a god, or, in one case, another kind of lord will be a "warrantor" (*guarant*) for his men, give them "warranty" (*guarant*), and "warrant" (*guarantir*) them.[5] Since *Roland* repeatedly implies that a king, a god, or a military leader would incur shame if he failed to meet this expectation, the poem presupposes recognition of a norm that a lord should be a warrantor for his men. If juridical concepts are in play in *Roland*, warranty is certainly one of them, as one can see from the many passages that use the noun *guarant* for warrantor or warranty or the verb *guarantir* for warranting.[6] Since the verb *guarir* is sometimes used interchangeably with *guarantir* in *Roland*, a study of warranty in the poem should also take account of passages using the first of these words. Early in the story, after Ganelon agrees to carry a message from Charlemagne to the Saracen king Marsile, he says that he will have no "warrantor" (*guarant*), just as two counts called Basan and Basile had had no warrantor when they went on a similar mission to Marsile, who took their heads.[7] Just before Ganelon leaves for the Saracen king's camp, Ganelon's uncle says that the emperor will neither "protect nor defend" (*guariz ne tensez*) his nephew Roland, who, the uncle implies, may well need protection and defence.[8] When the Franks in the rearguard of Charlemagne's army are fighting against their Saracen attackers, they claim Roland as their "warrantor" (*guarant*);[9] and they later claim as "warrantors" (*guarant*) all twelve of the peers of France, including Roland and his companion Oliver.[10] The Saracens, however, say that the twelve peers will have no "warrantor" (*guarant*),[11] while Marsile's nephew invokes Mohammad as his own "warrantor" (*guarant*).[12] In battle, King Corsablix taunts the Franks by saying that none of them will be "protected" (*guarit*) by Charlemagne.[13] The poet says that God "protected" (*guarit*) Oliver from a blow by one of the Sara-

5 Since *Roland* uses *guarant* and *guarantir*, these spellings are ordinarily used here, though Old French dictionaries give *garant* and *garantir* as the default spellings (see below, n. 36).

6 On the conflation of words with different roots, see Wolfgang G. van Emden, "'E cil de France le cleiment a guarant': Roland, Viven et le thème de guarant," *Olifant* 1 (1974): 21–47.

7 R 329: "J'i puis aler, mais n'i avrai guarant." On Basan and Basile losing their heads, see R 207–9.

8 R 354: "Charlemagne n'ert guariz ne tensez."

9 R 1161: "E cil de France le cleiment a guarant."

10 R 1469–70: "Suvent reclaiment Oliver et Rolland, / Les duze pers, qu'il lor seient guarant."

11 R 948: "Li duze per n'avrunt de mort guarant."

12 R 868: "Se Mahumet me voelt estre guarant."

13 R 1241: "Ja pur Charlun n'i ert un sul guarit."

cens.[14] The Franks pray to God that he "protect" (*guarisset*) Roland,[15] who recalls how God "protected" (*guaresis*) Daniel from the lions before praying that God "protect" (*guaris*) his soul from every peril.[16] Roland laments that he cannot "warrant or defend" (*tenser ne guarantir*) the men in the Frankish rearguard who are fighting under his leadership.[17] After killing the Saracen Estorgans, Oton tells him he will never have a "warrantor" (*guarant*).[18] The Franks praise their "warrantor" (*guarent*) Roland for striking well.[19] Archbishop Turpin tells them that Charlemagne will always be their "warrantor" (*guarant*).[20] Charlemagne calls on God to be the "warrantor" (*guarent*) of the souls of the Franks who die in battle.[21] The Franks call upon God to "warrant" (*guarantisez*) Charlemagne.[22] Following Charlemagne's defeat of Marsile's army, the emir Baligant sends word to Marsile's queen that he will be the "warrantor" (*guarant*) of King Marsile;[23] and after the emir has killed a number of Franks in battle, the Saracens say that they have a "warrantor" (*guarant*).[24] Baligant calls on those who want "protection" (*guarison*) from the Saracens' gods to pray to them.[25] According to a Saracen called Jangleu, the emir's gods will not be his "warrantors" (*guarant*).[26] In the clash between Baligant's army and Charlemagne's, the pagans call on their god Tervagant to be their "warrantor" (*guarant*).[27] At Ganelon's trial at the end of the poem, Thierry says that Roland's service to Charlemagne should have "protected" (*guarir*) him from Ganelon;[28] later, God protects Thierry from death in his battle with Ganelon's champion Pinabel.[29]

14 R 1316: "Deus le [Oliver] guarit, qu'el cors ne l'ad tuchét."
15 R 1837: "E prïent Deu qu'il guarisset Rollant."
16 R 2386–87: "E Danïel des lëons guaresis. / Guaris de mei l'amne de tuz perilz."
17 R 1864: "Jo ne vos pois tenser ne guarantir."
18 R 1303: "Ja n'i avrez guarant!"
19 R 1609 (1652): "Dïent Franceis: 'Ben fiert nostre guarent!'"
20 R 1254: "Carles, mi sire, nus est guarant tuz dis."
21 R 2518: "E prïent Deu qu'as anmes seit guarent."
22 R 3277: "Li nostre Deu, guarantisez Carlun!"
23 R 2726: "Marsilïun, ço dit, serat guarant, / Si l'en enveiet sun bastun e sun guant."
24 R 3472: "Ferez, baron, nus i avom guarant!"
25 R 3271: "Ki par noz deus voelt aveir guarison."
26 R 3514: "Ja vostre deu ne vos erent guarant."
27 R 2468–69: "Paiens recleiment un lur deu, Tervagant, / Puis saillent enz, mais il n'i unt guarant."
28 R 3828.
29 R 3923. The poem uses the word *garantir* once in the sense of "to guarantee the truth of something." After charging Ganelon with perjury and treason and judging that he should be hanged, Thierry says that he will immediately "warrant" this judgment with his sword (R 3835–36).

So what was a warrantor? What was warranty? What did it mean for a lord to warrant and/or protect a follower? The clearest analyses of warranty are those of historians of warranty of land in twelfth-century England. According to Paul Hyams, a lord's obligation to warrant a grant of land arises from an undertaking that

> he (and his family) would maintain [it] against outside challenge. They would defend their grantee's right against third parties and (probably) acquit him against anyone who tried to claim from him service other than that provided for in the original grant. If they were unable to do this, the grantee had to be compensated for his loss, as by an exchange (*escambium*) of an equivalent holding.[30]

In addition to associating warranty of land with "defence," "maintenance" and "acquittance," Hyams links these obligations to "good lordship" and to "a [more general] duty to support and protect in their material honour the vassals on whose support [the lord] depends."[31] Elsewhere, Hyams writes that "From the vassal's viewpoint, the lord's obligation to maintain him against those who would do him wrong seemed almost the most important attribute of good lordship."[32] In discussing "the language of warranty of land" in twelfth-century England, David Postles further explicates the relationship between warranty and good lordship by showing that twelfth-century charters sometimes represented a warrantor of land as a *protector*, *tutor*, or *defensor*, or as one who would "aid" his donee against all those who might try to use *violentia* against him or do him injury.[33] Similarly, John Hudson associates warranty of land "with various forms of protection a man sought from his lord," including "maintenance, a voluntary obligation to support vassals, in some cases if necessary by force."[34] Like Hyams, Hudson suggests that a warrantor was expected not only to warrant his grantees' land in court but also give them "protection against third parties." To illustrate this broader kind of "warranty," he cites a passage from *Raoul de Cambrai* about a king's duty to

30 Paul R. Hyams, "Warranty and Good Lordship in Twelfth-Century England," *Law and History Review* 5 (1987): 437–503, at 438.

31 Hyams, "Warranty," 439.

32 Paul R. Hyams, *Rancor and Reconciliation in Medieval England* (Ithaca: Cornell University Press), 150.

33 David Postles, "Seeking the Language of Warranty in Twelfth-Century England," *Journal of the Society of Archivists* 20 (1999): 209–22, at 215.

34 John Hudson, *Land, Law and Lordship in Anglo-Norman England* (Oxford: Oxford University Press, 1994), 53.

"warrant and defend" his men and two passages from *Roland* about warranty which were cited above.[35]

How close is the similarity between warranty in *Roland* and warranty of land in twelfth-century England? The latter evidently involved not only warranting the land by protecting it and supporting the grantee's claim to it in court, but also giving the donee, if the lord failed to warrant the land and it was lost, other land of equal value as an *escambium* in compensation. English legal historians typically treat warranty of land as an obligation of feudal lords generally, while *Roland* almost always invokes a norm that kings and gods should warrant their men. But the similarity between warranting land and warranting men may have involved more than the parallel between protecting a subordinate's land against attacks and claims by third parties, and protecting the subordinate himself from attackers. There may also be a parallel between giving compensation for the loss of land that a lord failed to warrant and providing compensation in the form of vengeance for losses of life and limb against which a god, a king, or another kind of lord could not protect his men. If so, one should think of a warrantor as a lord obliged to keep his men's lands and the men themselves under his warranty by providing either protection or compensation for loss. In *Roland* warranty in this double sense is so important to ideas of good lordship on earth and in supernatural realms that to cite or predict a lord's failure to warrant his men is to shame him and even deny his status as a lord.

What Hyams called "a [lord's] duty to support and protect in their material honour the [men] on whose support [the lord] depends" has its parallel in the expectation frequently articulated in *Roland* that a lord should warrant his men in what appears to be the sense of protecting them against physical attack by third parties. According to Wolfgang van Emden, the Old French word *guarantir* (or *garantir*) had a complicated etymology, being derived doubly from *guarant* (or *garant*), which can mean either "warranty" or "warrantor," and from *guarir*, meaning "to protect."[36] Moreover, *guarant* and *guarir* supposedly came from two different roots whose derivatives became confused: the Germanic WARJAN, meaning "to resist" or "to protect," and the Old Frankish WARJAN,

35 Hudson, *Land, Law and Lordship*, 54, citing R 1864 and 2354 and *Raoul de Cambrai*, ed. and trans. Sarah Kay (Oxford: Oxford University Press, 1992), lines 495–96.

36 A. Tobler and E. Lommatzsch, *Altfranzösisches Wörterbuch*, vol. 4: *G–J* (Wiesbaden: Franz Steiner Verlag, 1960), s.vv. "garant," "garanter," "garantie," "garantir," "garantison" (cols. 102–7); Frédéric Godefroy, *Dictionnaire de l'ancienne langue française*, vol. 4: *Filé–Listage* (1885; rpt. New York: Kraus Reprint, 1961), s.vv. "garant," "garanter," "garantie," "garantir," "garantisun" (pp. 218–19).

meaning "to warrant the truth of something."[37] It is possible that the double etymology of warranty has been retro-fitted to an imperfect understanding of the word whose etymology is being speculatively reconstructed because, in the context of warranting land at least, warranting the truth of a claim is tantamount to defending it against a challenge. Nevertheless, van Emden's philological analysis explains how *Roland* sometimes uses *guarantir* as well as *guarir* to refer to a superior's act of physically protecting an inferior from harm. When the poem represents the Franks as calling on Roland and on the twelve peers to be their "warrantors" and as praising their "warrantor" Roland for striking well,[38] one can think of a warrantor as a superior expected to provide physical protection to his men, just as God does when he defends Oliver from a blow from a Saracen and as God is expected to do when the Franks call on him to protect Roland. This is what God did when he defended Daniel from the lions.[39] Similarly, one may think of the Saracens' gods as failing to do what is expected of a warrantor when they fail to protect the Saracens from the Franks.[40]

Sometimes, a *guarant* in *Roland* is a protector or defender in the same sense in which a warrantor in Latin charters is thus a *protector*, a *tutor*, or a *defensor*, while *guarantir*, like *guarir*, may simply mean "to protect from harm." In other passages already cited, however, it is difficult or impossible to imagine a human warrantor, at least, as a superior expected to provide physical protection to his men, particularly in the cases where the warrantor is not or was not physically present to provide protection of this kind. Under such circumstances, to call a superior the warrantor of his men is to say that he has, or ought to have, his men under his protection. Fulfilling this responsibility may involve more than simply giving them physical protection from harm or providing leadership in battle. Instead, as Van Emden and other commentators on *Roland* have pointed out, it can entail avenging them if they are killed or suffer harm (*damage*) and/or loss (*perte*).[41] A warrantor is thus an avenger or, at least, someone expected to take appropriate revenge on third parties who have killed his men, sometimes by taking their heads, or who have brought them harm and loss, including the loss of other body-parts.

37 Van Emden, "Le thème de guarant," 37, citing the Old French dictionaries referred to in n. 36.

38 R 1161, 1470, 1652.

39 R 1316, 2386, 1837.

40 R 2468–69, 3514. Van Emden situates warrantors in a hierarchy that "begins with God, supreme warrantor of Christians ... as Mohamet is said to be of Saracens. The emperor [Charlemagne] is in his turn *guarant* of all his vassals and rear-vassals" (Van Emden, "Le thème de guarant," 39).

41 "Vengeance is implied in the lord's sworn duty of protection" (Cook, *Roland*, 217).

From the beginning of the Franks' first council scene to the end, there is a clear progression in the aspersions cast on Charlemagne's capacity as a warrantor, on the value of his protection, and thus on his capacity as a king and perhaps even his manliness. First, Roland says that Charlemagne should now avenge men whom, by implication, he has previously failed to avenge and thus failed to warrant. When Roland tells Charlemagne to avenge Basan and Basile, treacherously beheaded by Marsile when they were acting as the emperor's messengers (R 210–13), he is, in effect, telling his uncle to act as their warrantor; he may also be implying that Charlemagne should already have assumed this role, in which case his advice to the emperor comes close to being an insult. When, at the end of the same council scene, Ganelon, who has just defied Roland and the other peers of France in Charlemagne's presence (R 329–30), says that in carrying a message from Charlemagne to Marsile, he will lack a warrantor, just as Basan and Basile had lacked one, he is also saying that while executing Charlemagne's command, he will not be under the protection of the emperor, who, having previously failed to warrant Basan and Basile and having just dismissed Ganelon's challenge to the twelve peers (R 327), will not avenge him. To the extent that a king is, by definition, a warrantor to his men, what looks like a prediction by Ganelon is really an insult since it implies that Charlemagne is no king at all. So, in the *laisse* ("verse stanza") immediately following, when the emperor, ignoring the insult, holds out his right glove to Ganelon in a way that can be read as an acknowledgement of his obligation to warrant him, he may be either shaming himself by failing to respond to the insult or shaming Ganelon by taking no notice of the insult and treacherously promising warranty that he will never provide (R 331). If Charlemagne's gesture of holding out his right glove is an insult to Ganelon, then, when the latter lets the glove drop, though without actively dropping it, he is responding to one oblique insult with another (R 332–33). Again, he verges on denying Charlemagne as his king.

Both Roland's oblique statement about Charlemagne's failure as a warrantor and Ganelon's direct one, possibly supplemented by the gesture just mentioned, anticipate statements by Saracens and Franks that question or deny the emperor's capacity to warrant his men by protecting or avenging them. The Saracens' statements are mortal insults not just to Charlemagne, but to the Franks, who must avenge them since without an avenger to avenge them, they are worthless. No compensation in blood will be paid for their deaths. Moreover, the Saracens' statements that the Franks have no warrantor (e.g., R 1241) also imply that the Christian god will not warrant them either because he has abandoned them or because he is no god at all. Finally, these statements are threats as well as insults because they imply that the Franks, having no warrantor, may be killed with impunity.

To be sure, warranty in the form of revenge can be understood in functionalist terms as a kind of protection against future attacks because a lord will be in a better position to protect his men from being killed or harmed if he maintains a reputation for always avenging them. Here, a credible threat of retaliation by the lord serves as a deterrent to future attacks on his men. Conversely, a lord who is known for failing to avenge his men may have difficulty protecting them because his enemies may well construe his past failures as a warrantor as signs that they can kill his men without fear of paying for their homicides. Nevertheless, if vengeance was understood as "compensation using blood, not instead of money, but as a kind of money" and the vengeance taken in a particular case was carefully calibrated so as to balance the act to be avenged, then warranty in the form of the warrantor's vengeance for his man's loss of life was structurally similar to warranty in the form of the warrantor providing an exchange of equal value to compensate his man for his loss of land.[42]

Because *Roland* depicts so many homicides and severed body-parts of men and so much blood that drips and flows, it is easy to miss the precision with which the poem shows specific killings, dismemberments, and mortal insults balancing off other specific killings, dismemberments, and mortal insults. For example, although Ganelon's "vengeance," as he calls it, results in the deaths of his step-son Roland and thousands of other Franks, the poem represents it, for certain purposes, as the equivalent of the act of Roland's that Ganelon was avenging.[43] By nominating his step-father to carry a message from Charlemagne to Marsile, Roland, as Ganelon later says, nominated him for death and woe, because, by implication, Roland makes the nomination in the belief that Marsile would take Ganelon's head, just as he had taken the heads of the two counts, Basan and Basile, whom Charlemagne had previously sent on a mission identical to Ganelon's and whose deaths the emperor did not avenge. Later, when Ganelon proposes Roland to lead Charlemagne's rearguard, he, too, nominates his adversary for death and woe since he does so in the belief that Marsile would kill Roland. The poem brings out the equivalence of the two acts not only by representing them in identical terms, but also by suggesting that each of them is taken in anger.

With even greater precision, the *Roland*-poet describes the bloody battle between Charlemagne's rearguard, led by Roland, and the army of Marsile as a series of exchanges of individual killings and mortal insults. The battle goes through four stages. To begin with, each of the twelve Saracen peers presents himself to King Marsile, with several of them boast-

42 William Ian Miller, *Eye for an Eye* (Cambridge: Cambridge University Press, 2006), 25.

43 R 3868–78.

ing that they will kill Roland, among others, and/or insulting the absent Charlemagne for leaving his men in a vulnerable position where he could not warrant them by physically protecting them or by avenging them (*laisses* 69–78). All but the first of these men are then killed in order of appearance (*laisses* 93–106). First, Marsile's nephew Aelroth asks the king for permission to strike the first blow, vowing that he will kill Roland and end the war by re-conquering the territory previously taken by Charlemagne (R 860–70). Aelroth then asks to make up a group of twelve barons who will attack the twelve peers of France (R 874–78). The second member of the group is Marsile's brother Falsaron, who says that he will go with his nephew, Aelroth; it is ordained, he adds, that they will destroy Charlemagne's rearguard (R 879–84). Next, King Corsalis, skilled in black arts, presents himself (R 885–88). Fourth, Malprimis of Brigant boasts that he will kill Roland (R 889–93). The fifth peer, an emir from Balaguer, says that the twelve peers of France, including Roland, will die and that Charlemagne will abandon Spain (R 894–907). Sixth, the almaçor from Moriane tells Marsile that he will go with his men to Roncevaux and kill Roland, if he finds him (R 909–15). Turgis of Turteluse, the seventh peer, boasts that he will kill Roland and then predicts that the Franks will die and Charlemagne will lose his crown and suffer grief and shame (R 916–30). Eighth, Escremiz of Valterne says that if he finds Roland and Oliver, both will lose their heads; that all twelve peers are ordained to die and all the Franks as well; and that Charlemagne will lose his good "vassals" (R 931–39). After the ninth and tenth peers, Estorgans and his companion Estramariz present themselves to Marsile (R 940–41), all of the men assembled thus far repeat the same boasts about killing Roland, Oliver, and the other peers of France, and the same insult about their having no warrantor (R 948); they also predict death for the Franks and shame for Charlemagne (R 946–54). The eleventh to join the group is Margariz of Seville, who repeats all of the boasts and predictions just made (R 954–74). The twelfth is Chernubles of Munigre, who speaks to the same purpose (R 975–89).

In the second stage of the battle, each of the twelve Saracen peers, except for Margariz and Chernubles, pays with his life for what he said about the Franks in the order in which he was introduced, as he is cut down or cut in two in an individual encounter with a Frankish peer, Archbishop Turpin, or another Frankish horseman (*laisses* 93–106). The first of the Saracen peers, Marsile's nephew Aelroth, is killed by Roland, a peer of France, who also kills his adversary's horse (R 1188–1205). The second, Marsile's brother Falsaron, is killed by Oliver (R 1213), also a peer. The third peer, King Corsalis, is killed by Archbishop Turpin (R 1235–60), while the fourth, Malprimis of Brigant, is cut down immediately afterwards by Gerin (R 1261–68), also a peer. Now, Oliver kills the fifth Saracen peer, the emir from Balaguer (1269–74), and a Frank called Aimon the sixth, the almaçor from Moriane (1275–80). Anseis the peer kills the seventh Saracen peer, Turgis of Turteluse (1281); then Engeler, another peer of France, kills the eighth Saracen peer, Escremiz of Valterne (R 1289–96). The ninth, Estorgans, is killed by the peer Oton (R 1296–1303) and Berenger the peer kills the tenth Saracen peer, Astramariz (Estramariz) (R 1304–08). The eleventh, Margariz of Seville, survives after attacking Oliver (R 1311–19).

The third stage of the battle is less clearly organized. But two patterns come clear. On the one hand, the Franks commit various vengeance-killings. On the other, the Saracens kill all of the peers except Roland and Oliver, thereby evening the score with the Franks, who had previously killed ten out of the twelve Saracen peers who took on the twelve peers of France. First, Roland kills Chernubles of Munigre, one of the Saracen peers to have survived the second stage of the battle (R 1310, 1325). Oliver kills another Turgis as well as a Saracen called Esturguz (R 1351–59). Two other peers, Gerin and Gerier, kill a pagan called Timozel (R 1379–84), Engeler of Bordeaux kills Espervaris (R 1388–89), and Archbishop Turpin kills Siglorel (R 1390). However, Climborin breaks the Franks' momentum by killing Engeler, a peer of France, who had previously killed Espervaris (R 1388–89) and Escremiz of Valterne (R 1289–91). After taking revenge on Climborin (R 1505–09), who had previously given Ganelon a gift and exchanged kisses with him at Marsile's camp (R 627–33), Oliver kills Alphaien, a Saracen duke, and cuts off the head of another Saracen, Escababi (R 1511–12). However, Valdebrun, who, like Climborin, had given Ganelon a gift and a kiss (R 617), kills another peer of France called Samson (R 1519–34), whose death Roland then avenges by killing Valdebrun (R 1537–46). Next, an African called Malquiant kills Anseis (R 1550–61, 1593–1604), a peer of France (R 105, 796), who had previously killed a Saracen peer, Turgis of Turteluse (R 1279–84). The Saracen Grandonie kills Gerin (R 1613–22, 1570–79), a peer of France who had previously killed a Saracen peer called Malprimis of Brigant (R 1261–68), and, with help from his companion Gerer, the pagan Timozel (R 1379–84). Grandonie then kills Gerer, Guiun of Saxony, and Berenger the peer (R 1580–81, 1623–4), who had killed Estramariz (R 1304–8). Later, Turpin kills Abisme, said to be the worst felon in all of Marsile's army (R 1665–67).

By the end of the third stage of the battle, the Franks have killed all of the Saracen peers, save Margariz, who disappears from the story, while the Saracens have killed all the peers of France, minus Roland and Oliver. So all that remains to even the score, according to this way of counting, is for the pagans to kill off the two remaining peers. This takes a while, as both Oliver and Roland kill masses of pagans and Roland himself cuts off Marsile's arm before killing his son Jurfaleu. Eventually, the Saracens kill both Roland and Oliver, though it is Oliver who, while mortally wounded and unable to see Roland, gives him what may well be the last blow Roland receives before dying – one that cuts through his helmet down to the nasal, though without reaching his head (R 1989–97). In a sense, a balance has finally been achieved between Franks and Saracens since all of the Saracen peers are dead and so are all of the Frankish peers. However, both leaders of the opposing groups, Charlemagne and King Marsile, have particular scores to settle. The former's nephew is dead and the latter has lost not only his son but his right arm. Besides, the Christian god, at least, has scores to settle with the Saracens who have insulted him; and he has yet to fulfil completely his obligation to warrant Roland and the other peers, the Frankish army, or the emperor himself, who clearly needs a warrantor. Marsile, too, needs a warrantor and finds one in the person of Baligant and not any of the Saracens' gods. Finally, Charlemagne has at least one score to settle with Ganelon – and possibly more.

For a particularly revealing example of how in *Roland* warranty in the form of revenge provides compensation for loss of limbs as well as life, consider the undertaking that King Baligant makes to Marsile when, through a messenger, he promises to be his warrantor (R 2809): "For the loss of your arm, I will give you a head." What could this mean? Here is one possible interpretation. Since, earlier in the story, Ganelon has identified Roland as Charlemagne's right arm when talking with King Marsile about how Roland's death will undermine the emperor's power,[44] a dream of Charlemagne's about a bear that tears off his right arm clearly pre-figures the killing of Roland.[45] Later, Marsile predicts that Charlemagne will lose his right hand.[46] Since, in these ways, the poem has previously shown Roland to be of the same flesh as Charlemagne and thus a kind of surrogate son, the audience is prepared to see Roland as taking vengeance in advance for his own death when he cuts off Marsile's hand – or arm, as it sometimes is – and also kills Marsile's son Jurfaleu by taking his head.[47] In fewer than a hundred lines prior to Baligant's undertaking to take a head for the loss of his man's arm, the poem refers four times to this loss, for which the emir, as Marsile's warrantor, now promises to the loser an even more valuable body-part, namely a head, which is the kind of body-part that the Saracens have been taking since before the story even started.[48] Is Baligant offering Marsile Charlemagne's head? Moreover, the emir calls

44 R 596.

45 R 727. Reporting to Naimes another dream about Ganelon destroying Roland, Charles says that his nephew can never be replaced (R 836–40).

46 R 1195.

47 R 1903.

48 For references to Marsile's lost hand or arm, see R 2719–20, 2724–25, 2729, 2780–81.

attention to Marsile's loss of his right hand by sending him a right glove, which may serve as both a token of the compensatory vengeance that Baligant promises to take on the Franks by taking the head of one of them and as compensation of a sort for the hand because the glove will at least hide Marsile's shame. So when Baligant, Marsile's warrantor, speaks of giving him a head for his lost arm, he is talking about avenging the loss of his hand, at the hands of Roland, which was Roland's revenge for his own death, as metaphorically represented by the author, who also identified Ganelon as Roland's slayer metaphorically as well. However, Baligant fails to kill Charlemagne, who kills the emir, thereby appeasing the anger of the Franks, one of whom, Geoffrey of Anjou, angrily goads him into avenging his own shame on the pagans by saying that the emperor does not do so, he should not wear a crown (R 3537–79). Charlemagne hesitates, but rejects Baligant's offer of peace, receives reassurance from St Gabriel, and acts the part of a true warrantor by splitting the emir's skull (R 3579–3620).

At this point in the narrative, Charlemagne's remaining task is to take vengeance on Ganelon. But for what and in what measure? At Ganelon's trial, Charlemagne says that Ganelon had taken from him 20,000 Franks, his nephew Roland, Oliver, and the other ten peers of France (R 3753–56). What could possibly provide the emperor with compensation for these losses? Nothing could. So the emperor takes as much vengeance as possible. His revenge includes the killing of Ganelon's champion and kinsman Pinabel (R 3926–29), the hanging of Ganelon's thirty pledges (R 3958), and the death and dismemberment of Ganelon himself (R 3964–72) for a total of thirty-two dead bodies. However, since Ganelon's dismemberment by four horses presumably pulls four parts off his body, one may think of Charlemagne as securing thirty-six bodies or body-parts in compensation for his losses. What meaning could the number thirty-six possibly hold? None, perhaps. But it is still worth noting that thirty-six is three times the number of peers who died in Charlemagne's service and that under the Salic law, the payment for slaying a man who was in the service of the king was 24,000 *denarii*, which is precisely three times the payment due for killing a Frank.[49] In any case, the emperor does not impose punishment for wrongs. He takes revenge and perhaps even heads and body-parts; and his vengeance differs in scale but not in kind from the other acts of vengeance already considered. He also warrants the twelve peers, at least.

If warranty involves vengeance as well as protection, it is now easier to understand why both are essential to what Hyams calls "good lordship" and why, in *Roland*, it counts as a mortal insult to a lord to say that he has

49 K.A. Eckhardt, ed., *Die Gesetze des Merovingerreiches, 481–714*, vol. 1: *Pactus legis Salicae* (Göttingen: Musterschmidt-Verlag, 1955), chs. 41.1, 3.

not warranted, will not warrant, or cannot warrant his men. For the most part, the *Roland*-poet uses the language of warranty to point up the powerlessness of the pagans' gods, whose failure to warrant the Saracens is so striking as to show that the gods are no gods at all. Similarly, Roland's famous acknowledgement that he cannot defend or warrant the men fighting under his leadership certainly sounds like an acknowledgement of his failure to be a good leader or lord. Finally, because the emperor of the Franks and the god of the Christians ultimately take vengeance on the unfaithful, murderous, treacherous Saracens, one can certainly read *Roland* as a story about their double triumph as warrantors. But there is also the possibility of emphasizing how miserably they both fail in giving real protection to their men and how dilatory they are in taking vengeance on their men's behalf. If warranty of men, like warranty of land, involved giving physical protection and compensation of equal value for loss, then it is not clear how highly rated as a warrantor either Charlemagne or the Christian god would have been.

RICHARD KAEUPER
University of Rochester

Vengeance and Mercy in Chivalric *Mentalité*

That the lust for vengeance is a potent historical force cannot be doubted. Vengeance may rank among the most basic human emotions – after food and shelter, and perhaps standing closely tied with sex. Whether or not modern society has altered so blatantly evident an historical commitment remains an open question.

For the Middle Ages we can inquire if a cultural commitment to vengeance represented a straightforward and overwhelming fact of life, or if such notions produced doubts and fears among elite males. To be more precise, I want to inquire about the role of vengeance (and its allies) within a dominant high and late medieval chivalric *mentalité*. Among the knighthood was vengeance significantly feared and condemned, or was it rather considered (with apologies to Sellar and Yeatman) a Good Thing, a moral duty and a pillar of a justly ordered society?

To pose such questions about the chivalrous seems reasonable and important, given their power and prominence in medieval society. Such an inquiry should in a small way complement work of recent scholars, especially Paul Hyams and Stephen White, and may unearth additional and useful veins of ore spreading out in other directions beneath the surface of the medieval landscape.[1] All such digging, I must emphasize, can only be preliminary and will be limited to north-western Europe.

Vengeance is a tough topic, intellectually as well as morally. Evidence on the views clerics advanced is surely abundant, if complex, and must largely be taken for granted here, with only a brief glance. Many among the tonsured advanced a line of thought obviously contesting the practice of vengeance; they pressed a message of forgiveness and mercy upon the warriors with style and vigour. A flow of ideas on peace and forbearance

Essential help with word searches was conducted by Paul Dingman and Peter Sposato. I wish to thank them both for their assistance.

1 See White's essays collected as *Feuding and Peacemaking in Eleventh-Century France* (Aldershot: Ashgate, 2005) and Paul Hyams, *Rancor and Reconciliation in Medieval England* (Ithaca: Cornell University Press, 2003).

came insistently to the knights in the liturgy, in art, in sermons, in preparation for confession. Each time they repeated the Lord's Prayer they intoned a need for forgiveness of those who wronged them.

An especially telling source may be found in collections of short, memorable moral tales or *exempla* that knights would have heard in sermons and later read in handbooks produced for the laity.[2] Their potential impact can be assessed in an *exemplum* told repeatedly – I found nearly a dozen retellings in the beautiful manuscript books filled with *exempla* in the British Library.[3] The basic story (though there are multiple variants) presents a knight who has suffered a terrible wrong from another (in some versions this enemy has slain his father). He is now besieged in his castle by this same enemy. On Good Friday this wronged and besieged knight sees his hated foe riding past his castle. Suddenly infused with the forgiving spirit of Christ, our knight issues forth from the castle, not to attack, but to forgive his highly surprised enemy of all wrongs. In fact, they not only make peace on his initiative, but ride to church together. As the forgiving knight approaches the crucifix standing in the apse of the local church, miraculously the cross bows and the Crucified stretches out his arms to embrace and kiss the man who has proved himself truly Christ's knight through forgiveness. This merciful knight's tale must have been widely used in sermons, as some of its sources are handbooks of materials for the use of preachers.

Yet any reader of the abundant evidence knows that ecclesiastics did not uniformly and consistently condemn vengeance. Tensions in their views readily formed from the full range of sacred sources. Ancient stories told of God's own awesome vengeance, whether executed in a flash by divine fiat or through a people who acted on his behalf. As members of a veritable culture of vengeance medieval clerics could easily share its values and find

2 In London, British Library, MS Harley 268, fol. 173, one man has survived a murderous attack that killed his two brothers. Though reluctant, at the point of death he is finally convinced by a priest to forgive the killers. He is thus saved from Hell. In London, British Library, MS Additional 1128, fol. 78b, a death in tournament remains unforgiven until the Pope informs the vengeful man that he sees the Devil riding on his shoulder.

3 See the following London, British Library, manuscripts: Arundel 506, fol. 5; Arundel 406, fol. 26b, col 2; Additional 22283, fol. 14b, col 2; Additional 18351, fol. 12b, col 2; Additional 18346, fol. 117; Additional 27336, fol. 8; Additional 11384; Harley 2391, fol. 221; Harley 2385, fol. 65, col 2; Burney 361, fol. 154. Several Middle English manuals give the story for readers and priests hearing confessions. See Idelle Sullens, ed., *Robert Mannyng of Brunne* (Binghamton, NY: Medieval and Renaissance Texts and Studies, 1983), lines 3797–3916, and also Siegfried Wenzel, ed., *Fasciculus Morum: A Fourteenth-Century Preaching Handbook* (University Park: Pennsylvania State University Press, 1989), 134–35.

religious valorization for them. The problem arose, of course, because of the powerful New Testament emphasis on forgiveness and forbearance, standing against both tradition and human nature. If clerics sometimes transmitted a mixed message on vengeful prowess, they could scarcely ignore the peace and forgiveness infused into the central message of the founder of their religion.

Grasping clerical opinion in its entirety is thus challenging, but how much more difficult the case of the knighthood. Can we know much of their thought and how it translated into action? I will advance two working hypotheses. First, that we can learn much of what we need to know from chivalric literature – imaginative chansons and romances – works that the knights read, patronized, and sometimes wrote themselves. To this we can add vernacular manuals, chronicles, and biographies (that may be only slightly less imaginative). Elsewhere I have made a case that this literature is both prescriptive and descriptive, that the two modes can usually be sorted out, and that both are significant for analysis.[4] As a second hypothesis here, I think we should pay attention in our searching to a close family group of ideas related to vengeance. This means looking especially at prowess as it links to shame and honour. Although prowess is not identical with vengeance, of course, it is a first cousin and so often represents a vigorous response to a perceived wrong that carries a threat of shame, and thus a challenge to all-important honour. Wrath, one of the seven deadly sins, likewise joins this family circle. The relationships are significant: as the anthropologist Julian Pitt-Rivers noted decades ago, in a lapidary sentence, "the ultimate vindication of honour lies in physical violence."[5] Knighthood realized vengeance through acts of prowess aimed at wiping out shame (often while in a state of wrath). Wrongs disorder the world and stain the individual (and his kin) with shame. Blood calls for blood, wrong for wrong. Vengeance wipes the slate clean and reorders a disordered world.

Spade in hand, then, with two hypotheses hung in a bag slung over our back, we turn to digging in the literary fields for evidence. We might first approach the fertile soil of imaginative literature through that magnificent chanson, *Raoul de Cambrai*. The existing text combines a *Raoul I* written

4 The case is made most explicitly in "Literature as the Key to Chivalric Ideology," *Journal of Medieval Military History* 5 (2006): 1–15; a more general discussion appears in Richard W. Kaeuper, *Chivalry and Violence* (Oxford: Oxford University Press, 1999) and in my forthcoming book, *Holy Warriors* (Philadelphia: University of Pennsylvania Press).

5 Julian Pitt-Rivers, "Honour and Social Status," in *Honour and Shame: The Values of Mediterranean Society*, ed. J.G. Peristiany (London: Weidenfeld and Nicolson, 1965), 19–77; quotation at 30.

by the mid-twelfth century and revised probably in the late twelfth century and an expanded text known as *Raoul II* likely from the second decade of the thirteenth century.[6] To search for vengeance in *Raoul I* is to play the glutton at a smorgasbord. This is a poem of vengeance, repeatedly proclaimed as a virtue and exultantly described, until, as Sara Kay has noted, all the leading male characters having been killed, the text closes. There are, indeed, warnings against the "hom desreez," the man out of measure; but the drumbeat of the poem sounds for hot-blooded revenge. "Sir Raoul," his barons assure him, "it is small wonder if [Bernier] is angry. He has served you with his sword and you have ill requited him. You have burnt his mother in her church, and, as for him, you have broken his head. God's curse on anyone who blames him if he wishes to avenge himself."[7] But citing examples would quickly exceed the limits of this brief study.

Raoul II shows more ambiguity. Standard cries for revenge appear, but the contrast with the earlier text is striking in that calls for mercy and forgiveness also appear. Such forbearance is linked, significantly, with divine mercy in general and with the Passion of Christ particularly. Near the end of the epic Bernier, for example, recalls the forgiveness Christ gave Longinus, the Roman centurion whose lance pierced his own side on Calvary; Bernier cites it as his model for forgiving his hated enemy, Guerri the Red. What did contemporary warriors think as they heard this poem? It is not simply some clerical screed: there is enough highly valorized violence to satisfy the most avid.

Turning to the classic chivalric biography may not quite be leaving the sphere of imaginative literature. To what extent the *Histoire de Guillaume le Marechal* joins the category could spark a quite separate debate.[8] All that I want to establish here is how well this splendid source, too, informs our inquiry. Some form of the root VENG appears in the text seventeen times by my count; in sixteen cases the word expresses what a knight wanted to do or actually accomplished; the remaining case is an invocation to God to take divine vengeance on William's enemies himself. God also receives thanks for graciously allowing Marshal and his men to take vengeance on the French invaders under Prince Louis. In passing, the text notes that by their fighting, crusaders to the East, in turn, avenge the shame inflicted on God by unbelievers. Adjectives modifying the noun "revenge" include "violent," "rightful," and "savage." Causes for revenge include claims of harm, damage, and shame inflicted. Those men who fail under these af-

6 See the fine edition of Sara Kay for text and discussion of compositional periods: *Raoul de Cambrai* (Oxford: Clarendon Press, 1992).

7 Kay, *Raoul de Cambrai*, *laisse* 85.

8 A.J. Holden, S. Gregory and D. Crouch, eds., *History of William Marshal*, 3 vols. (London, 2002–6).

fronts to take revenge in the approved manner are characterized as "nanny goats" or the "lily-livered." References to mercy are not lacking; but they are less numerous and mainly relate to a quality that an individual, mindful of sin and wrong in himself, fervently hopes to find in God. At several points someone is said to be "in mercy," especially in the king's mercy or in William's mercy (i.e., totally at their will). Once or twice a man asks for mercy in God's name. Echoing *Raoul de Cambrai*, patience, forbearance and moderation are once at least declared to be admirable qualities; and the Marshal is himself praised as a generous man who shows mercy, for example, to those who opposed him in Ireland. He shows another sort of mercy to the poor fellow who tried to steal his great warhorse one dark evening while Marshal attended an urban eve-of-tournament party. Caught red-handed in a dark nearby street, the hapless thief suffers a blow from the Marshal's baton so severe that one of his eyes flies out; at which point he calls for mercy in God's name, as William's retainers suggest hanging him. But the Marshal mercifully says what he has already done is enough.[9] I believe this is the point of the story, and I think we will find this pattern interesting in a moment.

Briefly, and simply to get another voice emanating from active knighthood, I turned to an old acquaintance, Geoffroi de Charny and his mid-fourteenth-century *Livre de chevalerie* of 1351 – a vernacular manual on the practice of chivalry. The surprise was to find only one reference to vengeance in his manual. The significance of his single remark, however, lies in its very casualness. In listing desired characteristics in a knight Charny says in passing (almost as if it were obvious) that the knight will take "cruel vengeance" against his enemies. He lived by his words: a man who grievously betrayed him ended up in displayed quarters after capture.[10]

The sampling so far is admittedly slight and would need much support in order to indicate any trend. Yet it does at least point to the deep commitment of knighthood to hot-blooded vengeance, and suggests the possibility of more complex ideas at work in their minds. If the tension – perhaps rather the paradox – rises to the level of consciousness, how could they deal with it? Would they even try?

By far the richest source for unearthing plentiful evidence is the immense field of romance writing, and within that huge field the Vulgate or Lancelot-Grail cycle – all of it (five major romances and their continua-

9 The incident occupies lines 4319–4450 in Holden, Gregory, Crouch, *History of William Marshal.*

10 Richard W. Kaeuper and Elspeth Kennedy, *The Book of Chivalry of Geoffroi de Charny* (Philadelphia: University of Pennsylvania Press, 1996), 138–39, and 10–12 (for Charny's disposal of the enemy).

tions), thousands of pages on chivalric behaviour and ideals, a grand chivalric *summa* written in the early decades of the thirteenth century and widely copied and read.[11]

No reader of the Vulgate Cycle can miss the striking emphasis on vengeance in the five romances and their continuations. From awful majesty at the apex of the hierarchy of authority in the universe, God takes vengeance that will be long remembered by mere mortals. In fact, immediately after the most dramatic display in the cycle, that which follows the infamous "Dolorous Stroke" in the *Merlin Continuation* (to be considered in a moment), the divine wrath operates almost like an atom bomb, with concentric rings of devastation rolling outward, leaving behind a wasteland over three kingdoms. God is at this point appropriately named The Supreme Avenger (*sovrains vengieres*).[12] He demands, moreover, that humans (or at least the right humans) do their best to follow his example and carry out righteous vengeance themselves. However distantly, his good knights act on his behalf, as his instruments in a world beset by sin. In the *History of the Holy Grail* the Roman Vespasian is shown avenging Christ against the Jews; crusaders are seen as avenging the shame later done to Christ in that same Holy Land by Saracens. Early in the *Quest of the Holy Grail* God's vengeance on King Bademagu – for a rash act he has committed – comes in the form of a White Knight who roughly unhorses Bademagu before disappearing.[13] Divine vengeance on Christians is regularly seen as penance for sin, establishing a link of the first importance in an era placing renewed emphasis on penance (following the Fourth Lateran Council). Bertelay, a knight implicated in the treasonous False Guinevere episode in *The Story of Merlin*, stoically requests that King Arthur take terrible vengeance on his body, knowing that his earthly pains will reduce yet more terrifying torments that he must suffer in the afterlife, as divine vengeance is enacted.[14]

11 In the discussion that follows I will generally use the Old French edition of H. Oskar Sommer, *The Vulgate Version of the Arthurian Romances*, 8 vols. (Washington: Carnegie Institution of Washington, 1908–16), and will quote the lively English translations of a team of scholars working under the general editorship of Norris J. Lacy, *Lancelot-Grail: The Old French Vulgate and Post Vulgate Cycle in Translation* (New York: Garland Publishing, 1993–96); I will give the name of the translator of the particular work being quoted within parentheses.

12 Lacy, *Lancelot-Grail*, 4: 214 (Martha Asher). For the French, see Gaston Paris and Jacob Ulrich, eds., *Merlin: Roman en prose*, 2 vols. (Paris: Société des Anciens Texts Français, 1886), 2: 232.

13 Sommer, *Vulgate Version*, 6: 21–22.

14 Lacy, *Lancelot-Grail*, 2: 277 (Samuel N. Rosenberg); Alexandre Micha, *Lancelot: roman en prose du XIII*[e] *siècle*, 9 vols. (Geneva: Libraririe Droz, 1978–83), 1: 163.

Repeatedly, good vengeance is valorized. At the Castle Carcelois the Grail companions are suddenly attacked by knights whom they summarily slaughter. What follows is a little debate scene among the heroes about the morality of revenge. Though Bors thinks they have acted well, the great and good Galahad worries over their agency in slaughtering the knights whose bodies lie heaped about: "If they had wronged Our Lord, we would not be the ones to take revenge, but the Lord himself, who waits until the sinner recognizes his error."[15] His statement echoes the well-known divine Biblical claim: "vengeance is mine, I will repay, says the Lord" (Romans 12:19). Such scruples are quickly brushed aside by a priest in a white robe who suddenly appears in the castle courtyard – carrying the *corpus domini* in a chalice no less – to inform Galahad that his actions, and not his doubts, are correct. Among much else, he assures the Grail knights that they have accomplished the finest deed that a knight has ever done. God has directed them to this spot and this action and the slain were irremediably evil.

The setting, however, need not be a hyper-evil castle beset by unsurpassed Grail Companions. Most of the action throughout the Vulgate Cycle takes place in court or forest settings with rather quotidian combats; but even in these fights the vengeance is counted as righteous. Sagremore, late in the massive romance *Lancelot*, is sure that he would be wicked in the sight of God if he failed to take vengeance for a maiden in his care.[16] And, as we will see, concepts of earthly justice inform the vengeance-taking no less than conceptions of the divine will in which they are ultimately rooted.

Yet the motivation is by no means limited to such abstract principles. Hot-blooded wrath animates revenge time and again. Knights say they will die if they cannot take vengeance, or fear they will die too soon and miss the chance.[17] The sword of the model knight Bors in *The Story of Merlin* is tellingly named Wrathful (*couroucesse sespee*).[18] A wise old Master Elias in the *Lancelot* assures the great knight Galehaut that he knows a cure for a sick heart:

15 For the incident and quotations see Lacy, *Lancelot-Grail*, 4: 72–74 (E. Jane Burns); Sommer, *Vulgate Version*, 6: 163–65: "Mais il ont este par auenture vne gent mescreant. Si ont tant mesfait a nostre signor quil ne voloit mie quil fuissent plus en vie. Et por ce nous enuoia il chi por auș destruire . vous ne dites mie asses fait galaad . & sil mesfisent a nostre signor la veniance nest pas a nos a prendre. Mais a celi qui atent tant que li pec[h]ieres se reconnoisse."

16 Lacy, *Lancelot-Grail*, 3: 124 (Wukkuan W., Kibler).

17 Lacy, *Lancelot-Grail*, 3: 66 (Roberta L. Krueger).

18 Sommer, *Vulgate Version*, 2: 235. Sharp clerical attacks on the sin of wrath can be found readily. See, e.g., Woodburn O. Ross, ed., *Middle English Sermons*, EETS, o.s., 209 (London: Oxford University Press, 1940), 51.

> The sick heart is cured by avenging the wrong done to it, and then it is wholly changed and returned to health. Imagine that someone tomorrow mocked and insulted you; your heart would not find peace till it were freed of the shame, and that, by giving hurt for hurt. If it were well avenged, it would be rid of the filth and poison clogging it, just like a man freed of worry and anger.[19]

The impulse to vengeance is so clearly visceral, perhaps even glandular.

The evidence appears to be straightforward and clear: among powerful chivalrous ranks vengeance achieved through prowess ranks as an honourable right and duty for the *bellatores*; as God takes holy vengeance on humans for sin, his good warriors on earth wipe out wrongs, harm and shame inflicted on them, edged weaponry in hand. From this evidence it seems that no problem troubles them, no yawning gap appears between ideal and actual (to be seen as troublesome); no paradox seems to disturb the focus of their minds and strong sword-arms on the honourable taking of revenge.

What of the voices for mercy, then? Early in the first romance of the cycle the symbolism of the bishop's staff is explained in significant terms: "This crozier you are holding in your hand symbolizes two things, vengeance and mercy: vengeance because it is pointed at the bottom; mercy, because it is curved on top."[20] We need to look further in the massive *fonds* of evidence in the Vulgate Cycle. The architecture of several of the constituent romances makes strong statements about mercy as well as vengeance. The clearest case appears in the magnificent final romance, the *Death of King Arthur*. As the perceptive Jean Frappier has elegantly and convincingly argued, this work might with equal justification be entitled "The Spiritual Rise of Lancelot."[21] What drives this romance is a set of contrasting ideas about vengeance: Gawain relentlessly demands Lancelot's blood to avenge that of his brothers, spilled by Lancelot in his famous

19 Lacy, *Lancelot-Grail*, 2: 250 (Samuel N. Rosenberg); Sommer, *Vulgate Version*, 4: 20: "Ore y a autres maladies dont on prent medecines Car quant li cuers est malades dedens de duel et dire . ou daucune honte qui au cors a este faite si en puet on bien venir a garison par ueniance prendre del forfait. Car qui vous feroit vilonnie li cuers ne seroit iamais a aise deuant ce que vous en series vengies . Chest de rendre honte por honte Et lors series deliures de lordure et del venin qui en vous seroit . Aussi com li homs seroit fors des pensees quant il est aquites de ses detes."

20 Lacy, *Lancelot-Grail*, 1: 27 (Carol J. Chase); Sommer, *Vulgate Version*, 1: 38: "Chel baston que tu tiens en ta main senestre senefie . ij . coses . ueniance & misericorde . veniance por ce que il est poignans par desous . misericorde por ce que il est corbes desus."

21 Jean Frappier, *Étude sur la Mort le Roi Artu* (Geneva: Libraririe Droz, 1961).

rescue of Guenevere from the stake. In single combat Lancelot repeatedly frustrates Gawain's fury by purely defensive fighting. In the melee of general combat Lancelot even unhorses King Arthur; but against the strident advice of his brothers to end the king's life and thus end the great war, he mercifully does the disabled Arthur no harm and even helps him to remount. Lancelot had failed to achieve the ideal of celestial chivalry in the Grail Quest, but here he rises above the culture of vengeance to a level of spiritual nobility.

Was not at least the negative side of this message – the anti-vengeance theme – delivered earlier in the cycle in the infamous incident of the "Dolorous Stroke" involving vengeance and counter vengeance?[22] Against direct divine warning, the knight Balin seizes the holy lance of Longinus that had pierced Christ's side, completing the ultimate divine act of mercy, as it hovers miraculously in mid-air, dripping blood into a chalice – and rams it into the genitals of King Pellehan, the Grail keeper, who is coming at him furiously to avenge the killing of Garlan, the king's brother, in his own court. Balin has been lauded as the knight of greatest prowess earlier in the tale; he had taken what all would consider justified revenge on Garlan who, as an invisible foe, had put his lance through men under Balin's protection. And King Pellehan, the Grail keeper, would likewise be considered fully justified in smiting Balin for violating the peace of his court and killing his brother in his presence. Yet consider what happens. As noted before, something like an atomic explosion lays waste three kingdoms as God takes final vengeance, surely an act that challenges the two merely human acts of vengeance that preceded it (however much they are valorized by earthly standards). God's response has been sparked by Balin's rash and hot-blooded act: a profane man with blood on his hands uses the Holy Lance of redemption (we might almost say the Lance of non-violence) in a private quarrel. Certainly the results are disastrous as God ends the cycle of human violence with stunning revenge of his own, which by definition must be just.

What is more, throughout all the romances in the cycle the knights often associate God with mercy. God is said to be the fount of mercy, the father of pity and forgiveness. And it seems worthy of note that knights frequently swear they will achieve some goal "by God's mercy." Of course sometimes, just to complicate matters, it is revenge that they wish to achieve.

And this very term, mercy, in all of its uses in the cycle, serves as a window through which we can glimpse ideas at work in knightly minds. There is a pattern for the display of mercy infused into nearly all of the

22 See Lacy, *Lancelot-Grail*, 4: 211–14 (Martha Asher); Paris and Ulrich, *Merlin*, 2: 24–32.

romances, a pattern that is tirelessly repeated in individual combat – hundreds of times. Here is a classic case from the *Merlin Continuation*; in this instance the knight Tor works the formula on each of two knights whom he has just unhorsed, in jousting that has left his lance projecting through the shoulder of one opponent:

> When Tor saw them both on the ground, he took his sword, for he wanted to be able to bring them both to defeat. He ran at the first, who had already got up and gave him such a great blow on the helmet that he stunned him completely and made him fall on his two hands on the ground. Then he rode over him on horseback, bruising him severely and the knight fainted with agony. Tor, who did not want to stop until the other cried mercy, dismounted. When he had tied his horse to a tree, he ran to the man he had ridden down, tore his helmet off his head, threw it away, and cried that he would kill him if he did not own himself defeated. The other, who had come out of his faint and saw himself in danger of death, cried mercy, for he saw that otherwise he could not escape. "Now swear," said Tor, "to yield yourself prisoner where I will send you." He swore. Then Tor left him and ran to the other one, who was all bruised from the hard fall he had had, and he gave him such a great blow on his helmet with his sword held in both hands that he made his eyes start out of his head and stunned him completely, so that he fell face down on the green grass and had no strength to get up. Tor seized his helmet and pulled hard on it, but he could not pull it off his head because the laces were very good. When he saw this, he cut the laces with his sword and drew it off his head. When the other saw his head bare but for his mail cap, he was afraid to die and cried mercy, seeing himself overcome. "Now swear," said Tor, "to yield yourself prisoner where I will send you." He promised, seeing that he could not escape otherwise. Tor left him then and said to him and his companion, "My lords, you are my prisoners." "This is true," they said."[23]

23 Lacy, *Lancelot-Grail*, 4: 234 (Martha Asher); Paris and Ulrich, *Merlin*, 2: 103–4: "Quant il les voit ansdeus a terre, il met le main a l'espee, car il bee que il les peuust ansdeus mener a outranche, si keurt sus au premier qui ja estoit relevés et li doune par mi le hyaume si grant caup qu'il l'estourdist tout et le fait flatir a terre d'ambesdeus les paumes. Après li vait par dessus le cors tout a cheval si que tout le debrise, et cil se pasme de l'angoisse qu'il sent. Et Tor descent, qui a tant ne s'en vaurra mie tenir se il ne crie merchi. Et quant il est descendus et il a son cheval atachié a un arbre, il keurt a chelui qu'il avoit defoulet, se li esrache le hyaume de la teste et le giete en voies et li crie qu'il l'ochirra s'il ne se tient a outré. Et cil qui fu revenus de pasmisons et se vit en peril de mort si crie merchi, car il voit bien que autrement ne

Techniques vary: usually a text specifies that the ventail or neck armour is turned down to expose the throat; sometimes pounding of the exposed head and face with the pommel of the sword is considered effective. For those seeking mercy, a kneeling posture seems to be recommended, along with an address to the victor that begins, "Noble knight." But the results are similar. For one party, defeat precedes mercy; for the other party, mercy follows a display of victorious power. Mercy, it is important to note, does not mean forgiveness. Rather, it means that vengeance is taken only up to the point of securing honour, wiping out shame, and expending wrath through prowess. The process (with a few exceptions) stops short of death for the defeated. The bloodied opponent is reduced to begging, in shame, for his life, which is granted from a plenitude of physical power. There is a legal term hovering in the atmosphere, I think. To be in the king's mercy, of course, was to be amerced totally at the king's will. The defeated in romance regularly promise, kneeling or flat out on the ground, helmet gone, swordless, armour stripped from a bare neck, with the victor's sharp sword raised over them, that they will do whatever will satisfy the victor. But the dominant mode is social rather than legal: begging for mercy involves shame – unless, the texts make clear, one is begging God or Lancelot: the power of either is too overwhelming to impose any shame for defeat. Other exceptions occur. A false and forsworn knight need not be given mercy, but should be made to die in sorrow and shame. The door to interpretation is clearly left ajar. Yet the formula is routinely displayed in action, and is prescriptively invoked by the authors no less than the self-interested figures kneeling in fear of death before their conquerors.

I would like to term this general pattern of defeat and mercy the Romance Compromise and identify it as a constituent of knightly ideology. After all, it carries out important ideological work: the danger of a disruptive paradox between mercy and vengeance is averted. Knights can have their

porroit il eschaper. « Ore fiancé, » fait Tor « a tenir prison lau je t'envoierai. » Et cil li fianche. Et il le laist maintenant, et court a l'autre qui tous estoit debrisiés del dur cheoir qu'il ot fait, et il li donne de s'espee par mi le hyaume a deus puins si grant caup que il li fait les ieus estinceler en la teste et l'estourdist tout, si que chius chiet as dens sour l'erbe vert ne n'a pooir de soi relever, et il l'ahiert erramment au hyaume et tire fort, et ne li puet esrachier dou chief, car moult estoient boin li lach. Et quant il vit chou, il li trenche a l'espee les las et li oste del chief. Et quant cil voit sa test nue fors de sa coife de fer, il a paour de morir, si crie mierchi, conme cil ki se voit au desous. Et Tor li dist : « Tu n'avras ja mierchi se tu ne fiances a tenir prison la ou je t'envoierai. » Et cil li fiancé, qui bien voit qu'il n'en puet autrement eschaper. Et il le laisse maintenant et dist a lui et a son compaingnon : « Signeur, vous estes mi prison. » « Verités est, » font il."

vengeance – and by not killing their enemy with a final swift sword stroke, they can consider themselves blessed participants in an economy of mercy, imitating their ultimate Lord in their earthly combats.

How closely ideology linked with life will be the question naturally troubling all empirical minds. So serious an issue undoubtedly deserves more than the cursory glance possible at the end of this paper; yet the question cannot be completely shoved under the rug with the usual academic disclaimers. Does it matter that romance presents such a pattern?

One link between the Romance Compromise and a world of very real medieval warriors might be found in a phenomenon emphasized by Matthew Strickland and John Gillingham. Both have argued the increasing likelihood during the High Middle Ages that prisoners would not be slaughtered after their defeat in battle.[24] Did the compromise on vengeance and mercy form the religious and moral underpinnings for this significant phenomenon? Debate would focus on the relative weights of fairly abstract ideas and the pragmatic business of ransoms, military tactics – or prudence.

While leaving tough tactical issues to specialists more adept at their discussion, I remain convinced that ideas in general mattered to the knighthood and that it is important for us to try to understand how they worked in the chivalric world. The process cannot have been simple and unidirectional; if an analogy is needed, alternating current works better than direct current for the flow of ideas. We can well suspect (as in the case of William Marshal) that real-world knightly exploits and views made considerable contributions to the ideas represented in chivalric literature, even if the writer wore a tonsure. The relationship between the ideas of clerics and knights can only have been complex. All ideas did not originate in clerical minds, to be force-fed to thick warriors obstinately trying to remain secular. Nor were all knights simply loyal and unwaveringly obedient sons of Holy Mother Church. They assuredly had deeply-held ideals of their own, including religious and moral principles. At important points chasms divided essential elements of the knightly professional ethic from the demanding principles of their religion. The writers who composed for them and spoke to them in all the forms of their literature had their work cut out for them; they had to build bridges over the chasms.[25] We should strive to

24 Matthew Strickland, *War and Chivalry* (Cambridge: Cambridge University Press, 1996); John Gillingham, "1066 and the Introduction of Chivalry into England," in George Garnet and John Hudson, eds., *Law and Government in Medieval England and Normandy* (Cambridge: Cambridge University Press, 1996).

25 These themes feature in my forthcoming book, *Holy Warriors* (Philadelphia: University of Pennsylvania Press). A good example of this bridging work involving vengeance and mercy appears in an *exemplum* of Etienne de Bourbon in which a dead knight's body laid out on a marvellous ship comes to Arthur's court. The body

understand these ideological bridging structures and how well they worked. If we succeed we will ensure a more nuanced view of the lay elite within medieval society.

---

bears a message calling for vengeance on the killer. Etienne notes that although vengeance is not the letter of the Gospel, just revenge here should be taken, for Christ was himself "pugil noster in navicula crucis." See A. Lecoy de la Marche, ed., *Anecdotes historiques* (Paris, 1877), 86–87.

JOHN MCKINNELL
Durham University

The Ideology of Vengeance in Old Norse Mythology

Vengeance has long been familiar as a feature of heroic societies, and it has often been explained as a type of social protection – that is to say, the probability that vengeance would follow an outrage against a family or clan member acted as a deterrent to potential attackers. If this is correct, we should expect the social duty of vengeance to be felt most strongly in those societies where central authority was weakest, and there could hardly be a more extreme example of the absence of central power than the Icelandic Republic (930–1262), in which the *lǫgsǫgumaðr* or Law Speaker, who combined the roles of supreme judge and parliamentary chairman, was the only paid servant of the state. Indeed, the main reason for the submission of the Icelanders to the king of Norway in 1262 was the lack of any authority capable of guaranteeing the rule of law.[1]

In this paper, I want to look briefly at the provision for vengeance in *Grágás* ("Grey Goose"), the republican code of law,[2] and then to compare it with the attitudes that can be seen in the mythological and legendary poetry whose major manuscripts were being copied around the end of the period during which *Grágás* was in force.[3] It may be true that the provi-

1 See Jón Jóhannesson, *A History of the Old Icelandic Commonwealth, Íslendinga Saga*, trans. Haraldur Bessason (Winnipeg: University of Manitoba Press, 1974), 247–87. For a reflection of this idea in saga literature, where feud often functions as a curb on the aggression of *ójafnaðarmenn* "unjust men" or "men who lack moderation," see Jesse Byock, *Feud in the Icelandic Saga* (Berkeley: University of California Press, 1982), especially 24–30.

2 *Grágás* survives in two slightly different early versions, *Konungsbók* and *Staðarhólsbók*, while a third, *Skálholtsbók*, is somewhat later but probably enjoyed prestige because it was kept at the episcopal seat of Skálholt. Both *Konungsbók* and *Staðarhólsbók* seem to have been largely written by the same scribe, probably Þorarinn kaggi Egilsson, priest at Vellir in Svarfaðardalur, northern Iceland (d. 1283), probably between 1250 and 1270; *Konungsbók* is more likely the earlier of the two (see Gunnar Karlsson, Kristján Sveinsson, and Mörður Árnason, eds., *Grágás* [Reykjavík: Mál og Menning, 1997], Inngangur xi–xvi).

3 *Grágás* was superseded by *Járnsíða* ("Ironside," the first royal law) in 1271–73 (see Jón Jóhannesson, *Old Icelandic Commonwealth*, 45, 69); the Codex Regius, the

sions of *Grágás* about legal revenge were more often flouted than obeyed in the mid-thirteenth century, but they still show the ideals concerning the law that were held by leading Icelanders at that time. Equally, it is of course true that most Eddic poems are probably much older than the mid-thirteenth century, but that was the period in which they were copied into the surviving manuscripts, and such copying represented a large expense in time and resources, so again, it seems probable that the ideals represented in them still seemed important to the same circle of highly literate people who were most likely to be reading *Grágás*. The fact that many of the Eddic poems concern heathen gods in whom thirteenth-century people no longer believed does not diminish their symbolic usefulness any more than it does when Chaucer imports the classical gods into *The Knight's Tale*; indeed, their lack of religious authority may have made the mythological poems more useful, since they could be used to investigate personal and social problems without the need to import a preconceived "right answer" from Christian scripture and doctrine.

According to *Grágás*, a man was entitled to take vengeance at any time up to the next Alþingi (annual General Assembly) for killings of defined relatives, or for serious personal wounds or injuries to himself or a close relative:

> It is prescribed that a man on whom injury is inflicted has the right to avenge himself if he wants to up to the time of the General Assembly at which he is required to bring a case for the injuries; and the same applies to everyone who has the right to avenge a killing. Those who have the right to avenge a killing are the principals in a killing case.[4]

The definitions of major wounds and injuries are extremely precise,[5] and in any case involving a killing of one of his relatives, the avenger also had a legal duty to bring a case for manslaughter at the next Alþingi.

---

most important of the manuscripts of the *Poetic Edda*, was copied in Iceland around 1270, but most or all of its constituent poems must already have existed in written form by about 1240 (see Ursula Dronke, ed., *The Poetic Edda, I: Legendary Poems* and *II: Mythological Poems* [Oxford: Clarendon Press, 1969–97], I: xi–xiii).

4 "Þat er mælt. at maðr a sin at hefna ef hann vill sa er á verþr uɴit til þess alþingis er hann er scylldr at søkia of averkin oc sva þeir menn allir er vigs eigo at hefna. En þeir eigo vigs at hefna er vigsacar ero aðilia"; see Vilhjálmur Finsen, ed., *Grágás: Konungsbók*, 2 vols. (1852; repr. Odense: Odense University Press, 1974), ch. 86, I: 147; trans. Andrew Dennis, Peter Foote, and Richard Perkins, *Laws of Early Iceland: Grágás I* (Winnipeg: University of Manitoba Press, 1980) (trans. of *Konungsbók*, with some additions from *Staðarhólsbók*), 141.

5 See *Grágás, Konungsbók*, ch. 86 (ed. Finsen, I: 145, 147–48); trans. Dennis, Foote and Perkins, *Laws of Early Iceland*, 140, 141.

A man was also entitled to take vengeance for rape of or improper sexual relations with his wife, daughter, mother, sister, foster-daughter or foster-mother:

> There are six women a man has the right to kill for. One is a man's wife, two a man's daughter, three a man's mother, four is his sister, five is the foster-daughter a man has brought up, six is the foster-mother who brought a man up. It is prescribed that if a man arrives to find another man forcing a woman to lie with him there, a woman he has the right to kill for, and the man has forced her down and lowered himself down upon her, then he has the right to kill on her account there at that place; or likewise if he finds him in the same bed as the woman ... then a man has the right to kill on her account in both instances even if intercourse has not taken place. ... [But if the wrongful intercourse took place, a man has the right to kill on that account up to the next General Assembly.][6]

The evidence required to demonstrate rape or improper sexual relations is thus equally carefully specified, and the male participant seems always to have been held solely responsible whether the woman consented or not.

There was also a more limited right to take vengeance on the spot, but not afterwards or elsewhere, in cases of attempted rape or improper intercourse, lesser assaults and attempted assaults (which are carefully defined to include actual or attempted cuts, thrusts, shootings, throwing of objects, striking with a weapon, knocking a person down, shaking, wresting objects from one's grasp or throttling),[7] killings of thralls (slaves, which could be

6 "Sex ero konor þær er maðr avigt vm. Ein er kona manz. ii. dóttir manz. iii. moðir manz. iiii. er systir. v. er fostra su er maðr hefir fødda. vi. er fostra su er maN hefir føddan. Þat er mælt. ef maðr kemr at þar er aNAR maðr brytr kono þa til svefnis er hann a vigt vm. þar a þeim vetvangi oc hafe hann fellda hana oc látet afallaz oc a hann þa vigt vm þar a þeim vetvangi eða sva ef hann fiðr hann i sama sæing konoNE. ... oc a maðr þar vigt vm ihvaromtvEGia stað þott misrøþan hafe eigi tekiz ... [Þar er legorðz söc hefir tekiz. þa a maðR vígt vm til ens næsta alþingis]"; see *Grágás, Konungsbók*, ch. 90 (ed. Finsen, I: 164); trans. Dennis, Foote, and Perkins, *Laws of Early Iceland*, 154 and 216, note 63. The provision for revenge until the next Alþingi if the sexual act took place is not in *Konungsbók*, but is added from Vilhjálmur Finsen, ed., *Grágás: Staðarhólsbók* (1879; repr. Odense: Odense University Press, 1974), 332 (ch. 293).

7 For definition of lesser assaults, see *Grágás, Konungsbók*, ch. 86 (ed. Finsen, I: 144–45), trans. Dennis, Foote, and Perkins, *Laws of Early Iceland*, 139, 208. *Konungsbók* specifies that a man who commits such an assault loses his immunity, but the right of revenge on the spot is only made explicit in *Staðarhólsbók* (ch. 265; ed. Finsen, I: 297).

avenged either by the slave's master or by his or her relatives),[8] or raiding or theft against a person's property (which had to be legally proved afterwards).[9] "On the spot" was defined as within a bowshot in all directions from the place where the original assault had taken place.[10] It usually seems to be assumed that vengeance will be lethal, but there are exceptions, as when provision is made for what should happen when a blow is (presumably illegally) avenged by a blow.[11]

At first sight, the scope of legally justified vengeance may look considerable, but in fact it is considerably less than one might have expected. *Grágás* is generally a very prescriptive code, imposing legal duties on people in many different situations (in this case, the obligation to bring legal cases for the injuries they have suffered). But there is no *duty* of vengeance anywhere in the law, and *Grágás* seems constantly concerned to limit rather than to encourage it; for example, an addition to the law insists that when a person against whom vengeance can be legally taken is being shielded by others but not on the scene of the original offence, then the vengeance cannot be extended to them (i.e., they do not lose their legal immunity to being attacked).[12] The law always prescribes limits to when and where vengeance may be taken, and it must always be replaced by legal process by the time of the next Alþingi (i.e., within, at most, just under a year). This impulse to limit the permitted scope of vengeance is no doubt partly due to the influence of Christianity, but there was probably also a sense that vengeance was socially destructive in a small, oligarchic society in which every householder could call on his *goði* (chieftain) for support, and opposing *goðar* were very likely to be related to each other.

It seems, therefore, that "justified" vengeance was a concept that the writers of *Grágás* did their best to minimize, but which they could not completely disallow because it was too deeply rooted in the traditional

8 *Grágás, Konungsbók*, ch. 111 (ed. Finsen, I: 190), trans. Dennis, Foote, and Perkins, *Laws of Early Iceland*, 172.

9 *Staðarhólsbók* only: see ch. 367 (ed. Finsen, 384); trans. Dennis, Foote, and Perkins, *Laws of Early Iceland*, 231–32. *Staðarhólsbók* adds that revenge can only be taken for the act of theft that has just taken place on the spot, not for any earlier thefts.

10 *Grágás, Konungsbók*, ch. 86 (ed. Finsen, I: 148); trans. Dennis, Foote, and Perkins, *Laws of Early Iceland*, 141–42. A "new law" added in *Staðarhólsbók* defines a bowshot range as two hundred legal fathoms and twelve roods on level ground = 240 fathoms, or about 480 metres (*Staðarhólsbók* ch. 321 [ed. Finsen, 352], and see Dennis, Foote, and Perkins, *Laws of Early Iceland*, 30, n. 22).

11 *Grágás, Konungsbók*, ch. 89 (ed. Finsen, I: 157–58); trans. Dennis, Foote, and Perkins, *Laws of Early Iceland*, 149.

12 *Staðarhólsbók*, ch. 271 only (ed. Finsen, 300–301); trans. Dennis, Foote and Perkins, *Laws of Early Iceland*, 209.

culture. All the same, they distinguish between those offences for which vengeance is only permissible when taken in the heat of the moment (assault, raiding, theft or killing a slave) and those where it was considered reasonable to take revenge in cold blood, though only until the next Alþingi (killing, serious wounding, and rape or improper sexual relations). The latter group are clearly seen as giving the most serious grounds for vengeance, but even here, *Grágás* merely tolerates revenge rather than giving it any encouragement.[13]

Vengeance in literature, however, is quite another matter. The number of instances of it in the sagas is very large, and when one turns to legendary and mythological poetry, vengeance on behalf of one's kin, or to maintain one's own self-respect, becomes a pressing moral duty. In *Reginsmál* 15, when Reginn has just urged Sigurðr to kill the dragon Fáfnir, the hero responds:

> Loudly Hundingr's sons will laugh,
> they who deprived Eylimi of life,
> if the prince [i.e., Sigurðr himself] prefers to seek
> ruddy rings rather than vengeance for a father.[14]

Sigurðr is not refusing to fight Fáfnir, and he certainly has no aversion to the dragon's treasure, but he insists that first things must come first, and that it will be disgraceful and worthy of mockery if he does not avenge his father's killing before he tries to do anything else.

Mockery for not avenging one's father was clearly a powerful slur, and it did not even have to be fair. Þórr has no answer when Loki taunts him in *Lokasenna* 58:

> Earth's son has now come in here –
> why are you raging so, Þórr?

13 For another convenient summary of legal vengeance in *Grágás* (in Danish), see Vilhjálmur Finsen, ed., *Grágás: Skálholtsbók m. m.* (1883; repr. Odense: Odense University Press, 1974), 695.

14 Hátt muno hlæia Hundings synir,
þeir er Eylima aldrs synioðo,
ef meirr tiggia munar at sœkia
hringa rauða enn hefnd fǫður.
(*Reginsmál* 15, N-K 177)

All translations of quotations from Eddic poems in this article are by the present author, but alternative translations can be found in *The Poetic Edda*, trans. Carolyne Larrington (Oxford: Oxford University Press, 1996); in this case, see p. 154.

but you won't dare to, when you ought to be fighting the wolf,
and he swallows Óðinn completely.[15]

Þórr might reasonably have objected that he will be rather busy fighting the World Serpent just at that moment, but the traditional taunt is so powerful that no answer to it seems sufficient.

And in the heroic lays it is not only the mockery of one's enemies that enforces vengeance. In a stanza of *Guðrúnarhvǫt* which is probably derived from the now damaged *Hamðismál*, Guðrún tells her sons Hamðir and Sǫrli about the death of their sister Svanhildr at the hands of King Jǫrmunrekkr, and continues:

You've not become such men as Gunnarr,
nor with a mind, either, like Hǫgni had;
you would have tried to avenge her
if you'd had the courage of my brothers
or the firm mind of the Hunnish kings.[16]

Vengeance is in this case equivalent to suicide, but their mother is still prepared to force Hamðir and Sǫrli to attempt it by suggesting that unlike her brothers and husband, they lack the courage that male members of her family ought to have. It is true that Hamðir then points out that his mother was less eager to praise her brothers' courage when they murdered her husband Sigurðr (*Hamðismál* 7, N-K 270), and that her own vengeance against Atli (by killing their young sons) damaged herself as well as him (*Hamðismál* 8), but once she has urged vengeance and called their courage in question, there is no point in arguing. Sǫrli laconically comments: "I don't want to bandy words with mother" (*Vilcat ec við móður málom scipta; Hamðismál* 9: 3–4), and concludes:

15 Iarðar burr er hér nú inn kominn:
hví þrasir þú svá, Þórr?
enn þá þorir þú ecci, er þú scalt við úlfinn vega,
oc svelgr hann allan Sigfǫður.
(*Lokasenna* 58, N-K 108; cf. Larrington, *Poetic Edda*, 94)

16 Urðoa iþ glíkir þeim Gunnari,
né in heldr hugðir, sem var Hǫgni;
hennar myndoð iþ hefna leita,
ef iþ móð ættið minna brœðra
eða harðan hug Húnkonunga.
(*Guðrúnarhvǫt* 3, N-K 264; cf. Larrington, *Poetic Edda*, 235)

you'll weep for both of us too, Guðrún,
doomed as we sit here on our horses – far away we shall die.[17]

Although *Hamðismál* is a very early poem (probably from the late ninth century),[18] one might reasonably argue that it does not altogether endorse vengeance – Hamðir and Sǫrli have good reason to object to the way that their mother is throwing their lives away. But the real point is that once she has demanded vengeance and questioned their courage, there is no more to be said – vengeance has become an unavoidable duty, however hopeless the circumstances.

The alternative to vengeance – legal process, negotiation and compensation – never appears in the legendary lays of the Poetic Edda, possibly because those against whom it might be directed are usually seen as independent rulers who are too powerful for legal proceedings against them to be possible. But strangely enough, there are a few cases of implied legal proceedings or compensation in myths about the gods. One is when the giantess Skaði comes among the gods seeking vengeance for the killing of her father Þjazi, but is diverted into accepting compensation instead. According to Snorri's *Skáldskaparmál*, this took the form of being allowed to choose a husband from among the gods and being entertained by Loki with an indecent spectacle that ended with him falling into her lap.[19] The poet of *Lokasenna* suggests an even more base reason for Skaði's failure to avenge her father; after she has expressed her hatred of Loki for his role in Þjazi's death, he retorts:

You were milder in words to Laufey's son [i.e., Loki himself]
when you invited me into your bed;
we'll have to mention such things if we must clearly
reckon up our faults.[20]

17 ocr scaltu oc, Guðrún, grāta báða,
er hér sitiom feigir á mǫrom, fiarri munom deyia.
(*Hamðismál* 10: 5–8, N-K 270; cf. Larrington, *Poetic Edda*, 239)

18 See Dronke, *Poetic Edda*, I: 214–17 for a demonstration that *Hamðismál* was probably known to Torf-Einarr, Jarl of Orkney, when he composed his occasional verses (*lausavísur*) around 890.

19 Anthony Faulkes, ed., *Snorri Sturluson, Edda: Skáldskaparmál*, 2 vols. (London: Viking Society for Northern Research, 1998), I: 2 (ch. G56); trans. Anthony Faulkes in Snorri Sturluson, *Edda* (London: Dent, 1987), 61.

20 Léttari í málom vartu við Laufeyiar son
þá er þú léz mér á beð þinn boðit;
getið verðr oss slícs, ef vér gorva scolom
telia vǫmmin vár.
(*Lokasenna* 52, N-K 106; cf. Larrington, *Poetic Edda*, 93)

Here there is no doubt at all that Skaði should have pursued honourable vengeance for her father, and accepting compensation is linked with disgraceful sexual self-indulgence – but then, what can you expect of a giantess?

Two other references to legal process in mythological poetry are in seduction cases, in which vengeance would again be permitted by *Grágás*. One is in *Lokasenna* 40, where Loki is abusing the god Týr:

> Shut up, Týr! It happened to your wife
> that she had a child by me;
> you never got a scrap of cloth nor a penny
> in compensation for this, you wretch.[21]

One might perhaps explain this allusion to compensation by saying that since Týr only has one hand, he cannot be expected to avenge his wife's disgrace, but he should at least have pursued a legal claim. But that explanation cannot apply in *Hávamál* 109–10, when the giant Suttungr comes seeking satisfaction for the seduction of his daughter Gunnlǫð. In this case, the giant probably does want vengeance on the seducer, whom he knows as Bǫlverkr ("evil-doer"), but he fails to realize that this was in fact Óðinn in disguise. The poet imagines him imposing an oath on Óðinn that he is not harbouring the miscreant:

> I think Óðinn has taken an oath on the ring –
> how can his word be trusted?
> He left the banquet with Suttungr deceived
> and Gunnlǫð reduced to tears.[22]

But both *Lokasenna* and this part of *Hávamál* are probably the work of twelfth-century Christians, at least in their present forms,[23] and neither

21 Þegi þú, Týr! Þat varð þinni kono,
at hon átti mǫg við mér;
ǫln né penning hafþir þú þess aldregi
vanréttis, vesall.
(*Lokasenna* 40, N-K 104; cf. Larrington, *Poetic Edda*, 91)

22 Baugeið Óðinn hygg ec at unnit hafi,
hvat scal hans trygðom trúa?
Suttung svikinn hann lét sumbli frá
oc grœtta Gunnlǫðo.
(*Hávamál* 110, N-K 34; cf. Larrington, *Poetic Edda*, 29)

23 The date of *Lokasenna* has been much debated, and some critics (such as Dronke, *Poetic Edda* II: 355 and Jónas Kristjánsson, *Eddas and Sagas: Iceland's Medieval Literature*, trans. Peter Foote [Reykjavík: Hið íslenska bókmenntafélag, 1997], 39)

case can be taken seriously. Both reduce the gods to the status of quarrelsome human householders, and both seem to assume that in normal circumstances the preferred option would be revenge. Only physical incapacity or gullibility can excuse or explain the resort to legal process, and neither of them can be admired.

In earlier mythological poetry, it is usually assumed that resort to the law is not an option – the only disagreement is over the question of whether "justified" revenge is admirable, or merely an inevitable duty. There are two avengers whose deeds are central to Old Norse mythology: Váli, who slays Hǫðr in revenge for his unwitting killing of the god Baldr, and Víðarr, who will in the future kill the wolf Fenrir at Ragnarǫk ("the downfall of the gods") as vengeance after the wolf has swallowed Óðinn himself. Both avengers are sons of Óðinn and of a giantess, and both were probably thought to have been begotten purely for their roles as avengers, since the sources agree that Óðinn has prophetic knowledge both of Baldr's death and of his own.

Both of them appear in two poems that probably date from before the Conversion to Christianity: the wisdom-contest poem *Vafþrúðnismál*, which may date from the mid- or later tenth century, and the prophetic monologue *Vǫluspá*, which was probably composed at the very end of the tenth century or the beginning of the eleventh. But the two poems show very different attitudes towards the two avengers. In *Vafþrúðnismál* they are named first among those who will inhabit the new world that will appear after Ragnarǫk:

> Víðarr and Váli will dwell in the gods' shrines
> when Surtr's fire is slaked;

continue to see it as a pre-Conversion poem, but it seems difficult to maintain this in view of its ironic quotations from a number of other Eddic poems (e.g., *Lokasenna* 53: 1–3, where Sif is about to protest her sexual purity, looks like a sarcastic echo of *Skírnismál* 37: 1–3, in which Gerðr expresses her sexual submission to Freyr), and Loki's role as accuser in this poem seems probably influenced by that of the devil at the Last Judgement. (Further on these arguments, see Maria Elena Ruggerini, ed., *Le Invettive di Loki* [Rome: Istituto di Glottologia dell'Università di Roma, 1979], 154–62; Barbro Söderberg, "Formelgods och Eddakronologi," *Arkiv för nordisk filologi* 101 (1986): 50–86; John McKinnell and Maria Elena Ruggerini, *Both One and Many* [Rome: Il Calamo, 1994], 46–55.) The seduction episodes in *Hávamál* give a light-hearted view of the mutual treachery of men and women towards each other in sexual matters, and probably draw on the concept of the Wheel of Fortune and on some *dicta* derived from Ovid and Virgil, both of which would require a good education in literary Latin, which was not available in Iceland or Norway until around 1100 (see John McKinnell, "*Hávamál B*: A Poem of Sexual Intrigue," *Saga-Book* 29 [2005]: 83–114, at 92–100).

Móði and Magni will possess Mjǫllnir
and work when the battle is over.[24]

According to this view, the sons of the two major gods will survive the battle and succeed their fathers in the re-born world. But they are also ideologically meaningful: *Móði* and *Magni* are "the brave one" and "the strong one," while Víðarr and Váli represent those who have fulfilled their obligation of vengeance for father or brother. The poet suggests that courage, strength and the resolute performance of vengeance are the qualities that deserve to survive into the re-born world. It is hard to know how old this mythological motif was: Víðarr at least may be a creation of the last stages of heathenism, since his name does not appear in skaldic verse, though it does also occur in *Grímnismál* 17 and *Lokasenna* 10, his mother Gríðr ("Violence") is mentioned in Eilífr Goðrúnarson's skaldic poem *Þórsdrápa* (ca. 990), and he may be depicted on the Gosforth Cross in Cumbria and perhaps on the Ovingham Stone in Northumberland, both of which date from the tenth century.[25] But the clear meaning of his name ("the widely ruling one")[26] suggests that his return in the re-born world was probably an original part of his myth. Váli is also known only from Eddic verse (*Baldrs draumar* 11, *Hyndluljóð* 29, both possibly influenced by *Vǫluspá*),[27] although Óðinn's seduction of his mother Rindr is mentioned by the skaldic poet Kormákr Ǫgmundarson (*c.*960),[28] but he may be an older figure, since his name is of obscure origin and can no longer have made sense to Norse speakers of the Conversion period. Its likeliest etymology, from Primitive Germanic **waihalaʀ*, cf. Gothic *waihjō* 'battle', suggests the meaning "little warrior,"[29] so the story of his ability to fight at one night old may always have been part of his myth.

Vǫluspá, by contrast, shows an attitude more like that of *Hamðismál*, in which vengeance is an unavoidable feature of the life of men and gods,

24 Víðarr oc Váli byggia vé goða,
þá er slocnar Surtar logi;
Móði oc Magni scolo Miǫllni hafa
oc vinna at vígþroti.
(*Vafþrúðnismál* 51, N-K 54–55; cf. Larrington, *Poetic Edda*, 48)

25 See Richard N. Bailey, *Viking Age Sculpture* (London: Collins, 1980), 126–28, 133–34.

26 Jan de Vries, *Altnordisches Etymologisches Wörterbuch*, 3rd ed. (Leiden: Brill, 1977), 659; Rudolf Simek, *Dictionary of Northern Mythology*, trans. Angela Hall (Cambridge: D.S. Brewer, 1993), 359–60.

27 See N-K 278–79, 293.

28 *Sigurðardrápa* 3,4 (Finnur Jónsson, ed., *Den Norske-Islandske Skjaldedigtning I–II A–B* [København, Kristiania: Gyldendal, Nordisk Forlag, 1908–15], I B, 69).

29 De Vries, *Altnordisches Etymologisches Wörterbuch*, 641.

but is not idealized. Here, Váli's precocious killing of Hǫðr at one night old and his binding of Loki are the subject of stt. 32–34, while Víðarr's revenge for his father Óðinn is told in st. 55:

> Then comes the great son of victory's Father [i.e., of Óðinn],
> Víðarr, to fight the slaughtering beast;
> he makes a sword stand in Hveðrung's son [i.e., the wolf Fenrir],
> a blade in his heart – then his father is avenged.[30]

This may sound like admiration, but neither Víðarr nor Váli appears in the re-born world of *Vǫluspá*. Instead, the battle purges away all who take part in it, and those who will return are the innocent, notably Baldr and his unwitting killer Hǫðr, who will inhabit Óðinn's dwellings together (*Vǫluspá* 62: 5–6, N-K 14). This suggests a quite different ideal from that of *Vafþrúðnismál*, one which sees vengeance as a cruel necessity in the present world, but which replaces it with reconciliation in the ideal world that will follow Ragnarǫk. This view is, no doubt, influenced by Christianity, although I do not think *Vǫluspá* is actually a Christian poem.

Clearly, vengeance for slayings or injuries to one's self or one's kin was a deeply ingrained feature of Old Norse society which could not be eradicated, however much pragmatic thinkers like the *Hamðismál* poet might point to its self-defeating outcomes, or Christian lawyers might seek to limit it and mitigate its effects. But was it really a mechanism for upholding the personal security of aristocratic fathers and brothers, the sexual integrity of their female relatives, and the security of their property, as is often assumed? If so, it was, like any other deterrent, one that had already failed whenever vengeance actually had to be taken, and the evidence of historical writings, imaginative literature and the law all suggest that this happened very frequently. If, then, it was so inefficient, why was it such a powerful feature of Norse ideology? To suggest an answer to this question, I would like to look at a few myths in which the gods appear not as the agents of vengeance, but as the potential victims of it.

Returning to Váli and Víðarr, it is worth noticing that both were conceived as the result of acts that would in *Grágás* have justified the taking of revenge against Óðinn. Kormákr Ǫgmundarson (*c.*960) says that Óðinn used illegal magic (*seiðr*) to seduce Váli's mother Rindr, while Saxo Grammaticus gives him a long and disgraceful wooing of her that culminates in

30 Þá kømr inn micli mǫgr Sigfǫður
Víðarr, vega at valdýri;
lætr hann megi Hveðrungs mund um standa
hiǫr til hiarta, þá er hefnt fǫður.
(*Vǫluspá* 55, N-K 13; cf. Larrington, *Poetic Edda*, 11)

rape.[31] *Baldrs draumar* 11 (N-K 278–79) adds that Rindr will bear Váli in halls in the west (i.e., among the gods, implying that Óðinn also abducted her). Less is known about the details of Óðinn's begetting of Víðarr on the hag Gríðr, but her seduction would still be an act that justified legal vengeance. The same is true of Óðinn's seduction of Jǫrð to beget Þórr, the essential defender of gods and men, and of Gunnlǫð in order to steal the mead of poetry.[32]

But the gods are liable to vengeance for killings as well as for acts of seduction and theft. *Vǫluspá* 25–26 (N-K 6) refers briefly to the story of the Giant Builder whom the gods hired to rebuild the giant-proof wall of Ásgarðr, and it is explained more fully by Snorri in *Gylfaginning* ch. 42:[33] on Loki's advice, the gods agreed to pay the Giant Builder the sun, the moon and Freyja (who is equivalent to sexual fertility) if he could complete the wall by the first day of summer, but then they threatened Loki into tricking the builder out of his reward, and when he went into a giant rage, Þórr killed him with his hammer, in defiance of the oaths of safe-conduct that had been given to him.

Even earlier in the mythological history of the gods, they had created the earth by killing the primeval giant Ymir, as Óðinn himself is made to say in *Grímnismál*:

From Ymir's flesh the earth was shaped,
  but from his blood the sea,
rocks from his bones, trees from his hair,
  but sky out of his skull.

But from his brows the blessed powers made
  middle earth for the sons of men;
but from his brains those threatening
  clouds were all created.[34]

31 Kormákr, *Sigurðardrápa* 3,4 (Finnur Jónsson, *Den Norske-Islandske Skjaldedigtning*, I B, 69); Saxo, *Gesta Danorum* III.iv (ed. J. Olrik and H. Ræder, *Saxonis Gesta Danorum I–II* (Copenhagen: Levin and Munksgaard, 1931–37), I: 70–73; trans. P. Fisher, ed. Hilda Ellis Davidson, as *Saxo Grammaticus, The History of the Danes I–II* (Cambridge: D.S. Brewer, 1979–80), I: 76–79 and commentary II: 56–58.

32 Further on Óðinn as seducer, see John McKinnell, *Meeting the Other in Norse Myth and Legend* (Cambridge: Boydell & Brewer, 2005), 152–71.

33 Ed. Anthony Faulkes, *Snorri Sturluson, Edda: Prologue and Gylfaginning* (Oxford: Clarendon, 1982), 34–36; trans. Faulkes, *Snorri Sturluson, Edda* (London: Dent, 1987), 35–36.

34 Ór Ymis holdi   var iǫrð um scǫpuð,
  enn ór sveita sær,

This was probably a traditional piece of verse, as a shorter variant of it appears in *Vafþrúðnismál* 21 as the giant's answer to Óðinn's first question, about the origins of the earth and sky. In this context it is a deliberate insult, since Vafþrúðnir is one of Ymir's immediate descendants; if the giant only realized it, the one on whom he could legitimately take vengeance is standing in front of him as he answers the question. The killing of Ymir must have been a well-known myth, and a number of skaldic poets refer to it, including Ormr Barreyjarskáld in the later tenth century.[35]

All these myths have two things in common: first, the central gods commit acts that would justify the giants in taking vengeance against them; second, they are forced into these deeds by necessity, and we human beings are the beneficiaries and accomplices of their actions. Without the killing of Ymir the earth would not exist; without the killing of the Giant Builder there would be no sun and moon and no bearing of children. Without the seduction of Jǫrð, Þórr would not exist and the giants would overrun the earth – and so on. All these acts were necessary, but they are collectively the probable explanation of why it was thought axiomatic that the giants wish to destroy gods and men, and why they will finally attack us at Ragnarǫk; in heathen times, this vengeance was undoubtedly thought certain to come about at some time in the future.

These myths do not suggest a world in which vengeance is a deterrent to attack, but one in which one may be forced by harsh necessity to make oneself into the potential object of revenge. The moral is not "don't do it, for fear of vengeance," but rather "do what must be done, and be prepared to take the consequences." The psychological preparedness to "do the deed and abide it," as William Morris put it,[36] seems to have lain at the root of what gave people individual and family self-respect, and this was recognized even in slaves. Acts of vengeance could provide an assertion of one's human dignity, both for the avenger and, more surprisingly, often for his victim as well, as he stoically accepted the probability that he would

---

biǫrg ór beinom,   baðmr ór hári,
    enn ór hausi himinn.

Enn ór hans brám   gerðo blíð regin
    miðgarðr manna sonom;
enn ór hans heila   vóro þau in harðmóðgo
    scý ǫll um scǫpuð.

(*Grímnismál* 40–41, N-K 65; cf. Larrington, *Poetic Edda*, 57)

35 Finnur Jónsson, *Den Norske-Islandske Skjaldedigtning*, I B, 135.

36 Brynhild's words to Sigurd in William Morris, *The Story of Sigurd the Volsung*, 4th ed. (London: Reeves and Turner, 1887), II: 143.

become its victim, but neither they nor anything else could guarantee protection or peace in the turbulent and lawless Iceland of the mid-thirteenth century.

It is a pervasive idea of much Old Norse culture that everything worthwhile has to be paid for in one way or another. The assertion of self-respect through vengeance is no exception: lawyers might seek to limit its cost in terms of bloodshed, and anthologists and scribes could popularize the heroic poems that helped people to accept its consequences, but both were finally forced into a stoic recognition of its unavoidable nature and personal cost.

Index